Acknowledgments

The authors would like to thank the following people for their help: Publisher Susan Schwartz; Managing Editor Gene DeRoin; Editorial Assistant Michael Stoeger; Researcher Nancy Myers; and Art Director Sally Hughes. Special appreciations to Researchers Jon Crook, Ph.D., and to Nancy Bishop for her insights into this revision and her efforts in earlier editions. Thanks also are due to Sheila Collins for her loyal support.

Note to Our Readers

We, the authors and editors, have made every effort to supply you with the most useful, up-to-date information available to help you find the job you want. Each name, address, and phone number has been verified by our fact checkers, Diane Ruehl and Jennifer Minks. But offices move and people change jobs, so we urge you to call before you write, and write before you visit. And if you think we should include information on companies, organizations, or people that we've missed, please let us know.

CONTENTS

How To Get the Most
from This Book

So you want to get a job in the Dallas/Fort Worth area? Well, you've picked up the right book. Whether you're a recent graduate, new in town, or an old hand at the great Texas Job Search; whether or not you're currently employed; even if you're not fully convinced that you *are* employable—this book is crammed with helpful information.

It contains the combined wisdom of three top professionals: Dr. Richard Citrin, a psychologist and career development specialist who has been practicing in Dallas/Fort Worth for over 10 years; Tom Camden, a personnel professional who currently heads the nationally known consulting firm of Camden and Associates; and Dr. Bill Osher, Associate Director of Georgia Tech's Counseling and Career Planning Center and also affiliated with the Atlanta Area Clinical Service.

Tom and Bill contribute expert advice on both basic and advanced job-search techniques, from how to write a resume to suggestions for racking up extra points in an employment interview. Richard shares his knowledge of Dallas/Fort Worth's employment scene, developed through his years as a psychologist at Texas Christian University as well as his contacts with the scores of career hunters and job changers he has helped over the years. Whether you're looking for a job in the city or the suburbs, his extensive listings will save you hours of research time.

Dozens of other metro-area insiders have contributed tips, warnings, jokes, and observations in candid, behind-the-scenes interviews. We've done our level best to pack more useful information between these covers than you'll find anywhere else.

We would love to guarantee that this book is the only resource you will need to find the job of your dreams, but we are not miracle workers. This is a handbook, not a Bible. There's just no getting around the fact that finding work *takes* work. *You* are the only person who can land the job you want.

What we *can* do—and, we certainly hope, have done—is to make the work of job hunting in Dallas/Fort Worth easier and more enjoyable for you. We have racked our brains, and those of many others, to provide you with the most extensive collection of local resources in print.

To get the most from this book, first browse through the Table of Contents. Acquaint yourself with each chapter's major features, see what appeals to you, and turn to the sections that interest you the most.

It may not be necessary or useful for you to read this book from cover to cover. If you're currently employed, for example, you can probably skip Chapter 8—"What To Do If Money Gets Tight." If you have no interest in using a professional employment service, you'll only need to browse through Chapter 6.

There are certain parts of this book, however, that no one should overlook. One of them is Chapter 4—"Researching the Dallas/Fort Worth Job Market." Unless you're a professional librarian, we'd bet money that you won't be able to read this chapter without discovering at least a few resources that you never knew existed. We've tried to make it as easy as possible for you to get the inside information that can put you over the top in an employment interview.

Chapter 5 is another Don't Miss—especially our unique listing of organizations that you should know about to develop your network of professional contacts. We strongly suggest that you read Chapter 7, even if you think you already know all about how to handle an interview. And then, of course, there's Chapter 11—listings of the Dallas/Fort Worth area's top 1,150 employers of white-collar workers.

There's another thing you should know about in order to get the most from this book. Every chapter, even the ones you don't think you need to read, contains at least one helpful hint or insider interview that is set off from the main text. Take some time to browse through them. They contain valuable nuggets of information and many tips that you won't find anywhere else.

Keep in mind that no one book can do it all for you. While we've touched on the basic tasks of any job search—self-analysis, developing a resume, researching the job market, figuring out a strategy, generating leads, interviewing, and selecting the right job—we don't have space to go into great detail on each and every one of them. What we *have* done is to supply suggestions for further reading. Smart users of this book will follow those suggestions when they need to know more about a particular subject.

Dallas/Fort Worth in the '90s

What's the economic outlook for the metropolitan area over the next decade? We would love to be able to look into our crystal ball and tell you exactly what jobs have the most promising future, but it's not that easy.

Prospects look good for a more stable job market, as the Dallas/Fort Worth economy winds itself out of the recession of the late 1980s and the rash of military cutbacks and closings. Metroplex communities are looking for new ways to change from industries relying on older manufacturing capabilities to more high technology information services.

Dallas/Fort Worth is still one of the top choices for corporate relocators. A recent article in *Investor's Daily* reported that Dallas is considered the top U.S. business city, with over 2,000 new companies having made Dallas their home. A look on the map will tell you why. By making a quick drive to the centrally located Dallas/Fort Worth International Airport, you can board a plane and be anywhere in the U.S. in a matter of three hours or less.

Companies such as J.C. Penney, GTE Corp., and Fujitsu have relocated their national headquarters to the area, citing other advantages: the area's central time zone, inexpensive office space, moderately priced housing, and favorable tax rates. J.C. Penney Chairman William Howell said, "When you start putting 1,400 pins on a map and six major catalog distribution centers, it makes your mind focus on the reality that the logical place to be with today's modern communication and transportation is somewhere in the center."

According to the Greater Dallas Chamber of Commerce's Dallas Partnership Group, Dallas, the eighth most populous city in the U.S., ranks fourth in the number of industrial and service companies located there. The Dallas/Fort Worth Metroplex is the ninth largest in the country. Thirty-one Fortune 500 companies call the Metroplex home, with twenty-six of them residing in Dallas itself.

Unlike Houston, which was so dependent on the energy industry, Dallas/Fort Worth has a diversified economy that has helped it recover faster from the downturn. Its strengths include a large number of high-tech, telecommunications, and electronics companies as well as its strong trade, retail, transporation, utilities, and medical industries. Civic boosters continue to work hard to attract new businesses and strengthen ones that are already here, such as the convention and tourism business that jumped from No. 3 to No. 2 in the nation, surpassed only by New York City.

North Dallas' high-tech corridor, sometimes referred to as the "Silicon Prairie," represents a major structural change in the city's economy. Despite some setbacks, the defense industry remains strong in North Texas, with many area companies holding major contracts. The biggest government contract holder is Texas Instruments, with General Dynamics, Bell Helicopter, E-Systems, and Rockwell International also receiving substantial government business.

Fort Worth came through the hard times of the 1980s in better shape than Dallas, Austin, or Houston. In fact, in 1989 *Newsweek* selected Fort Worth as one of America's best places to live and work. However, Fort Worth now faces major challenges, with cutbacks at the General Dynamics plant and the closing of Carswell Air Force Base in 1993. But don't count Fort Worth out on these projects. We've already seen an ad that G.D. is looking to hire 200 engineers, and the mayor has formed a task force to examine uses for Carswell. Fort Worth as a city offers stable neighborhoods, a solid working class population, a network of parks with total acreage second only to Chicago, and a place where rush-hour traffic jams are rare.

While there are still many inherent differences between buttoned-down, cosmopolitan Dallas and Fort Worth, which still bills itself as the "Place where the West begins," Fort Worth has many industrial as well as cultural attractions, with three of Texas' top art museums, a ballet company, and a symphony. The Fort Worth area receives more Defense Department contracts than any area of the country except St. Louis and Los Angeles. Fort Worth is home to General Dynamics,

American Airlines, and Alcon Laboratories. It's a diversified blend of aerospace, high-tech research and development, corporate management, manufacturing, and commercial activities.

The Fort Worth metropolitan area is ranked tenth among cities in manufacturing job growth. It has drawn such major businesses as Burlington-Northern, Motorola, and the U.S. currency plant. Future growth is expected to be buoyed by the Alliance Airport located in North Fort Worth, the nation's first industrial airport, which is expected to generate 5,000 jobs in the next couple of decades. Nearby Waxahachie, located to the south, will benefit Tarrant and Dallas counties with its Superconducting Supercollidor.

Many of the area's suburban cities have become more than bedroom communities. They've become employment centers for many major companies. Arlington led the way in the 1950s by attracting General Motors. The drive to broaden the business base in suburban cities continued on a grand scale with Las Colinas, a mini-downtown built near D/FW Airport, which is home to Kimberly-Clark, Exxon Corp., GTE Corp., and the Dallas Communications Complex.

The Metroport cities of Haslet, Roanoke, Keller, Southwest-Westlake, Grapevine, and Colleyville have become attractive places for major companies. IBM moved 2,000 employees from Las Colinas to a 900-acre office and retail park in Westlake/Southlake. Northeast Tarrant County is considered an economic hot spot because of the industrial development and accompanying boom in homebuilding.

The Mid-Cities' population is expected to increase to 1.1 million in 2010 from 821,150 in 1988, according to the North Central Texas Council of Governments. And the labor force will jump more than 80 percent to 622,135 from 341,717. The biggest increases will be in service, construction, government, and education, with a slight decline in retail, manufacturing, wholesale, and transportation.

The Dallas/Fort Worth job market will continue to see white-collar jobs outpace openings in blue-collar positions. There will be an increasing demand for skilled professionals and technical workers in high-tech industries, health care, and support services. The service sector will continue to grow, especially small companies with fewer than 20 people.

Workers can rest easy, knowing that the unemployment rate is expected to drop to 6 percent in the early 1990s. That's a welcome relief from the high of 9 percent and more in some areas during the late '80s, when consolidations, mergers, and company shutdowns produced major layoffs. The boom that peaked in the mid-1980s was unsustainable. The area paid the price for it later when dealing with an overbuilt real esate market and a rash of savings and loan and bank failures.

Growth will be slower than in the past, as indicated by the overall weakness in the banking, construction, and real estate industries. While Nic Santangelo, regional analyst for the Bureau of Labor Statistics Dallas office, is optimistic about overall prospects, he says the halcyon days of the Sun Belt are a thing of the past.

Nevertheless, we hope to provide you with the resources you need to find the job you want. Good luck—and happy hunting.

Need Help Finding Your Way Around the Dallas/Fort Worth Area?

Keep in mind that most Dallas/Fort Worth residents depend on their cars to get around the 1,748-square-mile metropolitan area. And there's a good reason why. Public transportation is available and has improved, but in some areas, especially the suburbs, service is slow and limited.

If you plan to be in the area for several days, your best bet is to rent a car. Automobile rental companies are available in and around the Dallas/Fort Worth International Airport and Love Field.

Dallas has beefed up its DART bus service in recent years. If you're downtown, however, don't think you're seeing things if a blue bus painted to look like a bunny pulls up. In fact, you might also see a red kangaroo bus or a green frog bus. It's one of the **Hop-A-Buses** that makes frequent runs around major hotels and businesses. Call (214) 979-1111 to find out bus routes and when and where the bus is scheduled to run. The schedule varies during weekdays and on weekends.

Depending on the route, **bus service in the Dallas area** is available from 5:45 a.m. to midnight Monday through Sunday, although the buses run less frequently on Sunday. You'll have a much easier time catching a bus during peak weekday business hours than on weekends or in the evening. And be sure to allow plenty of time to get from one destination to another. If you live in a suburban area not served by a bus route, you can call 742-2688 24 hours in advance and a van will pick you up and take you to your destination or to a bus stop. The charge is $1.75/way.

For **Fort Worth-area bus service,** call The T, (817) 871-6200, which operates from 5:20 a.m. to 9:15 p.m. Monday through Saturday and from 8:00 a.m. to 6:00 p.m. Sunday. An airport shuttle service is provided. Pickups are made at major downtown hotels, and a park-and-ride service, Airporter is located at 1000 Weatherford St.

Other **airport shuttle** services include the Super Shuttle, which provides door-to-door service: call (817) 329-2000.

Major **taxi companies** include Taxi Dallas (214) 631-8588, State Taxicab Co. (214) 371-0777, Republic Taxi (214) 631-5544, Richardson Cab Company (214) 235-3500, American Cab Co. (817) 332-1919, and Yellow Checker Cab (817) 534-5555.

Chambers of Commerce

Most major chambers of commerce have published material that is especially helpful to newcomers or anyone who wants to be better informed about the Dallas/Fort Worth area. These brochures and maps are available free or for a nominal charge and provide much of what you want to know about area businesses, city services, transportation, public schools, utilities, and entertainment.

If you have a question that is not answered in one of the publications, ask one of the Chamber's representatives. The two largest chambers in the area are:

Greater Dallas Chamber
1201 Elm St., Suite 2000
Dallas, TX 75270
(214) 746-6700 or 746-6600
For an orientation to Dallas, check out the newcomer's packet. It includes a Dallas Housing/New Resident Guide, a Dallas street map, Greater Dallas Business Guide, and other materials for a $5 fee that covers postage and handling. The Chamber also helps entrepreneurs with a source book called *How to Start a Business in the City of Dallas*. This book costs $7, including postage and handling. Ask the Chamber for its list of other resource materials that can be picked up at the main office downtown or mailed. Booklets are available on everything from the top 100 companies to foreign-owned companies in the Dallas/Fort Worth area.

Fort Worth Chamber of Commerce
777 Taylor St., Suite 900
Fort Worth, TX 76102
(817) 336-2491
Ask for the 'free newcomer's packet, which includes a booklet and map to help you find out more about Fort Worth. You can pick up this information at the downtown office or request that it be mailed to you free of charge. If you want information about starting a business or have questions about existing companies, check with the Economic Development Department. The Chamber's information department publishes many helpful booklets and guides, including *Major Employers in Fort Worth and Tarrant County*, and informative material on major manufacturers, area clubs, organizations, and associations.

Chambers of Commerce for Area Cities
Addison Chamber of Commerce: (214) 416-6600
Allen Chamber of Commerce: (214) 727-5585
Arlington Chamber of Commerce: (817) 275-2613
Balch Springs Chamber of Commerce: (214) 557-0988
Benbrook Area Chamber of Commerce: (817) 249-4451
Burleson Area Chamber of Commerce: (817) 295-6121
Carrolton Chamber of Commerce: (214) 416-6000
Cedar Hill Chamber of Commerce: (214) 291-7817
Colleyville Area Chamber of Commerce: (817) 488-7148
The Colony Chamber of Commerce: (214) 625-4916
Coppell Chamber of Commerce: (214) 416-6600
Crowley Chamber of Commerce: (817) 297-4211
Dallas Black Chamber of Commerce: (214) 421-5200.
Dallas Hispanic Chamber of Commerce: (214) 637-2420
Denton Visitors Bureau: (817) 430-8139 (toll free)
DeSoto Chamber of Commerce: (214) 224-3565
Duncanville Chamber of Commerce: (214) 298-6128
East Dallas Chamber of Commerce: (214) 321-6446
Everman Chamber of Commerce: (817) 293-3957
Farmer's Branch Chamber of Commerce: (214) 416-6600
Forest Hill Chamber of Commerce: (817) 535-7057
Fort Worth Hispanic Chamber of Commerce: (817) 625-5411
    (Minority Procurement Program: (817) 625-4331)
Fort Worth Jaycees: (817) 336-0696
Fort Worth Metro. Black Chamber of Commerce: (817) 531-8510
French American Chamber of Commerce: (214) 821-7475
Garland Chamber of Commerce: (214) 272-7551
Grand Prairie Chamber of Commerce: (214) 264-1558
Grapevine Chamber of Commerce: Metro (817) 481-1522
Hurst-Euless-Bedford Chamber of Commerce: (817) 283-1521 (metro:
    (817) 267-5111)
Hutchins Chamber of Commerce: (214) 225-8850
Irving Chamber of Commerce: (214) 252-8484
Keller Chamber of Commerce: (817) 431-2169
Kennedale Chamber of Commerce: (817) 483-6794
Lakewood Chamber of Commerce: (214) 827-8921
Lake Worth Area Chamber of Commerce: (817) 237-0060
Lancaster Chamber of Commerce: (214) 227-2579
Mansfield Chamber of Commerce: (817) 473-0507
Mesquite Chamber of Commerce: (214) 285-0211
Metrocrest Chamber of Commerce: (214) 416-6600
North Dallas Chamber of Commerce: (214) 368-6485
Northeast Tarrant County Chamber of Commerce: (817) 281-9376
Northwest Dallas County Chamber of Commerce: (214) 416-6600
Oak Cliff Chamber of Commerce: (214) 943-4567
Plano Chamber of Commerce: (214) 424-7547
Red Oak Chamber of Commerce: (214) 617-0906
Richardson Chamber of Commerce: (214) 234-4141
Roanoke Chamber of Commerce: (817) 491-1222
Rockwall Chamber of Commerce: (214) 771-5733
Saginaw Chamber of Commerce: (817) 232-0500

Seagoville Chamber of Commerce: (214) 287-5184
Southeast Dallas Chamber of Commerce: (214) 398-9590
Southlake Chamber of Commerce: Metro (817) 481-8200
Southwest Wise Co. Chamber of Commerce: (817) 636-2560
White Settlement Chamber of Commerce: (817) 246-1121

What If Your Company Transfers You

Imagine how lost and confused most people feel when their company first transfers them to the Dallas/Fort Worth area. They take a look at the two major cities and dozens of suburbs and wonder: Where's the best place to live? Where should I enroll my kids in school? And what about job prospects for my spouse?

The Relocation Center takes the guesswork out of getting settled through services offered by the service started by Larry Powers. Newcomers who have been transferred by their company are eligible to make an appointment to visit the Center, located in The Central Tower at Williams Square, 5215 N. O'Connor Blvd., Suite 1750, Irving, Texas.

The independent relocation service is primarily used by companies that seek help in transferring employees or settling new hires. Counselors discuss individual needs and direct people to area services and resources. For example, when the Kimberly-Clark Corporation moved its world headquarters from Neenah, Wisconsin, to Las Colinas, The Relocation Center coordinated weekend group orientation trips and met with individual families to assist with housing and "human needs."

The Center also assists spouses of transferred employees who are beginning a job search. They can browse through employment guides and watch a videotape produced by Karli and Associates on how to conduct a successful job hunt. For individual career counseling, The Relocation Center refers people to career counselors and consultants in the Dallas/Fort Worth area.

The Center provides a free education guide that lists basic information about area school districts, such as the tax rate, student/teacher ratio, talented and gifted program, special education services, and teacher pay scale. The Center also provides information about the National Child Care Association Services that provides referrals to day-care centers and offers suggestions on how to evaluate them.

Newcomers take a tour around The Relocation Center to see real estate company displays of available housing and apartments. They can also drop by a large magazine rack to pick up free publications and newcomers' guides. A residential leasing division provides information on short-term and long-term leasing. Another service assists in selecting a Realtor.

As newcomers leave the Center, Powers says he often hears a common remark: "Why didn't I come here first? I sure could have saved a lot of wasted time." To make an appointment for the free service, call (214) 869-3131.

Establishing an Objective: How To Discover What You Want to Do

One of the most common mistakes job seekers make is not establishing an *objective* before beginning the job search. Practically everyone wants a job that provides personal satisfaction, growth, good salary and benefits, prestige, and a desirable location. But unless you have a more specific idea of the kind of work you want, you probably won't find it. You wouldn't take off on your big annual vacation without a clear destination in mind. Well, you'll be spending a lot more time on the job than at the beach. As

David Campbell puts it, "If you don't know where you're headed, you'll probably wind up somewhere else."

Many of our readers already have a clear objective in mind. You may want a job as a systems analyst, paralegal, sales manager, or any of a thousand other occupations. (*The Dictionary of Occupational Titles*, available at your public library, lists 40,000 jobs!) If you know what you're looking for, you're to be commended because *establishing an objective is a necessary first step in any successful job search.*

But even if you have an objective, you can benefit from a thorough self-appraisal. What follows is a list of highly personal questions designed to provide you with insights you may never have considered and to help you answer the Big Question, "What do I want to do?"

To get the most from this exercise, you must write out your answers. Writing out your responses to these questions forces you to consider carefully the kind of person you are and what values and priorities you hold. You can always change your priorities later, but by putting them down on paper, you have a great beginning. Give yourself the benefit of responding to these questions over several days or a week-long time period. By allowing yourself time to complete the exercise, you won't feel rushed and will give your career and job search the attention it deserves. By the way, by carefully completing this exercise, you will find that you've made a great start on your resume!—a subject we'll discuss in more detail in the next chapter.

When you've completed the exercise, consider sharing your responses with a trusted friend, loved one, or a mentor. Ask these people to listen to your answers and not to criticize your responses. After you've shared your responses, ask them to respond to the questions as *they* see you, and tape record their responses. Although we think we know ourselves, we seldom have the objectivity to see ourselves clearly. By obtaining "friendly feedback," we can begin to evaluate our history and ourselves.

Remember to take your time—maybe just answering one question a day—but do so in an honest and forthright manner. And, of course, there are no right or wrong answers.

Questions About Me

1. What is my personality like?
   - Am I outgoing or more of a loner?
   - How well disciplined am I?
   - Am I quick tempered or easygoing?
   - Am I self-motivated or do I need to be jump-started?
   - How sensitive am I to other people's needs?

2. What kind of problem solver am I?
   Do I tend to take a conventional, practical approach to problems or am I more of an imaginative, experimental type person?
   Am I a leader or a follower?
   Do I feel challenged by problems or do I prefer more routine activities that tend to keep life easy and regular?
3. Do I like working closely with others or do I prefer to work alone?
4. What is my philosophy of life? And how does work enter into my philosophy?
5. How important are other people to me, and what kind of impact do I want to have on them?
6. What are my most important life achievements to date?
7. Where do I want to live and work? (choose a part of the country, or world, and when you've selected an area, identify how far you want to live from your workplace)
8. What role does money play in my value system? What is the minimum amount of money I want to make from work? What is the maximum I'd like to make?
9. Is my career the center of my life or just a part of it? Which should it be?
10. What are my main interests?
11. What do I enjoy most in life?
12. What displeases me most?

Questions About Your Job
1. Beginning with your most recent employment and then working back toward school graduation, describe *in detail* each job you had. Include your title, company, responsibilities, salary, achievements and successes, failures, and reason for leaving. (If you're a recent college graduate and have little or no career related work experience, you may find it helpful to consider your collegiate experience, both curricular and extracurricular, as your work history for questions 1, 2, 3, 8, 9, and 11.)
2. How would you change anything in your job history if you could?
3. In your career thus far, what responsibilities have you enjoyed most? Why?
4. What kind of job do you think would be a perfect match for your talents and interests?
5. What responsibilities do you want to avoid?
6. How hard are you really prepared to work?
7. If you want the top job in your field, are you prepared to pay the price?

8. What have your subordinates thought about you as a boss? As a person?
9. What have your superiors thought about you as an employee? As a person?
10. Can your work make you happier? Should it?
11. If you have been fired from any job, what was the reason?
12. How long do you want to work before retirement?

Your answers to these highly personal questions should help you to see more clearly who you are, what you want, what your gifts are, and what you realistically have to offer. They should also reveal what you *don't* want and what you *can't* do. It's important to evaluate any objective you're considering in light of your answers to these questions. If a prospective employer knew nothing about you except your answers to these questions, would he think your career objective was realistic?

People who are entering the job market for the first time, those who have been working for one company for many years, and those who are considering a career change need more help in determining their objectives. If you're still in college, be sure to take advantage of the free counseling and career planning services that are available on most campuses. Vocational analysis, also known as career planning or life planning, is much too broad a subject to try to cover here. But we can refer you to some excellent books.

CAREER STRATEGY BOOKS

Allen, Jeffrey. *How to Turn an Interview into a Job Offer.* New York: Simon & Schuster, 1988.

Applegath, John. *Working Free: Practical Alternatives to the 9 to 5 Job.* New York: AMACOM, 1984.

Baldwin, Eleanor. *300 Ways to Get a Better Job.* Holbrook, MA: Bob Adams, Inc., 1991.

Bastress, Frances. *Relocating Spouse's Guide to Employment,* 3rd ed. Chevy Chase, MD: Woodley Publications, 1989.

Beatty, Richard H. *The Complete Job Search Book.* New York: John Wiley & Sons, 1988.

Bly, Robert W., and Gary Blake. *Dream Jobs: A Selective Guide to Tomorrow's Top Careers.* New York: John Wiley and Sons, 1983.

Bolles, Richard N. *The Three Boxes of Life and How to Get Out of Them.* Berkeley, CA: Ten Speed Press, 1983.

Bolles, Richard N. *What Color Is Your Parachute?* Berkeley, CA.: Ten Speed Press, 1991. The Bible for job hunters and career changers, this book is revised every year and is widely regarded as the most useful and creative manual available. Try it! We think you'll like it.

Camden, Thomas M. *The Job Hunter's Final Exam.* Chicago: Surrey Books, 1990.

Clawson, James G., et al. *Self Assessment and Career Development.* Englewood Cliffs, NJ: Prentice-Hall, 1985.

Dubin, Judith A., and Keveles, Melonie R. *Fired for Success.* New York: Warner Books, 1990.
Figler, Howard. *The Complete Job-Search Handbook.* New York: H. Holt & Co., 1988.
Jackson, Tom. *Guerrilla Tactics in the Job Market.* New York: Bantam Books, 1981. Filled with unconventional but effective suggestions.
Lee, Patricia. *The Complete Guide to Job Sharing.* New York: Walker, 1983.
Morin, William J., and Colvena, James C. *Parting Company: How to Survive the Loss of a Job and Find Another Successfully.* San Diego, CA: HBJ, 1991.
Noble, John. *The Job Search Handbook.* Boston: Bob Adams, Inc., 1988.
Rushlow, Ed. *Get a Better Job.* Princeton, NJ: Peterson's Guides, 1990.
Scheele, Adele. *Making College Pay Off.* New York: Ballantine, 1983.
Shapiro, Michele. *Your Personal Career Consultant: A Step-by-Step Guide.* Englewood Cliffs, NJ: Prentice-Hall, 1988.
Wood, Orrin G. *Your Hidden Assets—The Key to Getting Executive Jobs.* Homewood, IL: Dow Jones-Irwin, 1984. Written by the co-founder of a job-changing workshop developed for Harvard Business School alumni; an upscale book.

If you're **still in college** or have **recently graduated,** the following books will be of particular interest:

Briggs, James I. *The Berkeley Guide to Employment for New College Graduates.* Berkeley, CA: Ten Speed Press, 1984.
La Fevre, John L. *How You Really Get Hired: The Inside Story from a College Recruiter,* 2nd ed. New York: Prentice Hall, 1989.
Osher, Bill, and Sioux Henley Campbell. *The Blue Chip Graduate: A Four Year College Plan for Career Succcess.* Atlanta: Peachtree Publishers, Ltd., 1987.
Tener, Elizabeth. *Smith College Guide: How to Find and Manage Your First Job.* New York: Pflume, 1991.

For those of you involved in a **mid-life career change,** here are some books that might prove helpful:

Allen, Jeffrey G. *Finding the Right Job at Midlife.* New York: Simon & Schuster, 1985.
Falvey, Jack. *What's Next? Career Strategies After 35.* Charlottesville, VT: Williamson Publishing Co., 1987.
Hecklinger, Fred J., and Bernadette M. Curtin. *Training for Life: A Practical Guide to Career and Life Planning.* Dubuque, IA: Kendall-Hunt, 1984.
Holloway, Diane, and Bishop, Nancy. *Before You Say "I Quit": A Guide to Making Successful Job Transitions.* New York: Collier Books, 1990.
Krannich, Ronald L. *The Educator's Guide to Alternative Jobs and Careers.* Woodbridge, VA: Impact Publications, 1991.
Nyman, Keith D. *Re-Entry: How to Turn Your Military Experience into Civilian Success,* 2nd ed., expanded. Harrisburg, PA: Stockpole Books, 1990.
Wolfer, Karen and Wong, Richard G. *The Outplacement Solution: Getting the Right Job after Mergers, Takeovers, Layoffs, and Other Corporate Chaos.* New York: Wiley, 1988.

For workers who are **nearing retirement age** or have already reached it, here are some books that might be useful:

Harty, Karen Herkstra. *50 and Starting Over: Career Strategies for Success.* N Hollywood, CA: Newcastle Pub. Co., 1991.

Strasser, Stephen, and Sena, John. *Transitions: Successful Strategies from Mid-Career to Retirement*. Hawthorne, NJ: Career Press, 1990.

And for **handicapped** job seekers, this title could prove helpful:

Lewis, Adele, and Edith Marks. *Job Hunting for the Disabled*. Woodbury, NY: Barrons, 1983.

For **women** in the work force, these titles will be of interest:

Catalyst Staff. *What to Do With the Rest of Your Life: The Catalyst Career Guide for Women in the '80s*. New York: Simon & Schuster, 1980.
Koltnow, Emily, and Dumas, Lynne S. *Congratulations! You've Been Fired: Sound Advice for Women Who've Been Terminated, Pink-Slipped, Downsized, or Otherwise Unemployed*. New York: Fawcett Columbine, 1990.
Morrow, Jodie B., and Myrna Lebov. *Not Just a Secretary: Using the Job to Get Ahead*. New York: Wiley Press, 1984.
Nivens, Beatrice. *The Black Woman's Career Guide*. New York: Anchor Books, 1987.
Thompson, Charlotte E. *Single Solutions—An Essential Guide for the Single Career Woman*. Boston: Branden Pub. Co., 1990.
Wyse, Lois. *The Six-Figure Woman (and How to Be One)*. New York: Linden Press, 1984. How to break into top corporate management.

Tips from career counselors for area newcomers

Many of the same job-hunting principles apply no matter if you're looking for a job in Dallas/Fort Worth, Los Angeles, or New York. But to really stand out in the local job market, here are some tips from career counselors. These will be especially helpful as you begin your job marketing campaign, particularly if you're a newcomer:

Taunee Besson, Career Dimensions: "People who come here and want to find work quickly locate the pivotal individuals in their fields. I've known people who have come to Dallas and in an afternoon get the whole place scoped out. Dallas has some well-established networks, and if you can plug into one of the networks, you can piggyback on it and get around to people you need to talk to.

"People who have similar interests enjoy helping each other out. Look up the local branch of a fraternal organization, sorority, or alumni club, or get involved in church. The fastest way to get plugged in is to get together with people of like minds. Those who are good at networking are going to be more successful."

Dr. Helen Harkness, Career Design Associates: "It is essential to project an image of being in charge and having a sense of direction because Dallas sees itself as a positive town. People in the area look for others who share this belief and have an air of confidence and self-assurance."

Dr. Jon Crook, Career Development Specialists: "Spend some time assessing your skills so you know what you can do: solve problems, reorganize to cut costs, create new markets. A candidate really impresses an employer when he or she can name their skills clearly and apply them specifically to the company's situation."

Bill Helton, an Arlington psychologist: "Organize in your mind the career areas which especially appeal to you. Then actively develop your own *network* as you participate in a number of *information interviews*. Don't hesitate to ask for names and referrals, and follow up on all possible leads. The Dallas-Fort Worth Metroplex has many people who will attempt to be helpful in your quest for information."

Robert Boudreaux, Rehabilitation Services Associates: "Motivated persons who want to work need to experience a variety of jobs in order to develop a career. Focusing on what you can do and want to do and marketing one's abilities related to these goals is essential in meeting the job objective." ■

Professional Vocational Analysis

It would be great if there were some psychological test that would confirm without a doubt who you are and precisely what job, career, or field best suits you. Unfortunately, there isn't. Professionals in vocational planning have literally dozens of tests at their disposal designed to assess personality and aptitude for particular careers.

There are basically two approaches to career assessment. The first measures *interests, values, and skills*. A variety of assessment tests evaluate these qualities and provide useful information for the career changer. This kind of assessment helps answer the questions, "What do I like to do?, What do I believe in?, and What have I developed some measure of expertise in?" These are vitally important questions since many people find that if they are doing what they enjoy and what is consistent with their beliefs and experiences, they will do well, excel, and have fun.

The second career assessment method measures *aptitudes*. Aptitudes are natural abilities in which you excel. These assessments may measure abilities ranging from manual dexterity to visual conceptualization (useful for interior design, for example). These types of assessments help answer the question, "What am I naturally good at?"

Remember that while it's important to engage in work that you have natural abilities in, many job skills are learned, developed, and refined in the work setting. It is therefore most important to do work that you enjoy. With the pleasure thus derived, you will find that your skill development increases.

The test most commonly used is probably the Strong-Campbell Interest Inventory (SCII). This multiple-choice test takes about an hour to administer and is scored by machine. The SCII has been around since 1933. The most recent revision, in 1981, made a serious and generally successful attempt to eliminate sex bias, and to introduce a theoretical orientation to career assessment.

The SCII offers information about an individual's interests on three different levels. First, the test provides a general statement about the test-taker's interest patterns. These patterns suggest not only promising occupations but also characteristics of the most compatible work environments and personality traits affecting work.

Second, the test reports how interested a person is in a specific work activity compared with other men and women who also completed the SCII. Finally, the occupational scales compare the test-taker with satisfied workers in some 90 different occupations. If you think you'd enjoy being a librarian, for example, you can compare yourself with other librarians and see how similar your likes and dislikes are. The occupational scales indicate how likely you are to be satisfied with the choice of a particular occupation.

Personality/vocational tests come in a variety of formats. Many are multiple choice; some require you to finish incomplete sentences; others are autobiographical questionnaires. No single test should ever be used as an absolute. Personality tests are important in evaluating your personal style and how well you might enjoy the work environment as well as for generating discussion and for providing data that can be used in making judgments.

In the Dallas/Fort Worth area, vocational guidance and testing are available from a variety of sources. The most comprehensive service is generally provided by private career counselors and career consultants. Their approaches and specialties vary greatly. Some primarily provide testing while others also offer long-term programs that include counseling, resume writing, preparing for the job interview, and developing a job marketing campaign. Fees usually range from $50 to several thousand dollars.

It's best to find a professional who specializes in the type of vocational help you need. You don't want to spend thousands of dollars on long-term psychotherapy when you only need several counseling sessions and tests. On the other hand, if you've had a history of employment problems or are feeling paralyzed in your job search, it is probably well to talk to a career counselor who is also qualified to conduct personal counseling.

The list that follows gives you some idea of what counselors and consultants offer. Telephone these professionals to find out whether their services fit your needs. Although the terms are often used synonymously, there is a difference between a career counselor and consultant. Most professionals can use the title *counselor* or *psychologist* only if they have fulfilled educational and professional requirements determined by the State of Texas in order to become a Licensed Psychologist or a Licensed Professional Counselor.

In Texas, you can provide career services without a license. Professionals who aren't licensed often call themselves career consultants. This field attracts people from a wide variety of backgrounds, education, and levels of competency. That's why it's important to talk to people who have used the service you are considering, and check with the Better Business Bureau to make sure you are getting the best possible help.

Because career counseling and consulting firms are private, for-profit businesses with high overhead costs, they usually charge more for testing than local community colleges or social service agencies. A fuller discussion of services offered by career consultants is provided in Chapter 6. Also in Chapter 6 is a list of social service agencies, some of which offer vocational testing.

Tips for women

"Looking for a job can be frustrating and can destroy self-esteem. People should realize there is a lot more out there than they thought," said Ann Midkiff, employment services director of **The Women's Center of Tarrant County.**

The Women's Center offers numerous programs to help people identify new employment opportunities. The Center's Job Search Club is a good place to begin because it's designed to help people improve job-search skills to find employment in a fairly short time. Programs start every two weeks. Anyone participating in the program can use a job bank, containing an average of over 3,000 current job openings each month.

Extra help is provided through the Center's Mentors Network, offering women an opportunity to receive advice from people in their field. Mentors are available from a variety of professions, ranging from fast-food managers, attorneys, and construction workers to hairdressers.

Other programs are designed to meet a variety of needs. Employment counseling may be sought by some who want special help, and others will want to check on self-sufficiency assistance for low-income parents.

"We offer services to help women get control over their lives and improve the quality of their lives," Midkiff said.

The employment services are provided free of charge and are available to women as well as men. About 15 percent of the participants are men. The Center is located at 1723 Hemphill St., Fort Worth, TX 76110, (817) 927-4050.

Here are five additional resource centers mainly oriented toward assisting women in job searches and counseling.

Adult Resource Center
Richland College

Crockett Hall, First Floor
12800 Abrams Rd.
Dallas, TX 75243
(214) 238-6034
Special personal and employment
counseling provided free of charge
to low-income single parents.
Referrals are made to special
courses and programs at the
community college.

Explore
Dallas County Phone: (214) 343-
0165
Tarrant County Phone: (817) 861-
4454
All-volunteer, non-profit
organization that offers eight-
week seminars for women who
want to boost their self-esteem,
grow professionally, and find
ways to accomplish their goals.

**Woman's Center in
Richardson**
515 Custer Rd.
Richardson, TX 75080
(214) 238-9516
Variety of free programs, sessions
on finding potential, considering
lifework planning, and preparing
for the job hunt. Three-part
program includes doing a
vocational self-assessment,
teaching job-search skills, and
exploring crossroads. Women-in-
Transition program helps women
who lose a spouse through death,
divorce, or separation reenter the
job market. Befrienders program
offers immediate job-search
assistance. Resource center and
informal network helps women
locate employment. When
requested in advance, child care is
provided for program participants.

Women's Center of Dallas
3505 Turtle Creek Blvd.
Dallas, TX 75219
(214) 521-9606
Mainly an advocacy program that sponsors special programs throughout the year on employment-related topics.

YWCA Women's Resource Center
4621 Ross Ave.
Dallas, TX 75204
(214) 821-9595
Employment services available at the YWCA's headquarters at 4621 Ross Ave. and at six branches in Dallas County. Services include individual career counseling, testing, job banks, support groups, quarterly YWCA Breakfasts, and bimonthly lunches with networking opportunities and guest speakers. The YWCA's Explore course is offered in the spring and fall. The self-discovery program includes eight sessions at several Dallas County locations.■

CAREER COUNSELORS AND CONSULTANTS

AIMS
12160 Abrams Rd., Suite 314, Lock Box 19
Dallas, TX 75243
(214) 234-8378
Non-profit research organization offering battery of tests to determine what career will be most satisfying according to aptitude. Works with all adults, college and high school students to help determine long-term career and educational goals. Fee: $525 for three half-day sessions that include counseling and evaluation.

Dr. Douglas Bellamy, Ed.D., Psychologist
12900 Preston Rd., 717 North Dallas Bank Tower
Dallas, TX 75230
(214) 404-8888
Individualized program that includes psychological testing to determine which careers are most likely to fit one's values, interests, personality characteristics, and aptitudes. Career alternatives explored; job-search strategies developed; and assistance and

guidance in implementation, including resume writing during
counseling sessions. Usually one to six sessions at $80 per hour.

Dr. Tim Branaman
670 W. Arapaho Rd., Suite 3
Richardson, TX 75080
(214) 669-1266
Career counseling, testing, and evaluation. Assistance provided for
many different needs, including graduating college students,
management and sales professionals, and women in transition.
Second office located at 309 Westpark Way, Euless, TX 76040.
Fee: Varies.

Career Action Associates
12655 N. Central Expwy., Suite 512
Dallas, TX 75243
Metro (214) 269-5106
Fort Worth (817) 763-9528
Contact: Rebecca Hayes, Licensed Professional Counselor
Provides full-service career assistance, including assessment, resume
writing, developing job-hunting strategies, interviewing, and
networking. Career/life planning, vocational assessment, and
vocational rehabilitation for disabled workers also available. Special
help provided for college students and high school students entering
the job market. Also conducts career/life-planning seminars. Fee: $80
an hour.

Career Development Specialists/Iatreia Institute
1152 Country Club Lane
Fort Worth, TX 76112
(817) 654-9600
Contact: Richard Citrin, Ph.D., or Jon Crook, Ph.D.
Counselors help clients develop specific career options through
testing, skills assessment, and individual counseling. Also provides
assistance in developing marketing plan for the job hunt and in
making contacts, resume writing, interview rehearsal, and salary
negotiations. Individualized career planning package, career
workshops, and seminars available. Fee: Varies.

Career Design Associates
2818 Country Club Rd.
Garland, TX 75043
(214) 278-4701
Contact: Dr. Helen Harkness
Comprehensive program for career planning and resources for
focusing, restructuring, or changing careers. Two programs are
available: Career Change—one-year retainer required for program
designed to include personal and extensive video taping, testing,
career information/resources, and complete job-hunting techniques;
Career Reappraisal—three-to-four-month program focusing on career
assessment and information. Prices vary according to need but range

from $1,500 to $4,900 with monthly pay-out available. First discussion is free. Client references provided.

Career Dimensions
6330 LBJ Frwy., Suite 136
Dallas, TX 75240
(214) 239-1399
Contact: Taunee Besson
Full-service career and life-planning program that includes a self-directed job search with emphasis on self-assessment, resume writing, job interviewing, researching job market, networking, salary negotiation. Offers special help to newcomers, career changers, and international transfers. Spouse network. Publishes free "Dimensions Associates" newsletter. Fee: $50 for exploratory session, $100 per hour for counseling, and $600 for 20-hour small-group program.

Career Focus Associates
1700 Coit Rd., Suite 220
Plano, TX 75075
(214) 596-1233
Contact: Jackie Statman
Comprehensive services that include 3-6-week programs for career self-assessment. Writing of resumes, cover letters, and thank-you notes. Skill training for information and job interviews, job-finding strategies, and negotiating salary offers. Fee: Varies.

Career Management Resources
5215 N. O'Connor Blvd., Suite 200
Irving, TX 75039
(214) 556-0786
Contact: Mary Holdcroft, Licensed Professional Counselor
Comprehensive career counseling service, including testing, skill assessment, resume preparation, and interviewing techniques. Identification of potential employers, networking, and introductions provided. Specialize in spouse relocation assistance, outplacement, individual career management, career/life planning, and facilitating successful career changes. Secretarial support provided, including resumes and job-search correspondence. Fee: Varies.

C.L. Carter, Jr. & Associates
811 S. Central Expwy., Suite 434
Richardson, TX 75080
(214) 234-3296
Career Evaluation and Assessment Program, resulting in 12-15 page analysis and report, including career counseling. Fee for total program is $750. Hourly fee for career counseling: $85.

Center for Counseling & Developmental Services
7525 John C. White Rd.
Fort Worth, TX 76112
Metro (817) 429-5050
Contact: Richard Cookerly, Ph.D.

Combines aptitude with vocational testing. Surveys area employment opportunities. Fee: Average cost is $150 and can vary according to needs.

Dr. Carrell Chadwell
3500 Oak Lawn, Suite 400
Dallas, TX 75219
(214) 526-3505
Contact: Carrell Chadwell, Ph.D.
Individualized career evaluation, testing, and counseling. Generally 2 to 6 sessions. Fee: Varies.

Corporate Dynamics
5215 N. O'Connor Blvd.
The Towers at Williams Square
Irving, TX 75039
(214) 869-2470
Contact: Linda Davidson or Richard Poth
In-depth personal assessment and career counseling for the professionl engaged in reevaluation of career and life direction. Individualized programs include assessment, counseling, resume writing, videotaping mock job interviews, researching the job market, and support throughout the job campaign. Fee: Varies.

Creative Career Counseling
703 Shadywood Lane
Richardson, TX 75080
(214) 235-4689
Contact: Joan Youngblood , certified career counselor
Customized counseling process designed for career changers, work-reality-shocked graduates, reentry homemakers, people who have lost a job, and others who are recareering. The program enables clients to define occupational direction, create a quantified, accomplishment resume, and connect with career resources: Fee: Sliding scale based on income.

Carol Duncan Enterprises
North Dallas Bank Tower
12900 Preston Rd., Suite 500
Dallas, TX 75230
(214) 385-1130
Contact: Carol Duncan, a licensed career counselor
Custom-designed program to fit individual needs. Included with career counseling is lifestyle planning, individual assessment through self-identity, job opportunities, resume writing, interview skills, salary negotiations, and follow-up support. Specialties include assisting people with a major career change, transitional counseling, helping women return to the workforce, and assisting graduating college students to develop strategies for their career and lifestyle. Fee: $60 per hour.

William Helton and Associates
Fielder Professional Park
721 N. Fielder Rd., Suite C
Arlington, TX 76012
(817) 460-5831
Contact: William M. Helton, Ph.D.
Offers career and life planning counseling, which emphasize assisting people in identifying their "essence"—those activities which naturally create a sense of satisfaction. A series of personal interviews is intertwined with an individualized battery of tests on personality, values, interests, and abilities to reveal future career and leisure options that lead to a balanced life.

Hour Savers Career Services
(214) 349-2992
Contact: Eleanor Baldwin
Package deal includes resume, improving job-hunting skills, and interviewing techniques. Also offers career workshops, outplacements, career and employment consultations, corporate outplacements, and public speaking on employment issues. Fee: $99-$259.

Texas Tip

Eleanor Baldwin recently published *300 New Ways to Get a Better Job*. It addresses what has changed in the job market and what you can do about it. Baldwin emphasizes the "womb to the tomb job is long gone." Contemporary job hunting moves from "project to project," and she encourages action on the individual's part. "When you see the ceiling cracking, you don't stand around waiting for the beams to fall." A consultant to the Texas Employment Commission, Baldwin often lectures to what she terms "stress professionals," suggesting they see "job hunting as theater."■

Johnson O'Connor Research Foundation
4950 N. O'Connor Blvd., Suite 250
Irving, TX 75062
(214) 541-0650
Metro (214) 791-0330
Contacts: Wendy Finan, Bill Stroud, or Bill Claunch
National non-profit educational organization that tests aptitude during three sessions. Interpretation of results helps clients make vocational and educational decisions. Fee: $450, which includes an additional counseling session within the first year after initial testing.

Professional Counseling Services
1221 Abrams Rd., Suite 227
Dallas, TX 75081
(214) 699-0774
Contact: Peggy Donohue
Offers vocational tests and helps clients prepare for job hunt by reviewing resume and preparing for job interview through role-playing. Marketing and job search strategies; job opportunities are explored. Fee: Negotiable.

Rehabilitation Services Associates
Dallas/Fort Worth Regional Office
3505 Turtle Creek Blvd., Suite 312
Dallas, TX 75219-9800
(214) 638-2586 or Metro (817) 261-3098
Contact: Robert Boudreaux, Carol Bennett, or Susan Laszynski
Assists the general public and persons with medical restrictions by providing counseling, vocational assessment, labor market information, job seeking skills, and job placement. Comprehensive program includes analyzing work history, helping clients in job seeking skills, resume writing, labor market surveys to identify openings in entry-level positions. Fee: $85 an hour.

Richland College Career and Life Planning Center
12800 Abrams Rd.
Dallas, TX 75243-2199
(214) 238-6020
Contact: Beverly G. Scott, CPC
Offers a Career Center designed for the adult professional in the business community who is dealing with issues surrounding career planning and changes. Serves all adults within the Dallas business community.

Margaret Thompson
3813 Crestwood Ter.
Fort Worth, TX 76107
(817) 626-7023
Contact: Margaret Thompson, Licensed Professional Counselor
Vocational testing and career assessments are primary services. Most appointments are scheduled on Saturday. Fee: Averages $300 for five hours of tests, report, and follow-up conference.

Dr. Jerry Weiss
7540 LBJ Frwy., Suite 510
Dallas, TX 75251
(214) 458-8111
Offers a scientifically developed program that uses particular interests, aptitudes, skills, and personality to help a person choose a career path that fits them. The two-step program begins with an assessment and then offers information about choosing the right career and pursuing it through job-hunting techniques, resume hints, and interviewing techniques. Fee: Varies.

**Who's good?
Who's not?**

A listing in this book does not constitute an endorsement of any consulting firm, search firm, or employment agency. Before embarking on a lengthy or expensive series of tests, try to get the opinion of one or more people who have already used the service you're considering.

In Texas, employment agencies and career consultants who charge individuals a fee for finding jobs must be licensed by the Texas Department of Labor. No license is required if the employer pays the cost. If you want to find out if a firm has a license, call the State of Texas, Department of Licensing and Regulation, Licensing Division, (817) 261-3800 or 1-800-252-8026.

Before hiring professional services, check with the Better Business Bureau. It's also a good idea to check with the City of Dallas Action Center or State Attorney General's office to find out if any complaints have been filed there. You can call, write, or drop by those offices for information.

Better Business Bureau of Metropolitan Dallas
2001 Bryan Tower, Suite 850
Dallas, TX 75201
(214) 220-2000

Better Business Bureau of Tarrant County
807 Sinclair Building
Fort Worth, TX 76102
(817) 332-7585

Action Center
City of Dallas
1500 Marilla St. C2/1N
Dallas, TX 75201
(214) 744-3600

State Attorney General
714 Jackson, Suite 700

Dallas, TX 75202
Toll free (214) 263-2685■

What To Expect from a Career Counselor

What kind of help can you expect from a career counselor that you can't find on your own?

The first thing you'd probably notice is that a counselor really listens to you. They are trained to understand, not to judge. You may find yourself being more candid with a counselor after 30 minutes than you would be with a friend you've know for 30 years. The result of this type of interaction is that you're likely to end up knowing yourself better.

While counselors are trained to understand and support you, they are not there simply to stroke your ego. Your mother or best friend might agree with your plan to change from sales to engineering. A counselor might point out that you've never managed to pass a course in mathematics.

A counselor will understand that career planning is an ongoing lifelong process that manifests itself differently in the various stages of human development that each of us must negotiate. It is a very different thing to hunt for a job at 21, 41, and 61. Tests aren't the whole answer, but they can be a part of the answer. Counselors know how to interpret tests.

Career counselors aren't locked in to outmoded job-search strategies. They can give you ideas on how to make more contacts, write a better resume, and interview with impact. They can spot where your approach needs beefing up more readily than a non-professional.

For most people, a job search is a demanding, if not downright stressful time. A counselor can provide both emotional support and expert advice. Career counselors and consultants provide many different types of services. When you're looking for professional help, make sure you find someone who can best meet your needs.

Career counselor Mary Holdcroft, who heads up Career Management Resources in Irving, suggests that individuals ask these questions when checking out services:

1. What type of individuals does the counselor work with most often?
2. What services are provided?
3. Does the counselor help focus on career selections, including research sources?
4. Does the counselor provide development and implementation of a job-search plan?
5. For newcomers to the area, how quickly can the plan be implemented?

Colleges Offering Vocational Testing and Guidance

Students don't often realize how much help is available through college and university career and placement centers. At several area community colleges, non-students can benefit as well. Several of the Dallas County Community College District campuses have extended services to assist everyone, whether or not they are enrolled. The extent of assistance varies from campus to campus.

Many of the colleges and universities offer non-credit and credit courses as well as special lectures and seminars to help individuals prepare for the job hunt and explore options in the work world. In recent years, schools also have offered more practical courses that are designed to help individuals acquire job skills or brush up on ones they already have.

Current or prospective students can also see what's available at career centers to help them plan what to do after graduation. By getting on track early, students can avoid the frustration of taking the wrong courses. After graduation, many colleges and universities continue to work with alumni through the placement office and in career centers.

Check with each school to find out what's available and who is eligible for assistance. Here's a list of area colleges offering vocational help and a description of basic services:

COLLEGES WITH VOCATIONAL PROGRAMS

Brookhaven College
3939 Valley View Lane
Farmers Branch, TX 75244
(214) 620-4830
Free counseling and testing for students enrolled in at least one credit course. Computer job bank located in the placement office. Credit and non-credit courses, seminars, and workshops assist individuals in many phases of career exploration. Adult center provides career symposiums, support programs, and resources for individuals, including single parents, displaced homemakers, and women returning to work. Call (214) 620-4849 for subsidized child-care information.

Cedar Valley College
3030 N. Dallas Ave.
Lancaster, TX 75134
(214) 372-8280
Free counseling, on academic level. Testing fees apply to non-students. Employment service for students and alumni only.

Computerized job listings. Human development credit courses assist individuals making career decisions.

Eastfield College
3737 Motley Dr.
Mesquite, TX 75150
(214) 324-7039
Career Planning and Placement Center offers free career counseling and testing for students and former students of the Dallas County Community College District. Career counseling and testing available for non-students for $40 through the Continuing Education Office (People Place/Adult Resource Center, (214) 324-7113). District computer job bank and employment listings available to students and former students. Career and job fair scheduled every April, along with employment seminars and other special programs.

El Centro College
Main and Lamar Sts.
Dallas, TX 75202
(214) 746-2415
Free career testing and counseling for students. Non-students pay fees for tests ranging from $5 to $25. Employment openings listed in computer job bank and on the career center bulletin board. Numerous references and books available in the Career Resource Center. Human development courses offered on career planning and exploration.

Mountain View College
4849 W. Illinois Ave.
Dallas, TX 75211
(214) 333-8606
Free testing for currently enrolled students and prospective students; $40 for non-students. Counseling and the Career Center's job bank are free and available to students and alumni.

North Lake College
5001 N. MacArthur Blvd.
Irving, TX 75062
(214) 659-5218
Free counseling for currently enrolled students and non-students at Career Planning and Placement Center. Testing available through a human development course. Counseling center has resource libarary and computer services for students and non-students. Job Placement Center assists alumni and students enrolled in credit and non-credit courses with job placement through a computerized job bank. Call Center for Returning Adults at (214) 659-5373 about brown-bag luncheons that are open to the public.

Richland College
12800 Abrams Rd.
Dallas, TX 75243
(214) 238-6106

Free career counseling and testing for currently enrolled students. The Career Resource Library has hundreds of resources on career planning, occupational research, and employment skill development. It also houses the student job placement computerized system and other computer-aided systems. The Career Resource Library is available free of charge to currently enrolled and former Richland College students. An educational and career-planning course is available through the Continuing Education Office. Special help provided in the Adult Resource Center to low-income single parents.

Southern Methodist University
P.O. Box 256
Dallas, TX 75275
(214) 692-2266
Services offered free to students and to alumni during two years after graduation. Other alumni pay $50 charge for six-month counseling and testing service. Computerized self-assessment program prepares individuals for exploring career options. Career Center offers individual and group counseling and information about job openings.

Tarrant County Junior College-Northeast Campus
828 Harwood Rd.
Hurst, TX 76053
(817) 656-6661
Free career counseling, testing, and placement for currently enrolled students and former students. $10 fee for applying for admission to service. SIGI and CASSI computer programs assist in making vocational choices. Non-students assisted through community college courses and spring job fair.

Tarrant County Junior College-Northwest Campus
4801 Marine Creek Pkwy.
Fort Worth, TX 76179
(817) 232-7788
Counseling and Career Placement Center offers free standard vocational tests and counseling for students and alumni. Also assists in helping locate part-time, seasonal, and full-time work. Special services provided for the handicapped. Students meet with professionals in their field through the Rotary Club Career Counseling Program.

Tarrant County Junior College-South Campus
5301 Campus Dr.
Fort Worth, TX 76119
(817) 531-4551
Comprehensive Career Planning and Placement Center. Some career and job search resources available to public. Career counseling for current, former, and prospective students. Special course in career planning for women in transition.

Texas Christian University
Career Planning and Placement Center
2800 S. University Dr., 220 Student Center

Fort Worth, TX 76129
(817) 921-7860
The Career Planning and Placement Center offers a full range of free
testing, counseling, and placement services for students and alumni.
Special programs include videotaping mock job interviews, career fairs
and summer job fairs, as well as more than 40 workshops on all
aspects of employment. Assistance in self-assessment and decision-
making provided by a computerized program. Job listings for students
and alumni are published weekly in *The Career Connection* bulletin.
Subscribers pay a minimal fee for postage.

Texas Wesleyan University

1201 Wesleyan St.
Fort Worth, TX 76105
Metro (817) 429-7104 or (817) 531-4432
Counseling and Testing Center provides free testing for currently
enrolled students; alumni pay a fee for testing. Special help offered
to those who are undecided about a major, going through a career
change, or want to pursue additional graduate studies. Placement
office regularly updates job listings on bulletin board, sponsors job
fairs, and sets up interviews with employers for graduating seniors.

The University of Texas at Arlington

800 S. Cooper St.
216 Davis Hall
Arlington, TX 76019-0156
(817) 273-3671
The Office of Counseling and Career Development assists current
UTA students and graduates with all phases of career exploration and
development. Seminars cover resume writing, interviewing skills, and
the job-search process. On-campus interviewing is conducted twice
each year—spring and fall—for full-time professional positions. A
weekly newsletter describing current, full-time job openings in the
metroplex is available to new graduates and alumni registered for this
service. A nominal fee is charged for use of these services. Student
Employment Services assists currently enrolled students and their
spouses with part-time, temporary, summer, internship, and co-op
positions. UTA holds a campus-wide career fair each spring and
participates in the Texas MBA Consortium, a "Hire-in" for MBA
students from 21 Texas universities.

University of Texas at Dallas

2601 Floyd Rd.
Richardson, TX 75080
(214) 690-2943
Office of Career Planning and Placement offers career counseling,
testing, and placement assistance for students and alumni. Nominal
fees charged for registration and vocational tests. Computerized
guidance information available. Special services include career
development library, career information fairs, job search seminars,
and information about employers. Students and alumni are
encouraged to bring

resumes and attend job fairs during fall and spring semesters. Job fairs are available to the public.

Thinking of starting your own small business?

Many basic questions about starting your own small company can be answered by the U.S. Small Business Administration. Ask for the *Directory of Business Development Publications* to find out for a nominal fee what information is offered by the SBA. Topics include everything from borrowing, recordkeeping, and marketing to managing employees.

Although simple questions can be answered by telephone, you'll learn more by dropping by one of the main offices to meet with staff members or volunteers from SCORE (Service Corps of Retired Executives). You will be matched up with a retired professional in your field who can share information that will help you get started. Special help is offered to veterans and women.

At area community colleges, SBA officials conduct seminars on how to start a business and how to manage a business. The Small Business Institute offers in-depth management assistance from senior and graduate-level business students.

The chambers of commerce in Arlington, Plano, Garland, and Richardson provide some SBA information. The full range of services are available at the following offices:

Dallas District Office
1100 Commerce St.,
Room 3C-36
Dallas, TX 75242
(214) 767-0605

Fort Worth Office
819 Taylor St., Room 8A32
Fort Worth, TX 76102
(817) 334-3613■

Writing a Resume That Works

Volumes have been written about how to write a resume. That's because, in our opinion, generations of job-seekers have attached great importance to the creation and perfection of their resumes. Keep in mind that *no one ever secured a job offer on the basis of a resume alone.* The way to land a good position is to succeed in the employment interview. *You have to convince a potential employer that you're the best person for the job. No piece of paper will do that for you.*

The resume also goes by the name of *curriculum vitae* (the course of one's life), or *vita* (life) for short. These terms are a little misleading, however. A resume cannot possibly tell the story of your life, especially since, as a rule, it shouldn't be more than two pages long. The French word *résumé* means "a summing up." But in the American job market, a resume is a concise, written summary of your work experience, education, accomplishments, and personal background—the essentials an employer needs to evaluate your qualifications.

A resume is nothing more or less than a simple marketing tool, a print ad for yourself. It is sometimes useful in generating interviews. But it is most effective when kept in reserve until after you've met an employer in person. Sending a follow-up letter after the interview, along with your resume, reminds the interviewer of that wonderful person he or she met last Thursday.

The Basics of a Good Resume

The resume is nothing for you to agonize over. But since almost every employer will ask you for one at some point in the hiring process, make sure that yours is a good one.

What do we mean by a good resume? First, *be sure it's up to date and comprehensive.* At a minimum it should include your name, address, and phone number; a complete summary of your work experience; and an education profile. (College grads need not include their high school backgrounds.)

In general, your work experience should include the name, location, and dates of employment of every job you've held since leaving school, plus a summary of your responsibilities and, most important, your accomplishments on each job. If you're a recent graduate, or have held several jobs, you can present your experience chronologically. Begin with your present position and work backward to your first job. If you haven't had that many jobs, organize your resume to emphasize the skills you've acquired through experience.

A second rule of resume-writing is to *keep the resume concise.* Most employers don't want to read more than two pages, and one page is preferable. In most cases your resume will be scanned, not read in detail. Describe your experience in short, pithy phrases. Use action words to describe your accomplishments. Avoid large blocks of copy. Your resume should read more like a chart than a short story.

There are no hard and fast rules on what to include in your resume besides work experience and education. A statement of your objective and a personal section containing date of birth, marital status, and so on, are optional. An employer wants to know these things about you, but it's up to you whether to include them in your resume or bring them up during the interview. If you have served in the military, you ought to mention that in your resume.

Your salary history and references, however, should not be included in your resume; these should be discussed in person during the interview.

Keep in mind that a resume is a sales tool. Make sure that it illustrates your unique strengths in a style and format *you* can be comfortable with. Indicate any unusual responsibilities you've been given, or examples of how you've saved the company money or helped it grow. Include any special recognition of your ability. For example, if your salary increased substantially within a year or two, you might state the increase in terms of a percentage.

Third, *keep your resume honest.* Never lie, exaggerate, embellish, or deceive. Tell the truth about your education, accomplishments, and work history. You needn't account for every single work day that elapsed between jobs, however. If you left one position on November 15 and began the next on February 1, you can minimize gaps by simply listing years worked instead of months.

Fourth, *your resume should have a professional look.* If you type it yourself or have it typed professionally, use a high-quality office typewriter with a plastic ribbon (sometimes called a "carbon" ribbon). Do *not* use a household or office typewriter with a cloth ribbon.

If your budget permits, consider having your resume typeset professionally or typed on a good quality word processor. In either case you have a choice of type faces, such as bold-face, italics, and small caps. You can also request that the margins be justified (lined up evenly on the right and left sides, like the margins of a book). If using a word processor, have the final draft laser printed.

No matter what method you use to prepare your resume, be sure to *proofread* it before sending it to the printer. A misspelled word or typing error reflects badly on you, even if it's not your fault. Read every word out loud, letter for letter and comma for comma.

Get a friend to help you.

Do *not* make copies of your resume on a photocopy machine. Have it printed professionally. The resume you leave behind after an interview or send ahead to obtain an interview may be photocopied several times, and copies of copies can be very hard to read. You should also avoid such gimmicks as using colored paper (unless it's very light cream or light gray) or using a paper size other than 8 1/2 x 11".

Our purpose here is not to tell you how to write the ideal resume (there is no such thing), but rather to provide some general guidelines. The following books are full of all the how-to information you'll need.

BOOKS ON RESUME WRITING

Beatty, Richard. *The Perfect Cover Letter*. New York: John Wiley and Sons, 1989.

Bostwick, Burdette. *Resume Writing: A Comprehensive How-To-Do-It Guide*. New York: John Wiley and Sons, 1990.

Coxford, Lola M. *Resume Writing Made Easy for High Tech*. Scottsdale, AZ: Gorsuch Scarisbrick, 1987.

Foxman, Loretta D. *Resumes That Work*. New York: John Wiley and Sons, 1989.

Jackson, Tom. *The Perfect Resume*. New York: Anchor/Doubleday, 1990.

Krannich, Ronald L., and William J. Banis. *High Impact Resumes & Letters*. Career Management Concepts, Inc., 1987.

Lewis, Adele. *How to Write a Better Resume*. Woodbury, NY: Barron's Educational Series, 1989.

Nadler, Burton Jay. *Liberal Arts Power: How to Sell It on Your Resume*. Princeton, NJ: Peterson's Guides, 1989.

Parker, Yana. *Damn Good Resume Guide: 200 Damn Good Examples*. Berkeley: Ten Speed Press, 1988.

Rosenburg, Arthur, and Hizer, David. *The Resume Handbook: How to Write Outstanding Resumes & Cover Letters for Every Situation*. Holbrook, MA: Bob Adams, 1990.

Smith, Michael Holley. *The Resume Writer's Handbook*. 2nd ed. New York: Harper & Row, 1987.

Wilson, Robert F., and Adele Lewis. *Better Resumes for Executives and Professionals*. New York: Barron's, 1983.

Yates, Martin. *Resumes that Knock 'em Dead*. Holbrook, MA: Bob Adams, 1988.

Should You Hire Someone Else to Write Your Resume?

In general, if you have reasonable writing skills, it's better to prepare your own resume than to ask someone else to do it. If you write your own job history, you'll be better prepared to talk about it in the interview. "Boiler plate" resumes also tend to look and sound alike.

On the other hand, a professional resume writer can be objective about your background and serve as a sounding board on what you should and shouldn't include. You might also consider a professional if you have trouble writing in the condensed style that a good resume calls for.

Here is a list of area firms that will assist you in preparing your resume. Remember that a listing in this book does not constitute an endorsement. Before engaging a professional writer, ask for a recommendation from someone whose judgment you trust—a personnel director, college placement officer, or a knowledgeable friend. Check with the Better Business Bureau and other consumer advocates listed in Chapter 2 to see if there have been any complaints made about the resume service you are considering.

PROFESSIONAL RESUME PREPARERS

A Better Answer
Gateway Tower II, Suite 787
Dallas, TX 75251
(214) 234-3833
Fee: $50 for up to 3 pages, and includes 10 copies.
Contact: Liz Moore or Glenda McKeehan

Accurate Type
1506 W. Pioneer Pkwy., Suite 105
Arlington, TX 76103
(817) 861-5695
Fee: $15 typesetting fee. Consulting and professional resume writing available. Offers laser printing.
Contact: Sherri Gay

Action Business Services
533 Hambrick Rd.
Dallas, TX 75218
(214) 348-0681
Fee: $10 and up per page for resumes and cover letters depending on needs. Evening appointments available.
Contact: Rubie Dawson

Career Pro
13601 Preston Rd., Suite 414W
Dallas, TX 75240
(214) 960-8363 or (800) 824-5858 for office nearest you.
Offers custom writing and career development sevice.
Complimentary consultations to assess individual needs. Electronic resume network. Several offices in Dallas-Fort Worth area.
Contact: Toni Stuffel

Executive Resume Service
4817 Brentwood Stair Rd., Suite F
Fort Worth, TX 76103
(817) 292-3307
Also: 4912 Westlake Dr.
Fort Worth, TX 76132
Fee: Averages $65-$100 for resume composition and printing.

Executive Services
1401 W. Pioneer Pkwy., Suite 112
Arlington, TX 76013
(817) 277-7643
Fee: $25 for one page, $35 for two pages. $5.50 for cover letter. $25 consultation fee.
Contact: Sandra Robinson

Hour Savers Career Services
(214) 349-2992

Package deal includes resume, improving job-hunting skills, and interview techniques. Also offers career workshops, outplacements, career and employment consultations, corporate outplacements, and public speaking on employment issues.
Fee: $99-$259.
Contact: Eleanor Baldwin

Resume Specialist of Arlington
1408 E. Mitchell St.
Arlington, TX 76016
Metro (817) 469-6500
Fee: $15 for typesetting. Minimum of $75 for full service, including resume counseling, marketing, composition, typesetting, and printing. Lifetime update.
Contact: Peter Ots

Resumes Plus
3201 Airport Frwy.
Bedford, TX 76021
(817) 283-2849
Other area offices.
Fee: $35 for one-page resume with 15 copies. Also provides cover and thank-you letters. Offers counseling, networking assistance, laser printing, typesetting, writing assistance, and brochure-style resumes.
Contact: Bill Mueller

Resumes That Win
845 E. Arapaho Rd., Suite 107
Richardson, TX 75081
(214) 234-2274
Offers a commitment to positive professional writing. Other area locations.
Fee: Ranges from $50-$200, depending on needs for composition and printing of resumes and cover letters.

Top O' The Stack
1300 E. Arapaho Rd., Suite 112
Richardson, TX 75081
(214) 907-8639
Fee: $12 and up for resume preparation and typing. Offers laser printing.

The Word Factory
2167 W. Seminary Dr.
Fort Worth, TX 76115
(817) 924-6720
Fee: $20 for one page, $10 for each additional page for resume typing and printing. Lifetime storage on computer disk.
Contact: Mike Hartley

How to choose a professional

Before engaging a professional to help you write your resume, run through the following checklist of questions.

What will it cost? Some firms charge a set fee. Others charge by the hour. Though many firms will not quote an exact price until they know the details of your situation, you should obtain minimum and maximum costs before you go ahead.

What does the price include? Does the fee cover only writing? Or does it include typesetting? Most firms will charge extra for printing.

What happens if you're not satisfied? Will the writer make changes you request? Will changes or corrections cost extra?

How do this writer's fees and experience stack up against others? It's wise to shop around before you buy writing services, just as you would when purchasing any other service.■

What NOT To Do with Your Resume Once You Have It Printed

Do not change your resume except to correct an obvious error. Everyone to whom you show the resume will have some suggestion for improving it: "Why didn't you tell 'em that you had a scholarship?" or "Wouldn't this look better in italics?" The time to consider those kinds of questions is *before* you go to the typesetter. Obviously, if you have saved your resume on a floppy disk, it will be easier to revise. Even then, it's probably not worth the trouble to make a lot of nitpicky changes. Remember, there is no such thing as a perfect resume. Except typographically.

The power of action verbs

Gary J. has been an engineer in Dallas for 20 years. During those years he has changed jobs seven times, enhancing his career with each move. Gary realized early that using powerful, action verbs to describe his accomplishments made his resume stand out. Here are some sample verbs that job seekers in various career areas should use to help build a more effective resume.

Management
Controlled
Headed
Implemented

Methods and Controls
Restructured
Cataloged
Verified
Systematized

Public Relations/ Human Relations
Monitored
Handled
Sponsored
Integrated

Creative
Devised
Developed
Originated
Conceived

Advertising/ Promotion
Generated
Recruited
Tailored
Sparked

Communications
Facilitated
Edited
Consulted
Disseminated

Resourcefulness
Rectified
Pioneered
Achieved

Negotiations
Engineered
Mediated
Proposed
Negotiated■

A second point to remember: DO NOT send out a mass mailing. If you send letters to 700 company presidents, you can expect a response of from 1 to 2 percent—and 95 percent of the responses will be negative. The shotgun approach is expensive; it takes time and costs money for postage and printing. You'll get much better results if you are selective about where you send your resume. We'll discuss this at greater length in Chapter 5. The important thing is to concentrate on known hiring authorities in whom you are interested.

The Cover Letter

Whether you are answering a want ad or following up an inquiry call or interview, you should always include a cover letter with your resume. If at all possible, the letter should be addressed to a specific person—the one who's doing the hiring—and not "To Whom It May Concern." You can generally track the right person down with a few phone calls to the company in question.

A good cover letter, like a good resume, is brief—usually not more than three or four paragraphs. No paragraph should be longer than three or four sentences. If you've already spoken to the contact person by phone, remind him or her of your conversation in the first paragraph. If you and the person to whom you are writing know someone in common, the first paragraph is the place to mention it. You should also include a hard-hitting sentence about why you're well qualified for the job in question.

In the next paragraph or two, specify what you could contribute to the company in terms that indicate you've done your homework on the firm and the industry.

Finally, either request an interview or tell the reader that you will follow up with a phone call within a week to arrange a mutually convenient meeting.

Remember that the focus of your job search is to sell yourself as a match to fit an employer's needs. You should emphasize that you match the company's needs throughout all your communication—your resume, any phone calls, and cover letters and follow-up letters.

Choosing a Resume Format

There are a number of different methods for composing a quality resume. Every career counselor and resume compiler has his or her own favorite method and style. As the person being represented by the resume, *you* must choose the style and format that best suits and sells you. Many resume books will use different terms for the various styles. We will highlight the three most popular types.

1. *The chronological resume* is the traditional style, most often used in the workplace and job search; that does not mean it is the most effective. Positive aspects of the chronological resume include the traditionalist approach that employers may expect. It also can highlight past positions that you may wish your potential employer to notice. This resume is also very adaptable, with only the reverse chronological order of items as the essential ingredient.

2.   *The functional resume* is most common among career changers, people reentering the job market after a lengthy absence, and those wishing to highlight aspects of their experience not related directly to employment. This resume ideally focuses on the many skills one has used at his or her employment and the accomplishments one has achieved. It shows a potential employer that you can do and have done a good job. What it doesn't highlight is where you have done it.

3.   *The combination resume* combines the best features of a functional resume and a chronological resume. This allows job seekers to highlight skills and accomplishments while still maintaining the somewhat traditional format of reverse chronological order of positions held and organizations worked for.

Here are some sample resumes and cover letters to help you with your own. The books listed earlier in this chapter will supply many more examples than we have room for here.

SAMPLE CHRONOLOGICAL RESUME

GEORGE P. BURDELL
200 Silicon Drive
Dallas, Texas 75204
(214) 555-4545

OBJECTIVE

Position in technical management.

WORK EXPERIENCE

SAMPO CORPORATION   1979-1992

Manager, Marketing & Management Planning (Taiwan)
1989-1992
- **Supervised** operations & staff of **new products development.**
- Instrumental in **making decisions** regarding **OEM new products** with clients such as: IBM, NCR, TI, Xerox, Quadram, etc.
- **Developed 4 new products:** Low-cost display monitor, oscilloscope, and two DEC-compatible terminals.
- Accomplishment: IPD **sales volume** in 1991: **$45,000,000; 50% increase** from 1989.

Manager, Southwestern Sales (Richardson, TX) 1987-1989
- Generated **$3,000,000 in sales** of OEM display monitors to IBM(NC), NCR(SC), Quadram, Digital Control, & other local accounts.

Sales Engineer (Garland, TX) 1985-1987
- Successfully collaborated with OEM engineers to **develop** monitors for computer & laser games such as Jungle King & Dragon's Lair.

Production Engineer (Dallas, TX) 1983-1985
- Member of team credited with building **Georgia's first TV manufacturing plant.**
- **Involvement in this $7,000,000** project ranged from conceptualization to production of 600, 19" color sets daily.

Circuit Design Engineer (Taiwan) 1980-1983
- **Designed** PIF, deflection & remote control circuit for color TV.

EDUCATION

Southern Methodist University: **MBA in Marketing,** 1985
University of Texas at Arlington: **BS in Electrical
Engineering,** 1979

REFERENCES

Furnished upon request.

SAMPLE FUNCTIONAL RESUME

KATHY JONES
4000 Greenwood Drive, NE
Dallas, TX 75238
(214) 555-5648

OBJECTIVE: Seek position as an **administrative assistant,** utilizing adminstrative, organizational, and computer skills.

SKILLS

Administrative
- Independently evaluated and restructured a major client's account for an advertising agency.
- Managed bookkeeping procedures for a non-profit corporation in excess of $80,000.
- Managed two rental properties.

Organizational
- Established procedure for assigned experiments and procured equipment for a research laboratory.
- Planned course syllabi, assessed weaknesses of individual students to facilitate learning.

Computer
- Managed data input and generated monthly reports.
- Completed courses in FORTRAN and BASIC.

EMPLOYMENT

Computer Operator, Woolco, Grand Prairie, TX	(1984-Present)
Trouble-shooter in accounting, The Bloom Agency/Dallas	(1982-84)
Instructor, Eastfield College Math Dept., Mesquite, TX	(1976-82)
Research Assistant, Harvard Medical School	(1972-74)

EDUCATION

M.S. Mathematics	University of Texas at Dallas	(1976)
B.A. Mathematics	Harvard University	(1975)
B.S. Physiology	Stanford University	(1972)

REFERENCES

Furnished upon request.

SAMPLE COMBINATION RESUME

SUSAN SKINNER
122 Pine Street
Fort Worth, TX 76262
(817) 555-0000

OBJECTIVE: Software development position.

EDUCATION: University of North Texas
M.S., Information and Computer Science;
GPA 3.7/4.0   12/88

Texas Christian University
B.A., Mathematics;
GPA 3.5/4.0   5/83

QUALIFICATIONS:

Career-related projects:
- Designed and implemented multi-tasking operating system for the IBM-PC.
- Implemented compiler for Pascal-like language.
- Implemented simulation project using tasking in Ada.
- Designed electronic mail system using PSL/PSA specification language.
- Designed menu-based interface for beginning UNIX users.

Languages and operating systems:
- Proficient in **Ada, Modula-2, Pascal, COBOL.**
- Familiar with C, Fortran, Lisp, Prolog, dBaseIII, SQL, QBE.
- Working knowledge of IBM-PC hardware and 8088 assembly language.
- Experienced in **UNIX, MS-DOS, XENIX,** CP/M operating systems.

WORK EXPERIENCE:

Neil Araki Programming Services—Fort Worth, TX—10/88-Present
- **UNIX Programmer**—Responsible for porting MS-DOS database applications to

IBM-PC/AT running Xenix System V. System administration.
Robert W. Woodruff Arts Center—Hurst, TX—10/85-9/88
▌ **Computer Programmer**—Performed daily disk backup on Burroughs B-1955 machine. Executed database update programs and checks.

From 8/83 to 9/85, held full-time positions as **Box Office Manager** and **Accountant** for arts organizations in Fort Worth.

REFERENCES:

Furnished upon request.

Universal Format

The following format will work for virtually all job seekers. But remember, there are no concrete rules in resume preparation. Modify this guide as necessary to make the most favorable impression.

NAME

Address	City, State, Zip	Phone

Job Objective: Vital piece of information. Many employers use as screening device or to signal job match; should grab attention and motivate employer to read further. If at all possible, the Objective should be tailored to the job you are seeking.

Employment: Place strongest of the two sections, Employment or Education, first. The more impressive your work history, the more prominently you should display it.

List jobs in reverse chronological order, putting the most promotable facts—employer or job title—first.

Give functional description of job if work history is strong and supports job objective.

Skills: You may embed these in employment section. Put skills section first for career changers. Choose skills that are most relevant to job objective.

Give short statements to support skills. Make support statements results oriented. Position most marketable skills first.

Education: List in reverse chronological order, putting the most promotable facts—school or degree—first. Mention any honors or achievements, such as high GPA or Dean's List.

Miscellaneous: Call this section anything applicable—
Interests, Activities, Accomplishments,
or Achievements. Give only information
that promotes your candidacy for the
position you're applying for.

You can also include community service
activities, whcih either enhance your
work skills or would bring credit to the
company.

References: Furnished upon request. (Don't waste
space on names and addresses. Keep on
separate sheet.)

SAMPLE COVER LETTER

3420 Rosedale Ave.
Fort Worth, TX 75421
June 26, 1991

Ms. Jacqueline Doe
Wide World Publishing Company
1400 Walnut Hill Lane, Suite 250
Dallas, TX 77237

Dear Ms. Doe:

As an honors graduate of The University of Texas at Arlington with two years of copy editing and feature writing experience with a community newspaper, I am confident that I would make a successful editorial assistant with Wide World.

Besides my strong editorial background, I offer considerable business experience. I have held summer jobs in an insurance company, a law firm, and a data processing company. My familiarity with word processing should prove particularly useful to Wide World now that you're about to become fully automated.

I would like to interview with you as soon as possible and would be happy to check in with your office about an appointment. If you prefer, your office can contact me between the hours of 11:00 a.m. and 3:00 p.m. at (817) 555-6886.

Sincerely,

Valerie Jones

SAMPLE COVER LETTER

May 14, 1991

2239 Forest Park Blvd.
Fort Worth, TX 76345

Box 1826
The Dallas Morning News
Communications Center
Dallas, TX 75265

Dear Employer:

Your advertisement in the May 13 issue of *The Dallas Morning News* for an entry-level bookkeeper seems perfect for someone with my background. I am about to graduate from Paschal High School in a business preparatory course that includes two semesters of accounting.

As you can see from my resume, my work experience consists mainly of miscellaneous summer employment and part-time jobs while in school. But I hope to offset my lack of experience with hard work, enthusiasm, and a desire to succeed.

My activities with Junior Achievement should give you an idea of my aptitude for business. I would appreciate the opportunity of an interview at your convenience.

Sincerely,

Jim Clark
(817) 555-4414

SAMPLE COVER LETTER

December 2, 1991

228 S. Meadowlark Lane
Dallas, TX 75116
(214) 555-9876

Dear Mike:

Just when everything seemed to be going so well at my job, the company gave us a Christmas present that nobody wanted—management announced that half the department will be laid off before the end of the year. Nobody knows yet just which heads are going to roll. But whether or not my name is on the list, I am definitely back in the job market.

I have already lined up a couple of interviews. But knowing how uncertain job hunting can be, I can use all the contacts I can get. You know my record—both from when we worked together at 3-Q and since then. But in case you've forgotten the details, I've enclosed my resume.

I know that you often hear of job openings as you wend your way about Dallas and Fort Worth. I'd certainly appreciate your passing along any leads you think might be worthwhile.

My best to you and Fran for the holidays.

Cordially,

Emily Noir

Seven ways to ruin a cover letter

1. Spell the name of the firm incorrectly.
2. Don't bother to find out the name of the hiring authority. Just send the letter to the president or chairman of the board.
3. If the firm is headed by a woman, be sure to begin your letter, "Dear Sir." Otherwise, just address it, "To Whom It May Concern."
4. Make sure the letter includes a couple of typos and sloppy erasures. Better yet, spill coffee on it first, then mail it.
5. Be sure to provide a phone number that has been disconnected, or one at which nobody is ever home.
6. Tell the firm you'll call to set up an appointment in a few days; then don't bother.
7. Call the firm at least three times the day after you mail the letter. Get very angry when they say they haven't heard of you.■

Researching the Dallas/Fort Worth Job Market

We've said the key to getting job offers is to convince employers that you match their needs. We'd add that the key to job satisfaction is finding a position whose responsibilities match your interests and abilities. This means you've got to know the job and the company.

Once you've figured out what kind of job you want, you need to find out as much as you can about which specific companies might employ you. Your network of personal contacts can be an invaluable source of information about what jobs are available where. But networking can't do it all; at some point, you'll have to do some reading. This chapter fills you in on the directories, newspapers, and magazines you'll need in your search, and notes the libraries where you can find them.

Libraries

Public libraries are an invaluable source of career information. Everything from books on resume writing to *Standard and Poor's Register of Corporations, Directors, and Executives* can usually be found in the business and economics sections.

DALLAS PUBLIC LIBRARY

The most extensive collection of job-hunting books and reference material can be found in this modern eight-floor downtown library located at **1515 Young St.** The 18 branch libraries carry many of the most frequently used guides and directories. Any book that isn't available in one library can be requested through the inter-library loan system.

At the main library, most of the major business directories, magazines, and books can be found in the **business and technology section** on the fifth floor. Few signs are posted, so ask at the main desk for directions on where to find what you're looking for and advice on where else to look for information. Underground parking is available and is convenient and usually safe.

Time invested in finding out as much as possible about a company before a job interview can pay off. For example, if you want to find out about a major business's financial outlook, check its annual report. Hundreds of annual reports, including those for most major Dallas companies, are on microfilm.

The Business Section also keeps an index of newspaper stories written about local companies. The **Infotrack** computer search system will identify stories about companies that have run in trade journals and other sources.

U.S. Securities and Exchange Commission reports on the sixth floor offer additional information about businesses. You may find even more revealing information than what is contained in annual reports, such as the profitability of different divisions within a company.

The sixth floor also includes many **government documents,** including U.S. Labor Department employment outlooks. You may wonder, for example, about the future for computer programmers during the next decade. Government publications can offer some predictions.

The first and eighth floors have stacks with general career books, such as *What Color Is Your Parachute?* and other popular guides. Information about government jobs and samples of tests are kept on the eighth floor.

Gail Bialas, the library's public relations director, highlights the library as an asset. "Lots of people tell us how helpful the library was in helping them find a job," Gail adds. "For one thing, it's one of the few resources that's free. And that can be a big help to someone who is out of work."

DALLAS BRANCH LIBRARIES:

Audelia Road: 10045 Audelia Rd. (214) 670-1350
Casa View: 10355 Ferguson Rd. (214) 670-8403
Dallas West: 2332 Singleton Blvd. (214) 670-6445
Forest Green: 9015 Forest Lane (214) 670-1335
Fretz Park: 6990 Belt Line Rd. (214) 670-6420
Hampton-Illinois: 2210 Illinois Ave. (214) 670-7646
Highland Hills: 3624 Simpson Stuart Rd. (214) 670-0987
Martin Luther King, Jr., Library-Learning Center: 2922 Martin Luther King, Jr., Blvd. (214) 670-0344
Lakewood: 6121 Worth St. (214) 670-1376
Lancaster-Kiest: 3039 S. Lancaster Rd. (214) 670-1952
North Oak Cliff: 302 W. Tenth St. (214) 670-7555
Oak Lawn: 4100 Cedar Springs Rd. (214) 670-1359
Park Forest: 3421 Forest Lane (214) 670-6333
Pleasant Grove: 1125 S. Buckner Blvd. (214) 670-0965
Polk-Wisdom: 7151 Library Lane (214) 670-1947
Preston Royal: 5626 Royal Lane (214) 670-7128
Renner Frankford: 6400 Frankford Rd. (214) 670-6400
Skyline: 6006 Everglade Rd. (214) 670-0938
Walnut Hill: 9495 Marsh Lane (214) 670-6376

How to conduct a rock-bottom computer search

Let's say you have an interview with the sales director of XYZ Corporation, a company that has the perfect job opportunity. You've done your homework by searching through the directories listed in this chapter, you've familiarized yourself with the appropriate trade magazines, and you have an information file with the XYZ Corporation's annual report and product brochures.

You know where the sales director went to college and even what sorority she joined. But you need more up-to-date information on what has happened to the company during the past six months.

One quick way to find out is through the Dallas Public Library's on-line search service available in the Information and Reference Section at (214) 670-1700. All reference questions are funneled through this department in the central library located at 1515 Young St.

The library has access to more than 200 databases, including DIALOG, Dun & Bradstreet, and Dow Jones. A computer search on XYZ Corporation will go through these databases and print out a bibliography of recent articles that have been written about that company.

The cost for the service is determined by the number of sources and time involved in doing the search. Minimum charge is $10. You first tell the librarian the maximum amount of money you can spend on the search. The public isn't charged for the librarian's time, making this offering one of the best values in town.∎

USING THE DALLAS PUBLIC LIBRARY'S ON-LINE INFORMATION SERVICE

You have hundreds of resources at your fingertips through the Dallas Public Library's community information database, called APL/CAT.

Say you want to find out the names of major professional organizations in your field of interest. Go to a computer terminal at any one of the Dallas city libraries and use the on-line information service to find more than 300 listings under professional organizations. You also will be given cross-reference listings for more sources.

APL/CAT can be especially useful to job seekers who may want to know about social services, employment agencies, women's programs, day-care centers for child care, and organizations that provide food and clothing for the unemployed. Dozens of major categories are listed in the information service that contains more than 6,000 single entries.

Printouts of some of the categories are available through the Urban Information Center on the sixth floor of the main library at 1515 Young St. Charges start at $10 and increase, depending on the number of listings. Call in advance to order the category you want.

Ask any librarian to help you learn to use APL/CAT. You can call the main reference desk at (214) 670-1700 to ask a librarian for information you need from the database. New listings are continuously added to APL/CAT. Most of the data is for the City of Dallas, although some entries are listed for Dallas County suburbs.

FORT WORTH PUBLIC LIBRARY

The downtown Fort Worth Public Library and its nine branches prove to be an invaluable resource for job hunters. Many library staff members go out of their way to help people who are looking for work.

The largest collection of material can be found in the **Business and Technology Section** in the lower level of the downtown library at **300 Taylor St.** Many of the 10-K reports on major corporations, government study guides, and self-help material are available. A list of City of Fort Worth job openings can be found here.

Limited information is provided by calling the Business and Technology section at **(817) 870-7727.** You'll gather much more from dropping by one of the libraries.

When you do, be sure to ask for a librarian's help. It's common for people to flounder if they aren't familiar with what's available in the library, says Sally McCoy, acting manager of the Business and Technology Section. That's why she likes to help point people in the right direction, so they can make the best use of the resources.

The main library and several of the branches have Adult Learning Centers that can be very useful to people who want to upgrade skills, prepare for taking the GED exam, or get help when English is their second language. The program, coordinated by the Fort Worth Independent School District, assists adults in getting the extra boost they need to find better jobs.

You can also find job-hunting information at the following Fort Worth branch libraries.

FORT WORTH BRANCH LIBRARIES

Diamond Hill/Jarvis: 1300 NE 35th St. (817) 624-7331
East Berry: 4300 E. Berry St. (817) 536-1945
Meadowbrook: 5651 E. Lancaster Ave. (817) 451-0916
North Side: 601 Park St. (817) 626-8241
Ridglea: 3628 Bernie Anderson Ave. (817) 737-6619
Riverside: 2913 Yucca Ave. (817) 838-6931
Seminary South: 501 E. Bolt St. (817) 926-0215
Shamblee: 959 E. Rosedale St. (817) 870-1330
Southwest Regional Library: 4001 Library Lane (817) 782-9853
Wedgwood: 3816 Kimberly Lane (817) 292-3368

MAJOR SUBURBAN LIBRARIES

Arlington: 101 E. Abram St. (817) 459-6900
Balch Springs: 4301 Pioneer Rd. (214) 286-8856
Bedford: 1805 L. Don Dodson Dr. (817) 685-2160
Burleson: 216 SW Johnson Ave. (817) 295-6131
Carrollton: 2001 Jackson Rd. (214) 466-3353
Cedar Hill: 502 Cedar Hill Rd. (214) 291-7323
DeSoto: 300 Lion St. (214) 223-8406
Duncanville: 103 E. Wheatland Rd. (214) 780-5052
Euless: 201 N. Ector Dr. (817) 685-1480
Everman: 118 W. Trammell (817) 551-0726
Farmers Branch: 13613 Webb Chapel Rd. (214) 247-2511
Forest Hill: 6619 Forest Hill Dr. (817) 483-9811
Garland Nicholson Memorial Library: 625 Austin St. (214) 205-2500
Grand Prairie: 901 Conover Dr. (214) 264-1571
Grapevine: 307 W. Dallas Rd. (817) 481-0336
Haltom City: 3201 Friendly Lane (817) 831-6431
Highland Park: 4700 Drexel Dr. (214) 521-4150
Hurst: 901 Precinct Line Rd. (817) 284-5931
Hutchins-Atwell: 300 N. Denton St. (214) 225-4711
Irving: 801 W. Irving Blvd. (214) 721-2606
Lake Worth: 4000 Merrett Rd. (817) 237-9681
Lancaster: 220 W. Main St. (214) 227-1080
Mansfield: 110 S. Main St. (817) 473-4391
Mesquite: 300 Grubb Dr. (214) 216-6220
Newark: Ramhorn Hill Rd. (817) 489-2224
North Richland Hills: 6720 NE Loop 820 (817) 581-5700
Richardson: 900 Civic Center Dr. (214) 238-4000
Richland Hills: 6724 Rena Dr. (817) 595-6630
River Oaks: 4900 River Oaks Blvd. (817) 626-5421
Rowlett: Main St. at Skyline Dr. (214) 475-3010
Sachse: 3033 6th St. (214) 530-8966
Saginaw: 404 Saginaw Blvd. (817) 232-2100, ext. 44
Seagoville: 702 N. Hwy. 175 (214) 287-7720
Sunnyvale: 402 Tower Place (214) 226-4491
Watauga: 7105 Whitley Rd. (817) 428-9412
White Settlement: 214 Meadow Park Dr. (817) 367-0166
Wilmer: 205 E. Belt Line Rd. (214) 225-6620

Directories

When you're beginning your homework, whether you're researching an entire industry or a specific company, there are four major sources of information with which you should become familiar.

Standard and Poor's **Register of Corporations, Directors, and Executives** (Standard and Poor's Publishing Co., 25 Broadway, New York, NY 10004) is billed as the "foremost guide to the business community and the executives who run it." This three-volume directory lists more than

50,000 corporations and 70,000 officers, directors, trustees, and other bigwigs.

Each business is assigned a four-digit number called a Standard Industrial Classification (S.I.C.) number, which tells you what product or service the company provides. Listings are indexed by geographic area and also by S.I.C. number, so it's easy to find all the companies in Texas that produce, say, industrial inorganic chemicals.

You can also look up a *particular* company to verify its correct address and phone number, its chief officers (that is, the people you might want to contact for an interview), its products, and, in many cases, its annual sales and number of employees.

If you have an appointment with the president of XYZ Corporation, you can consult Standard and Poor's *Register* to find out where he or she was born and went to college—information that's sure to come in handy in an employment interview. Supplements are published in April, July, and October.

The **Thomas Register of American Manufacturers** and the **Thomas Register Catalog File** (Thomas Publishing Co., One Penn Plaza, New York, NY 10119) are published annually. This 23-volume publication is another gold mine of information. You can look up a particular product or service and find every company that provides it. (Since this is a national publication, you'll have to weed out companies that are not in the Dallas/Fort Worth area, but that's easy.) You can also look up a particular company to find out about branch offices, capital ratings, company officials, names, addresses, phone numbers, and more. The *Thomas Register* even contains five volumes of company catalogs. Before your appointment with XYZ Corporation, you can bone up on its product line with the *Thomas Register*.

Moody's Complete Corporate Index (Moody's Investor Service, 99 Church St., New York, NY 10007) gives you the equivalent of an encyclopedia entry on more than 20,000 corporations. This is the resource to use when you want really detailed information on a particular company. Moody's can tell you about a company's history—when it was founded, what name changes it has undergone, and so on. It provides a fairly lengthy description of a company's business and properties, what subsidiaries it owns, and lots of detailed financial information. Like the directories above, **Moody's** lists officers and directors of companies. It can also tell you the date of the annual meeting and the number of stockholders and employees.

The **Million Dollar Directory** (Dun & Bradstreet, Inc., 3 Century Drive, Parsippany, NJ 07054) is a three-volume listing of approximately 160,000 U.S. businesses with a net worth of more than half a million dollars. Listings appear alphabetically, geographically, and by product classification and include key personnel. Professional and consulting organizations such as hospitals, engineering services, credit agencies, and financial institutions other than banks and trust companies are not generally included.

So much for the Big Four directories. The following list contains more than five dozen additional directories and guides that may come in handy. Many are available at area libraries.

OTHER USEFUL DIRECTORIES

Accounting Employers of Texas
(Texas Society of CPA's Education Fund, 1421 W. Mockingbird Ln., Suite 100, Dallas, TX 75247.) A directory of company profiles.

Accounting Firms and Practitioners
(American Institute of Certified Public Accountants, 1211 Avenue of the Americas, New York, NY 10036.) Covers about 25,000 certified public accounting firms belonging to the Institute, as well as member accountants with independent practices.

Advertising Research Foundation Yearbook
(Advertising Research Foundation, 3 E. 54th St., New York, NY 10022.) Lists 375 member advertising agencies, research organizations, trade associations, advertisers, academic institutions, and broadcasting and publishing firms.

Adweek Agency Directory
(A/S/M Communications, Inc., 49 E. 21st St., New York, NY 10010.) Lists ad agencies, media and media buying services, key personnel, major accounts.

The Almanac of American Employers: A Guide to America's 500 Most Successful Large Corporations
(Contemporary Books, 180 N. Michigan Ave., Chicago, IL 60601.) Alphabetical profiles of major corporations, including information about benefits, job turnover, and financial stability.

Apparel Trades Book
(Dun & Bradstreet, One Diamond Hill Rd., Murray Hill, NJ 07974.) Lists about 175,000 apparel retailers and wholesalers. Separate editions for each.

Bacon's Publicity Checker
(Bacon's Publishing Company, 332 S. Michigan Ave., Chicago, IL 60604.) Covers over 7,800 trade and consumer magazines,

1,700 daily newspapers, and 8,000 weekly newspapers in the United States and Canada.

Billion Dollar Directory: America's Corporate Families
(Dun and Bradstreet, Inc., 3 Sylvan Way, Parsippany, NJ 07054-3896.) Lists 7,800 U.S. parent companies and their 44,000 foreign and domestic subsidiaries. Organized alphabetically by name of parent company.

Book of Lists
(Dallas Business Journal, 4131 N. Central Expwy., Suite 310, Dallas, TX 75204.) Lists of the top 25 companies in all major industries, along with the 100 largest public companies and 50 largest employers for Dallas, Tarrant, and Austin counties.

Career Guide: Dun's Employment Opportunity Directory
(Dun's Marketing Services, 3 Sylvan Way, Parsippany, NJ 07054-3896) Designed for those beginning a career; describes job prospects at hundreds of companies.

Consultants and Consulting Organizations Directory
(Gale Research Co., 835 Penobscot Bldg., Detroit, MI 48226; $85.) Contains descriptions of 16,000 firms and individuals involved in consulting; indexed geographically.

Corporate Technology Directory
(Corporate Technology Information Services, Inc., 12 Alfred St., Suite 200, Woburn, MA 01801) Profiles of 23,000 high-technology corporations, manufacturers, and developers in the U.S., including address, phone, ownership, history, brief description, sales, number of employees, executives, and products. Indexed by company names, geography, technology, and product.

Dallas Chamber of Commerce Publications
(Greater Dallas Chamber Information Department, 1201 Elm St., Suite 200, Dallas, TX 75270.) The following publications are available:

Directory of Foreign-Owned Companies lists Dallas/Fort Worth foreign-owned companies by country of origin, including year of local establishment and area employment.

Directory of High-Technology Firms lists high-technology firms in the Dallas/Fort Worth area.

Dallas at a Glance

Greater Dallas Business and Industry Guide

Greater Dallas Office Real Estate Journal

Minority Business Development Handbook

Dallas Area Employment Trends and Economic Indicators

Dallas County Business Guide

(Business Extension Bureau, 4802 Travis St., Houston, TX 77002.) Major Dallas-area businesses listed alphabetically and according to business category.

Data Sources: Hardware-Data Communications Directory and Data Sources: Software Directory

(Ziff-Davis Publishing Co., 20 Brace St., Suite 110 Cherry Hill, NJ 08034.) Two-volume guide to most products, companies, services, and personnel in the computer industry.

Dictionary of Occupational Titles

(U.S. Dept. of Labor, Washington, DC 20210.) Occupational information on job duties and requirements; describes almost every conceivable job.

Directories in Print

(Gale Research Company, 835 Penobscot Bldg., Detroit, MI 48226.) Contains detailed descriptions of all published directories: what they list, who uses them, and who publishes them.

Directory of Chain Restaurant Operators

(Business Guides, Inc., 425 Park Ave., New York, NY 10022.) Listings of chain restaurants, chain hotels, and food services.

Directory of Community Resources for Fort Worth and Tarrant County

(United Way of Metropolitan Tarrant County, 210 E. 9th St., Fort Worth, TX 76102.) Major social service agencies in Tarrant County listed alphabetically.

Directory of Construction Associations

(Metadata, Inc., Box 585, Locust, NJ 07760.) Lists about 2,500 local, regional, and national professional societies, technical associations, trade groups, manufacturer bureaus, government agencies, labor unions, and other construction information sources. Arranged by topic.

Directory of Services

(Community Council of Greater Dallas, 2121 Main St., Suite 500, Dallas, TX 75201.) Lists agencies and services for residents of Dallas and Collin counties and the Lewisville Independent School District.

Directory of Texas Manufacturers

(Bureau of Business Research, The University of Texas, P.O. Box 7459, Austin, TX 78712.) Texas manufacturers listed alphabetically and according to SIC number and major product.

Electronic News Financial Fact Book and Directory

(Fairchild Publications, Inc., 7 E. 12th St., New York, NY 10003.) Background and financial information about leading companies in the electronics industry.

Encyclopedia of Associations: National Organizations in the U.S.
(Gale Research Co., 835 Penobscot Bldg., Detroit, MI 48226.) Lists 14,000 local and national associations, professional clubs, and civic organizations by categories; includes key personnel. Indexed geographically.

Encyclopedia of Business Information Sources
(Gale Research Co., 835 Penobscot Bldg., Detroit, Detroit, MI 48226.) Lists each industry's encyclopedias, handbooks, indexes, almanacs, yearbooks, trade associations, periodicals, directories, computer databases, research centers, and statistical sources.

Everybody's Business
(Doubleday, 10 E. 53rd St., New York, NY 10022; available at bookstores for $10.) Candid profiles of 400 American manufacturers of well-known brand-name products.

Fairchild's Financial Manual of Retail Stores
(Fairchild Books, Fairchild Publications, Inc., 7 E. 12th St., New York, NY 10003.) Lists 275 publicly held companies in the U.S. and Canada that deal partly or exclusively in retail sales. Arranged alphabetically.

Fairchild's Textile and Apparel Financial Directory
(Fairchild Books, Fairchild Publications, Inc., 7 E. 12th St., New York, NY 10003.) Lists 275 publicly owned textile and apparel corporations. Arranged alphabetically.

Fort Worth Chamber of Commerce Membership Directory & Buyer's Guide
(Fort Worth Chamber of Commerce, 777 Taylor St., Suite 900, Fort Worth, TX 76102.) Membership roster, classified listings, and business index.

Fortune Double 500 Directory
(Time, Inc., Time & Life Bldg., Rockefeller Center, New York, NY 10020.) Lists the 500 largest corporations, as well as the 500 largest U.S. non-industrial coporations and the top 100 service companies in diversified financial services and banking. Arranged by annual sales.

Gale Directory of Publications
(Gale Research, Inc., 835 Penobscot Bldg., Detroit MI 48226-4094) Lists national, local, and trade magazines alphabetically and by state.

Gale Directory of Publications and Broadcast Media
(Gale Research Inc., 835 Penobscot Bldg., Detroit, MI 48226.) Lists 35,000 publications and broadcast stations as well as the feature editors of major daily newspapers.

Greater Dallas Chamber Membership Directory and Business Guide
(Greater Dallas Chamber Information Dept., 1201 Elm St., Suite 200,

Dallas, TX 75270.) Chamber of Commerce members listed alphabetically and according to products and services.

Guide to Special Issues and Indexes of Periodicals
(Special Libraries Association, 235 Park Ave. S., New York, NY 10003.) Alphabetical listing of consumer, trade, and technical periodicals.

Hispanic Media & Markets Directory
(Standard Rate & Data Service, 3004 Glenview Rd., Wilmette, IL 60091.) Provides company, subsidiary, and branch names, addresses, phone, and key personnel for over 600 Spanish-language publications and broadcast stations.

Hispanic Media USA
(Media Institute, 3017 M St. NW, Washington, DC 20007.) Provides company name, address, phone, and names of key personnel for 250 print, TV, and radio stations whose primary language is Spanish.

Hotel and Motel Management—Buyer's Directory
(Harcourt Brace Jovanovich, Inc., 757 Third Ave., New York, NY 10017.) Lists about 2,100 companies that supply goods and services to the lodging market; includes separate sections for hotel chains, related associations, manufacturers' representatives, franchise and referral organizations, consulting firms, personnel agencies, publishers, and schools.

International Advertising Association—Membership Directory
(IAA, 342 Madison Ave., Suite 2000, New York, NY 10017.) Covers 2,700 member advertisers, advertising agencies, media, and other firms involved in advertising. Arranged geographically and by function or service.

International Association for Personnel Women— Membership Roster
(IAPW, P.O. Box 969, Andover, MA 01810) Lists 1,500 members-at-large and members of affiliated chapters.

International Television and Video Almanac
(Quigley Publishing Company, Inc., 159 W. 53rd St., New York, NY 10019; $42.) Lists television networks, major program producers, major group station owners, cable television companies, distributors, firms serving the industry, equipment manufacturers, casting agencies, literary agencies, advertising and publicity representatives, and television stations.

National Directory of Magazines
(Oxbridge Communications, Inc., 150 Fifth Ave., New York, NY 10011.) Profiles 29,000 magazines by interest categories; includes key staff names, circulation, and description. Cross-indexed by subject. Indexed alphabetically by title.

National Directory of Women-Owned Business Firms
(Business Research Services, Inc., 2 E. 22nd St., Suite 202, Lombard, IL 60148.) Lists 20,000 women-owned firms, providing name, address, phone, products and services, and name and title of contact.

National Trade and Professional Associations
(Columbia Books, Inc., 1212 New York Ave. NW, Suite 3000, Washington, DC 20005; $30.) Lists all associations and labor unions in the U.S. and Canada; indexed geographically and by key words.

Newsletters in Print
(Gale Research Co., 835 Penobscot Bldg., Detroit, MI 48226.) Reference guide to national and international information and financial services, association bulletins, and training and educational services.

Occupational Outlook Handbook
(Bureau of Labor Statistics, 441 A St. NW, Washington, DC 20212.) Describes in clear language what people do in their jobs, the training and education they need, earnings, working conditions, and employment outlook.

O'Dwyer's Directory of Public Relations Firms
(J.R. O'Dwyer & Co., 271 Madison Ave., New York, NY 10016.) Describes 1,500 public relations firms in the U.S., their key personnel, local offices, and accounts; indexed geographically.

Oil & Gas Directory
(Geophysical Directory, Inc., P.O. Box 130508, Houston TX 77219.) Directory of 5,200 producers, purchasers, gatherers, transporters, and other oil service companies worldwide.

Peterson's Job Opportunities for Engineering, Science, and Computer Graduates
(Peterson's Guides, Inc., P.O. Box 2123, Princeton, NJ 08540; $13.25.) Describes 1,000 government agencies, technical firms, and manufacturers that hire engineers, computer scientists, and physical scientists.

The Red Book of Housing Manufacturers
(McGraw-Hill, 24 Huntwell Ave., Lexington, MA 02173) Listings of companies involved in the production of everything from dwelling units to small components.

Reference Book of Corporate Management
(Dun & Bradstreet, Inc., 3 Century Dr., Parsippany, NJ 07054.) National directory of 2,400 companies with at least $20 million in sales; listed by name. Also lists biographies of key personnel and directors, including schools attended and past jobs.

Rotan-Mosle/Paine-Webber Guide
(Scholl Communications, Inc., P.O. Box 560, Deerfield, IL 60015;
$26.95.) Directory of major publicly held corporations and financial
institutions headquartered in Texas and Oklahoma.

Sheldon's Department Stores
(Phelon, Sheldon & Marsar, 15 Industrial Ave., Fairview, NJ 07022.)
Directory of the largest department stores, women's specialty stores,
chain stores, and resident buying offices. Geographical listings, plus
alphabetical index.

The Sibbald Guide to the Texas Top Two-Fifty
(The Sibbald Guide, 5725 E. River Rd., Suite 575, Chicago, IL 60631.)
Profile of the state's leading public companies and financial
institutions.

Standard Directory of Advertising Agencies
(National Register Publishing Co., 3004 Glenview Rd., Wilmette, IL
60091.) The Red Book of 5,000 advertising agencies and their 60,000
accounts.

Texas Almanac and State Industrial Guide
(A.H. Belo Corp., Communications Center, Dallas, TX 75265.)
Information on business and industry, transportation, education, and
other essential facts.

Texas Association of Realtors Referral Directory
(Texas Association of Realtors, P.O. Box 14488, Austin, TX 78761.)
Texas Association of Realtors members listed by city.

Texas Banking Red Book
(Bankers Digest, Inc., 6440 N. Central Expwy., Suite 215, Dallas, TX
75206; $15.75.) Lists banks, federal deposit insurance corporations,
holding companies, and other banking institutions.

Texas Fact Book
(Bureau of Business Research, University of Texas at Austin, Austin,
TX.) Includes economic profiles, business information, employment,
and manufacturing. Begins in 1989 with yearly supplements.

Texas Food Industry Association Directory
(Texas Retail Grocers Association, 7333 Hwy. 290 East, Austin, TX
78723.) List of Texas Retail Grocers Association members, sponsors,
exhibitors, and advertisers.

Texas Insurance Directory (North and South)
(Insurance Field Co., 4325 Old Shepherdsville Rd., Louisville, KY
40218.) Annual list of facilities and services of licensed property,
liability, and life companies, and agencies in Texas.

Texas Savings & Loan Directory
(Texas Savings & Loan League, 408 W. 14th St., Austin, TX 78701.)
Includes statistical information, regulatory agencies, industry
associations, annual reports, and members.

Texas Trade and Professional Associations
(Bureau of Business Research, The University of Texas at Austin.) Lists
trade and professional associations.

**Ward's Business Directory of U.S. Private and Public
Companies**
(Gale Research Inc., 835 Penobscot Bldg., Detroit, Mich 48226.)
Covers nearly 85,000 privately owned companies representing all
industries.

Yearbook of International Organizations
(Union of International Associations and International Chambers of
Commerce, Rue Washington 40, B-1050, Brussels, Belgium.) Lists
27,000 truly international organizations (active in at least 3
countries); indexed by name, address, and description.

Newspapers

Answering want ads is one of several tasks to be done in any
job search, and generally among the least productive.
According to *Forbes* magazine, only about 10 percent of professional and technical people find their jobs through want
ads. Like any other long shot, however, answering want ads
sometimes pays off. Be sure to check not only the classified
listings but also the larger display ads that appear in the
Sunday business sections of the major papers. These ads are
usually for upper-level jobs.

Help-wanted listings generally come in two varieties: open
advertisements and blind ads. An open ad is one in which the
company identifies itself and lists an address. Your best bet is
not to send a resume to a company that prints an open ad.
Instead, you should try to identify the hiring authority (see
Chapter 5) and pull every string you can think of to arrange
an interview directly.

The personnel department is in business to screen *out* applicants. Of the several hundred resumes that an open ad in a
major newspaper is likely to attract, the personnel department will probably forward only a handful to the people who
are actually doing the hiring. It's better for you to go to those
people directly than to try to reach them by sending a piece
of paper (your resume) to the personnel department.

Blind ads are run by companies that do not identify themselves because they do not want to acknowledge receipt of resumes. Since you don't know who the companies are, your
only option in response to a blind ad is to send a resume. This

is among the longest of long shots and usually pays off only if your qualifications are exactly suited to the position that's being advertised. Just remember that if you depend solely on ad responses, you're essentially conducting a passive search, waiting for the mail to arrive or the phone to ring. Passive searchers usually are unemployed a long time.

Newspaper business sections are useful not only for their want ads but also as sources of local business news and news about personnel changes. Learn to read between the lines. If an article announces that Big Bucks, Inc., has just acquired a new vice-president, chances are that he or she will be looking for staffers. If the new veep came to Big Bucks from another local company, obviously that company may have at least one vacancy and possibly several.

MAJOR NEWSPAPER RESOURCES

The Dallas Morning News
Communications Center
Dallas, TX 75265
(214) 977-8222
The *News* purchased the *Dallas Times Herald* in late 1991, making Dallas a one-newspaper city. The *News* carries an extensive Sunday classified section. A bulldog Sunday edition is sold on Saturday. Extensive business coverage is carried in the daily business sections.

Fort Worth Star-Telegram
400 W. 7th St.
Fort Worth, TX 76101
Metro (817) 429-2655
The *Star-Telegram* publishes a "Tarrant Business" section on Monday, which includes news and features for Fort Worth and the Mid-Cities area.

National Business Employment Weekly
Box 300
Princeton, NJ 08540
(609) 520-4305
The weekly is published every Sunday by *The Wall Street Journal*. It reprints recruitment ads from the *Journal's* four regional editions as well as articles and editorials about the business community.

The Wall Street Journal
1233 Regal Row
Dallas, TX 75247
(214) 631-7250
The nation's leading weekday business publication carries a Southwest edition, which is published locally. Its classified section usually carries ads for mid- to upper-level management positions. The *Journal* only covers news about the business community—everything from the

economy to personnel changes in the country's major corporations. If you really want to do your homework on the business community, the *Journal* is the place to start.

SUBURBAN AND COMMUNITY NEWSPAPERS
Most of the following newspapers carry want ads.

Addison/North Dallas Register
4950 Keller Springs Rd., Suite 160
Addison, TX 75248
(214) 385-3547
Published on Thursday.

Arlington Citizen-Journal
1111 W. Abram St.
Arlington, TX 76012
(817) 548-5400
Thursday and Sunday publications inserted in the Arlington edition of the *Fort Worth Star-Telegram*.

Arlington News
1000 Ave. H East
Arlington, TX 76011
Metro (817) 695-0500
Published Thursday, Friday, and Sunday by the Dallas/Fort Worth Suburban Newspapers.

Carrollton Chronicle
1712 Belt Line Rd.
Carrollton, TX 75006
(214) 446-0303
Published on Wednesday.

Cedar Hill Chronicle
708 Cedar St.
Cedar Hill, TX 75104
(214) 291-4223
Published on Thursday.

The Colony Leader
4916 FM 423
Frisco, TX 75056
(214) 625-6397
Published on Wednesday.

Coppell Gazette
102 Lewisville Leader Professional Bldg., Suite 100
Lewisville, TX 75067
(214) 446-0303
Published on Wednesday.

Dallas Downtown News
2908 McKinney Ave.
Dallas, TX 75204
(214) 826-7661
Published on Monday for the Central Business District, Oak Lawn,
Fair Park, North Oak Cliff, East Dallas, and the Market Center area.

Dallas Post Tribune
2726 S. Beckley Ave.
Dallas, TX 75224
(214) 946-7678
Published on Thursday. A good resource for the minority community.

Duncanville Suburban
606 Oriole
Duncanville, TX 75116
(214) 298-4211
Published on Thursday.

El Sol De Texas
4260 Spring Valley Rd.
Dallas, TX 75244
(214) 386-9120
Spanish language newspaper published on Thursday, with news about
Dallas, Fort Worth, and Latin countries.

Farmers Branch Times
1712 Belt Line Rd.
Carrollton, TX 75006
(214) 446-0303
Published on Wednesday.

Garland Daily News
613 State St.
Garland, TX 75040
(214) 272-6591
Published Thursday, Friday, and Sunday by the Dallas/Fort Worth
Suburban Newspapers.

Grand Prairie Daily News
1000 Ave. H East
Arlington, TX 76011
Metro (817) 695-0500
Published Thursday, Friday, and Sunday by the Dallas/Fort Worth
Suburban Newspapers.

Grapevine Sun
332 Main St.
Grapevine, TX 76051
(817) 488-8561
Published Thursday and Sunday.

Irving Daily News
1000 Ave. H East
Arlington, TX 76011
Metro (817) 695-0500
Published Thursday, Friday, and Sunday by the Dallas/Fort Worth
Suburban Newspapers.

Lancaster News
303 W. Pheasant Run
Lancaster, TX 75146
(214) 227-6033
Published on Thursday.

Lewisville Daily Leader
102 Lakeland Plaza
Lewisville, TX 75067
(214) 436-3566
Published Wednesday and Saturday.

Lewisville News
131 W. Main St.
Lewisville, TX 75067
(214) 436-5551
Published Wednesday, Friday, and Sunday.

Mesquite News
303 N. Galloway Ave.
Mesquite, TX 75149
(214) 285-6301
Published Sunday.

Metrocrest News
1430 Valwood Pkwy., Suite 125
Carrollton, TX 75006
(214) 243-0194
Published on Thursday, Friday, and Sunday by the Dallas/Fort Worth
Suburban Newspapers for Carrollton, Farmers Branch, Addison, and
Coppell.

Mid-Cities Daily News
1000 Ave. H East
Arlington, TX 76011
Metro (817) 695-0500
Published Thursday, Friday, and Sunday for Hurst, Euless, Bedford,
Haltom City, North Richland Hills, and Richland Hills by the
Dallas/Fort Worth Suburban Newspapers.

Oak Cliff Tribune
2303 W. Ledbetter Professional Bldg., Suite 200
Dallas, TX 75208
(214) 339-3111
Published on Thursday.

Park Cities News
6060 N. Central Expwy., Suite 134
Dallas, TX 75206
(214) 369-7570
Published on Thursday for Highland Park and University Park.

Park Cities People
6116 N. Central Expwy., Suite 230
Dallas, TX 75206
(214) 739-2244
Published on Thursday for Highland Park and University Park.

Plano Daily Star-Courier
801 E. Plano Pkwy., Suite 100
Plano, TX 75074
(214) 424-6565
Published Wednesday through Sunday, with a special "Working Section" on Sundays.

Richardson Daily News
613 State St.
Garland, TX 75040
(214) 272-6591
Published Thursday, Friday, and Sunday by the Dallas/Fort Worth Suburban Newspapers.

Seagoville Suburbia News
115-A Hall Rd.
Seagoville, TX 75159
(214) 287-3277
Delivered Thursday for Balch Springs, Combine, Crandall, and Seagoville.

Suburban Tribune
1838-B S. Buckner Blvd.
Dallas, TX 75217
(214) 398-1456
Published Thursday and mailed to residents in the Southeast Dallas area.

The White Rocker News
10809 Garland Rd.
Dallas, TX 75218
(214) 327-9335
Published on Thursday for the White Rock area.

General Business Magazines

The smart job seeker will want to keep abreast of changing trends in the economy. These periodicals will help you keep up with the national and Dallas/Fort Worth business scenes.

Business Week
1221 Avenue of the Americas
New York, NY 10020
(212) 997-1221
Weekly.

Dallas Business Journal
4131 N. Central Expwy., Suite
310
Dallas, TX 75204
Metro (214) 520-1010
Weekly business publication
(Fridays).

Forbes
60 5th Ave.
New York, NY 10011
(212) 620-2200
Bi-weekly.

Fort Worth Business Press
501 Jones St.
Fort Worth, TX 76106
(817) 336-8300
Weekly business publication
(Fridays).

Fortune
Time & Life Bldg., Rockefeller
Center
New York, NY 10020
(800) 621-8000
Published 26 times per year.

Money
Time & Life Bldg., Rockefeller
Center
New York, NY 10020
(800) 633-9970
Monthly.

Newsweek
444 Madison Ave.
New York, NY 10022
(800) 631-1040
Weekly. Includes business
coverage.

Success
230 Park Ave.
New York, NY 10169
(800) 234-7324

Time Magazine
1271 Avenue of the Americas
New York, NY 10022
(212) 586-1212
Weekly. Includes business
coverage.

Venture
521 Fifth Ave.
New York, NY 10075
(212) 682-7373
Monthly.

Working Woman
230 Park Ave.
New York, NY 10169
(212) 551-9500
Monthly.

Job-Hunt-Related Publications

The following newspapers and magazines contain only job
listings and job-related information and advice.

AAR/EEO Affirmative Action Register
8356 Olive Blvd.
St. Louis, MO 63132
(314) 991-1335

"The only national EEO recruitment publication directed to females, minorities, veterans, and the handicapped." Monthly magazine consists totally of job listings.

Career Pilot
Future Aviation Professionals of America
4959 Massachusetts Blvd.
Atlanta, GA 30337
(800) JET-JOBS
Monthly magazine outlines employment opportunities for career pilots. Organization provides hiring information, salary surveys, monthly job reports, and counseling to prepare for interviews.

Community Jobs
50 Beacon St.
Boston, MA 02108
(617) 720-5627
The employment newspaper for the non-profit sector.

Contract Engineer Weekly
CE Publications, Inc.
P.O. Box 97000
Kirkland, WA 98083
(206) 823-2222
Weekly magazine of job opportunities for contract engineers.

Federal Jobs Digest
310 N. Highland Ave.
Ossining, NY 10562
Elaborate listing of job opportunities with the federal government. Published bi-weekly.

Legal Employment Newsletter
P.O. Box 36601
Grosse Point, MI 48236
Newsletter lists open legal positions as well as career opportunities in the public-private sector.

National and Federal Legal Employment Report
1010 Vermont Ave., NW
Washington, DC 20005
(202) 393-3311
Monthly in-depth listings of attorney and law-related jobs in federal government and with other public and private employers throughout the U.S. Lists 99.9% of available positions for attorneys.

Local Trade and Special Interest Magazines

Every industry or service business has its trade press—that is, editors, reporters, and photographers whose job it is to cover an industry or trade. You should become familiar with the magazines of the industries or professions that interest you, especially if you're in the interviewing stage of your job search. Your prospective employers are reading the industry trade magazines; you should be too.

Trade magazines are published for a specific business or professional audience; they are usually expensive and available by subscription only. Many of the magazines we've listed here are available at major Dallas/Fort Worth area libraries. For those not to be found at the library, call up the magazine's editorial or sales office and ask if you can come over to look at the latest issue.

The following magazines have editorial offices in the Dallas/Fort Worth area, reporting area news about the people and businesses in their industry. Many carry local want ads and personnel changes. For a complete listing of the trade press, consult the *Ayer Directory of Publications* at the library.

Adweek/Southwest
2909 Cole Ave., Suite 220
Dallas, TX 75204
(214) 871-9550
Weekly advertising, public relations, and marketing trade publication.

Bankers Digest
6440 N. Central Expwy., Suite 215
Dallas, TX 75206
(214) 373-4544
Weekly Texas banking publication.

The Cattleman
1301 W. 7th St.
Fort Worth, TX 76102
(817) 332-7155
Monthly cattlemen's magazine.

Cotton Gin and Oil Mill Press
3638 Executive Blvd.
Mesquite, TX 75149
(214) 288-7511
Bi-weekly cotton industry publication.

Farm Journal
811 S. Central Expwy., Suite 525
Richardson, TX 75080
(214) 231-6033
Regional editorial office for monthly farm industry publication.

Greenhouse Manager
120 St. Louis Ave.
Fort Worth, TX 76104
(817) 332-8236
Monthly worldwide publication for greenhouse growers.

Impressions
15400 Knoll Trail Dr., Suite 112
Dallas, TX 75248
(214) 239-3060
Monthly publication for the imprinted sportswear and textile screen printing industries.

The Insurance Record
2730 Stemmons Frwy., Suite 507
Dallas, TX 75207
(214) 630-0687
Bi-weekly insurance trade publication.

Journal of Petroleum Technology
222 Palisades Creek Dr.
Richardson, TX 75080
(214) 669-3377
Monthly publication for drilling, exploration, production engineers, and managers.

Nursery Manager
120 St. Louis Ave.
Fort Worth, TX 76104
Metro (817) 429-1494
Monthly worldwide publication for nursery industry.

Oil & Gas Journal
4849 Greenville Ave., Suite 660
Dallas, TX 75206
(214) 739-3338
Weekly petroleum industry publication.

Performance
1203 Lake St., Suite 200
Fort Worth, TX 76102
(817) 338-9444
Weekly international touring talent magazine.

Petroleum Engineer International
10300 N. Central Expwy., Bldg. 5, Suite 580
Dallas, TX 75231
(214) 691-3911
Monthly petroleum engineers' publication.

Pipeline & Gas Journal
10300 N. Central Expwy., Suite 580
Dallas, TX 75231
(214) 691-3911
Monthly petroleum industry publication.

SAF-The Center for Commercial Horticulture
120 St. Louis Ave.
Fort Worth, TX 76104
Metro (817) 429-1494
Monthly florist industry publication.

Texas Contractor
2510 National Dr.
Garland, TX 75041
(214) 271-2693
Weekly publication and daily newsletter for heavy construction industry.

General Interest Magazines and Newspapers

In your job search, you'll find it helpful to know as much about the Dallas/Fort Worth area as possible. The following publications will help you become better informed:

American Way
P.O. Box 619640
DFW Airport, TX 75261
Metro (817) 967-1804
American Airlines' semi-weekly inflight magazine.

Aura of Fort Worth
2917 Morton
Fort Worth, TX 76107
(817) 332-3548
Bi-monthly magazine for Tarrant County.

Baptist Standard
2343 Lone Star Dr.
Dallas, TX 75212
(214) 630-4571
Weekly publication for
Southern Baptists.

Buddy Magazine
5705 Ovam
Dallas, TX 75206
(214) 826-8742
Monthly music magazine with a
special edition for the
Dallas/Fort Worth area that
includes entertainment listings.

D Magazine
3988 N. Central Expwy., Suite
1200
Dallas, TX 75204
(214) 827-5000
Monthly city magazine that
explores trends in area politics,
business, education, lifestyle,
entertainment, and dining.

Daily Commercial Record
706 Main St.
Dallas, TX 75202
(214) 741-6366
Dallas County legal news
published Monday through
Friday.

Dallas Business Journal
4131 N. Central Expwy., Suite
310
Dallas, TX 75204
Metro (214) 520-1010
Weekly business publication.

Dallas Child
3330 Earhart Dr., Suite 102
Carrollton, TX 75006
(214) 960-8474
Monthly magazine for parents.

Dallas Cowboys Weekly
Cowboys Center
1 Cowboys Pkwy.
Irving, TX 75063
(214) 556-9972
Dallas Cowboys publication,
distributed weekly during
football season and monthly
during off-season.

Dallas Observer
3211 Irving Blvd., Suite 110
Dallas, TX 75247
(214) 637-2072
Weekly entertainment,
lifestyles, and current events
publication.

Detour Magazine
3100 Carlisle St.
Dallas, TX 75204
(214) 520-9777
Fashion, art, and feature
publication issued 10 times a
year.

Fort Worth Business Press
501 Jones St.
Fort Worth, TX 76106
(817) 336-8300
Weekly business publication
(Fridays).

Fort Worth Magazine
777 Taylor St., Suite 900
Fort Worth, TX 76102
(817) 336-2491
Quarterly Fort Worth Chamber
of Commerce publication.
General interest, with a
business slant.

Key Magazine
3626 N. Hall St., Suite 508
Dallas, TX 75219
(214) 528-5070
Monthly visitor's magazine.

Private Clubs
3030 LBJ Frwy., Suite 600
Dallas, TX 75234
(214) 243-6191
Bi-monthly magazine for Club
Corporation of America
members.

SR Texas
11551 Forest Central Dr., Suite
305
Dallas, TX 75243
(214) 341-9429
Monthly publication for
people over the age of 50.

**The Texas Catholic
Newspaper**
3915 Lemmon Ave.
Dallas, TX 75219
(214) 528-8792
Bi-weekly publication with
local and international news for
Catholics.

Texas Jewish Post
11333 N. Central Expwy., Suite
213
Dallas, TX 75243
(214) 692-7283
Weekly publication with local
and international news for the
Jewish faith.

The Texas Lawyer
1 Ferris Plaza
400 S. Record St., Suite 1400
Dallas, TX 75202
(214) 744-9300
Weekly publication for the
legal profession.

Travelhost Magazine
8080 N. Central Expwy.
Dallas, TX 75206
(214) 891-8200
A guide placed in 22,000 area
motel rooms, with advertising
for entertainment and
restaurants along with some
real estate ads.

Vitality Magazine
8080 N. Central Expwy., Suite
1500
Dallas, TX 75206
(214) 691-1480
Weekly travel magazine, with
features on real estate,
entertainment, health,
wellness, and dining available
at area hotels.

Telephone Job Banks

Here's a way to find out about job openings by "letting your fingers do the walking." Just dial any one of the numerous telephone job banks and listen to the taped recordings that describe available positions and how to apply.

There is no charge for most of these job hotlines other than what you might spend for a telephone call. The following is a list of area telephone job banks.

City of Dallas (214) 670-5908
City of Fort Worth (817) 870-7760
Communicators' Job Bank (214) 978-8070
Dallas County Community College District (214) 746-2438
Federal Job Information Line (214) 767-8035
Network of Hispanic Communicators and DFW ABC Job
   Line (214) 977-6635
Southern Methodist University (214) 692-2157

Tarrant County Junior College (817) 335-6721
Texas Christian University (817) 921-7791
Texas Instruments (214) 995-6666

The right job may be only a phone call away

The Communicators' Job Bank, (214) 978-8070, is a joint service project of the local International Association of Business Communicators (IABC) and the Public Relations Society of America (PRSA). Each week, job bank coordinator Cami Hardee updates a 6-minute recording that relays information about openings in public relations, advertising, marketing, design, and related fields. She describes the job, qualifications, and salary range, but no company name is disclosed.

To apply for openings through the Communicators' Job Bank, you request that your resumes be sent to the job listings of your choice. To register with the Communicators' Job Bank, a small fee is charged that covers the cost of mailing your resumes to an unlimited number of employers during a three-month period. IABC and PRSA members pay $5, and non-members are charged $10.

An average of 30 jobs are usually on file each week. Hardee, who volunteers her time for the project, can testify to its benefits. She found her own job through the service.■

Developing a Strategy:
The ABCs of Networking

The successful job search doesn't happen by accident. It's the result of careful planning. Before you rush out to set up your first interview, it's important to establish a strategy, that is, to develop a plan for researching the job market and contacting potential employers.

This chapter and Chapter 7 will cover specific techniques and tools that you'll find useful in your search. But before we get to them, a few words are in order about your overall approach.

It's Going to Take Some Time

Looking for a new job is no easy task. It's as difficult and time-consuming for a bright young woman with a brand-new MBA as it is for a fifty-year-old executive with years of front-line experience. Every once in a while someone lucks out. One of Tom's clients established a record at Camden and Associates by finding a new position in four days. But most people should plan on two to six months of full-time job-hunting before they find a position they'll really be happy with.

According to *Forbes* magazine, the older you are and the more you earn, the longer it will take to find what you're looking for—in fact, up to six months for people over 40 earning more than $40,000. People under 40 in the $20,000-$40,000 bracket average two to four months.

Your line of work will also affect the length of your search. Usually, the easier it is to demonstrate tangible bottom-line results, the faster you can line up a job. Lawyers, public relations people, and advertising executives are harder to place than accountants and sales people, according to one top personnel specialist.

Be Good to Yourself

Whether or not you're currently employed, it's important to nurture your ego when you're looking for a new job. Rejection rears its ugly head more often in a job search than at most other times, and self-doubt can be deadly.

Make sure you get regular exercise during your job search to relieve stress. You'll sleep better, feel better, and perhaps even lose a few pounds.

Take care of your diet and watch what you drink. Many people who start to feel sorry for themselves tend to overindulge in food or alcohol. Valium and other such drugs are not as helpful as sharing your progress with your family or a couple of close friends.

Beef up your wardrobe so that you look and feel good during your employment interviews. There's no need to buy an expensive new suit, especially if you're on an austerity budget, but a new shirt, blouse, tie, pair of shoes, or hairstyle may be in order.

Maintain a positive outlook. Unemployment is not the end of the world; few people complete a career without losing a job at least once. Keep a sense of humor, too. Every job search has its funny moments. It's OK to joke about your situation and share your sense of humor with your friends and family.

Life goes on despite your job search. Your spouse and kids still need your attention. Try not to take out your anxieties, frustrations, and fears on those close to you. At the very time you need support and affirmation, your friends may prefer to stay at arm's length. You can relieve their embarrassment by being straightforward about your situation and by telling them how they can help you.

Put Yourself on a Schedule

Looking for work is a job in itself. Establish a schedule for your job search and stick to it. If you're unemployed, work at getting a new job full-time—from 8:30 a.m. to 5:30 p.m., five days a week; and from 9 a.m. to 12 noon on Saturdays. During a job search, there is a temptation to use "extra" time for recreation or to catch up on household tasks. Arranging two or three exploratory interviews will prove a lot more useful to you than washing the car or cleaning out the garage. You can do such tasks at night or on Sundays, just as you would if you were working.

Don't take a vacation during your search. Do it after you accept an offer and before you begin a new job. You might be tempted to "sort things out on the beach." But taking a vacation when you're unemployed isn't as restful as it sounds. You'll spend most of your time worrying about what will happen when the trip is over.

Even if you're currently employed, it's important to establish regular hours for your job search. If you're scheduling interviews, try to arrange several for one day so that you don't have to take too much time away from your job. You might also arrange interviews for your lunch hour. You can make phone calls during lunch or on your break time. You'd also be surprised at how many people you can reach before and after regular working hours.

Tax-deductible job-hunting expenses

A certified public accountant offers the following tips on deducting job-hunting expenses on your income tax form. To qualify for certain deductions, you must hunt for a job in the same field you just left, or in the field that currently employs you. For example, someone who has worked as a public school teacher could not be compensated for the cost of getting a real estate license and seeking a realtor's job.

If you are unemployed or want to switch jobs, expenses can be itemized on Schedule A of Form 1040. Expenses you can deduct include preparing, printing, and mailing resumes; vocational guidance counseling and testing; and you can take the standard government reimbursement for miles driven to and from job interviews. Telephone, postage, and newspaper expenses are also deductible.

While seeking work out of town, additional deductions are allowed for transportation, food, and lodging.

Another good bit of advice: tax laws are subject to change, so always check with your local Internal Revenue Service office. ■

Watch Your Expenses

Spend what you have to spend for basic needs such as food, transportation, and housing. But watch major expenditures that could be delayed or not made at all. The kids will still need new shoes, but a $200 dinner party at a fancy place could just as well be changed to sandwiches and beer at home.

Keep track of all expenses that you incur in your job search, such as telephone and printing bills, postage, newspapers, parking, transportation, tolls, and meals purchased during the course of interviewing. These may be tax deductible.

Networking Is the Key to a Successful Job Search

The basic tasks of a job search are fairly simple. Once you've figured out what kind of work you want to do, you need to know which companies might have such jobs and then make contact with the hiring authority. These tasks are also known as researching the job market and generating leads and interviews. Networking, or developing your personal contacts, is the best technique for finding out about market and industrial trends and is unsurpassed as a way to generate leads and interviews.

Networking is nothing more than asking the people you already know to help you explore the job market and meet the people who are actually doing the hiring. Each adult you know has access to at least 300 people you do not know. Of course, a lot of them will not be able to do much in the way of helping you find a job. But if you start with, say, 20 or 30 people, and each of them tells you about 3 other people who may be able to help you, you've built a network of 60 to 90 contacts.

Mark S. Granovetter, a Harvard sociologist, reported to *Forbes* magazine that "informal contacts" account for almost 75 percent of all successful job searches. Agencies find about 9 percent of new jobs for professional and technical people, and ads yield another 10 percent or so.

Here's an example of a networking letter

Box 7457
The University of Dallas
Irving, TX 75033

April 11, 1992

Dr. Norman Hartman
President
Combined Opinion Research
300 Progress Ave.
Irving, TX 75008

Dear Dr. Hartman:

Dr. Obrigon Partito, with whom I have studied these past two years, suggested that you might be able to advise me of opportunities in the field of social and political research in the Dallas/Fort Worth area.

I am about to graduate from the University of Dallas with a B.A. in American History, and am a member of Phi Beta Kappa. For two of the last three summers, I have worked in the public sector as an intern with Citizens for a Better Government and with Senator Kerry in Washington. Last summer I worked as a desk assistant at Newsweek's Dallas office.

I am eager to begin work and would appreciate a few minutes of your time to discuss employment possibilities in the field of social and political research. I will be finished with exams on May 24 and would like to arrange a meeting with you shortly thereafter.

I would appreciate an opportunity to visit with you about your firm and its activities and will call next week. Dr. Partito sends his warmest regards.

Sincerely,
Steven Sharp
(214) 555-2468 ■

How to Start

To begin the networking process, draw up a list of all the possible contacts who can help you gain access to someone who can hire you for the job you want. Naturally, the first sources, the ones at the top of your list, will be people you know personally: friends, colleagues, former clients, relatives, acquaintances, customers, and club and church members. Just about everyone you know, whether or not he or she is employed, can generate contacts for you.

Don't forget to talk with your banker, lawyer, insurance agent, dentist, and other people who provide you with services. It is the nature of their business to know a lot of people who might help you in your search. Leave no stone unturned in your search for contacts. Go through your Christmas card list, alumni club list, and any other list you can think of.

On the average, it may take 10 to 15 contacts to generate one formal interview. It may take 5 or 10 of these formal interviews to generate one solid offer. And it may take 5 offers before you uncover the exact job situation you've been seeking. You may have to talk to a minimum of 250 people before you get the job you want. The maximum may be several hundred more.

Don't balk at talking to friends, acquaintances, and neighbors about your job search. In reality, you're asking for advice, not charity. Most of the people you'll contact will be willing to help you, if only you tell them *how*.

The Exploratory Interview

If I introduce you to my friend George at a major downtown bank, he will get together with you as a favor to me. When you have your meeting with him, you will make a presentation about what you've done in your work, what you want to do, and (most importantly) you will ask for his advice, ideas, and opinions. That is an exploratory interview. As is true of any employment interview, you must make a successful sales presentation to get what you want. You must convince George that you are a winner and that you deserve his help in your search.

The help the interviewer provides is usually in the form of suggestions to meet new people or contact certain companies. I introduced you to George. Following your successful meeting, he introduces you to Tom, Dick, and Mary. Each of them provides additional leads. In this way, you spend most of your time interviewing, not staying at home waiting for the phone to ring or the mail to arrive.

A job doesn't have to be vacant in order for you to have a successful meeting with a hiring authority. If you convince an employer that you would make a good addition to his or her staff, the employer might create a job for you where none existed before. In this way, networking taps the "hidden job market."

To make the most of the networking technique, continually brush up on your interviewing skills (we've provided a refresher course in Chapter 7). Remember, even when you're talking with an old friend, you are still conducting an exploratory interview. Don't treat it as casual conversation.

Developing Professional Contacts

Friends and acquaintances are the obvious first choice when you're drawing up a list of contacts. But don't forget professional and trade organizations, clubs, and societies—they are valuable sources of contacts, leads, and information. In certain cases, it isn't necessary for you to belong in order to attend a meeting or an annual or monthly lunch, dinner, or cocktail party.

Many such groups also publish newsletters, another valuable source of information on the job market and industry trends. Some professional associations offer placement services to members, in which case it may be worth your while to join officially. At the end of this chapter, we've provided a list of selected organizations that might prove useful for networking purposes.

If you're utterly new to the area and don't as yet know a soul, your job will naturally be tougher. But it's not impossible. It just means you have to hustle that much more. Here are some first steps you should take. Start attending the meetings of any professional society or civic organization of which you've been a member in the past. Find a church, temple, or religious organization that you're comfortable with and start attending. Join a special interest group. It could be anything from The Sierra Club to Parents Without Partners.

If you're just out of college (or even haven't finished yet), work through your alumni association to find out who else in the area attended your alma mater. If you were in a fraternity or sorority, use those connections. If you're not a member of any of the groups mentioned above, now's the time to join— or to investigate some of the networking groups that follow.

Once you've taken the trouble to show up at a meeting, be friendly. Introduce yourself. Tell people you talk to what your situation is, but don't be pushy. You've come because you're interested in this organization and what it stands for. Volunteer to serve on a committee. You'll get to know a smaller number of people much better, and they'll see you as a responsible, generous person, a person they'll want to help. Do a bang-up job on your committee and they'll want to help all the more.

You've already got lots of contacts

Networking paid off for Liz, a young woman eager to make her way in banking or a related industry. She told us why she's glad she took the time to talk with her friends and neighbors about her job search.

"I was having dinner with close friends and telling them about my job search," says Liz. "During the conversation, they mentioned a banker friend they thought might be hiring. As it turned out, the friend didn't have a job for me. But he suggested I come in, meet with him, and discuss some other possibilities. He put me in touch with an independent marketing firm, servicing the publishing industry. The owner of the firm was looking for someone with my exact qualifications. One thing led to another, and pretty soon I had landed exactly the position I wanted." ■

Keeping Yourself Organized

The most difficult part of any job search is getting started. A pocket calendar or engagement diary that divides each work day into hourly segments will come in handy.

You will also want to keep a personal log of calls and contacts. You may want to develop a format that's different from the one shown here. Fine. The point is to keep a written record of every person you contact in your job search and the results of each contact.

Your log (it can be a notebook from the dime store) will help keep you from getting confused and losing track of the details of your search. If you call someone who's out of town until Tuesday, say, your log can flag this call so it won't fall between the cracks. It may also come in handy for future job searches.

Your log's "disposition" column can act as a reminder of additional sources of help you'll want to investigate. You'll also have a means of timing the correspondence that should follow any interview.

CALLS AND CONTACTS

Date	Name & Title	Company	Phone	Disposition
2/10	Chas. Junior, V.P. Sales	Top Parts	(214) 689-5562	Interview 2/15
2/10	E. Franklin Sales Manager	Frameco	(214) 876-0900	Out of town until 2/17
2/10	L. Duffy Dir. Marketing	Vassar Inc.	(817) 744-8700	Out of office. Call in aft.
2/10	P. Lamm Sls. Dir.	Golfco Ent.	(817) 834-3000	Busy to 2/28 Call then.
2/10	E. Waixel VP Mktg. & Sales	Half'n'Half Foods	(214) 342-1200	Call after 2

If you're unemployed and job-hunting full time, schedule yourself for two exploratory interviews a day for the first week and three to five networking phone calls per day. Each meeting should result in at least three subsequent leads. Leave the second week open for the appointments you generated during the first. Maintain this pattern as you go along in your search.

We can't emphasize too strongly how important it is that you put yourself on a job-searching schedule, whether or not you're currently employed. A schedule shouldn't function as a straight jacket, but it ought to serve as a way of organizing your efforts for greatest efficiency. Much of your job-hunting time will be devoted to developing your network of contacts. But you should also set aside a certain portion of each week for doing your homework on companies that interest you (see Chapter 4), and for pursuing other means of contacting employers (we'll get to these in a minute).

As you go through your contacts and begin to research the job market, you'll begin to identify certain employers in which you're interested. Keep a list of them. For each one that looks particularly promising, begin a file that contains articles about the company, its annual report, product brochures, personnel policy, and the like. Every so often, check your "potential employer" list against your log to make sure that you're contacting the companies that interest you most.

Go for the Hiring Authority

The object of your job search is to convince the person who has the power to hire you that you ought to be working for him or her. The person you want to talk to is not necessarily the president of the company. It's the person who heads the department that could use your expertise. If you're a salesperson, you probably want to talk with the vice president of sales or marketing. If you're in data processing, the vice president of operations is the person you need to see.

How do you find the hiring authority? If you're lucky, someone you know personally will tell you whom to see and introduce you. Otherwise, you'll have to do some homework. Some of the directories listed in Chapter 4 will name department heads for major companies in the Dallas/Fort Worth area. If you cannot otherwise find out who heads the exact department that interests you, call the company and ask the operator. (It's a good idea to do this anyway since directories go out of date as soon as a department head leaves a job.)

Use an introduction wherever possible when first approaching a company—that's what networking is all about, anyway. For those companies that you must approach "cold," use the phone to arrange a meeting with the hiring authority beforehand. Don't assume you can drop in and see a busy executive without an appointment. And don't assume you can get to the hiring authority through the personnel department. If at all possible, you don't want to fill out any personnel forms until you have had a serious interview. The same goes for sending resumes (see Chapter 3). In general, resumes are better left behind, *after* an interview, than sent ahead to generate a meeting.

Telephone Tactics

Cold calls are difficult for most job seekers. Frequently, a receptionist or secretary, sometimes both, stands between you and the hiring authority you want to reach. One way around this is to call about a half-hour after closing. There's a good chance that the secretary will be off to happy hour, and the boss will still be finishing up the XYZ project report. Only now there will be no one to run interference for him or her.

Generally, you're going to have to go through a support staffer, so the first rule is to act courteously and accord him or her the same professional respect you'd like to be accorded yourself. This person is not just a secretary. Often, part of his or her job is to keep unsolicited job hunters out of the boss's hair. You want this intermediary to be your ally, not your adversary. If possible, sell what a wonderfully qualified person you are and how it is to the company's advantage to have you aboard.

If you're not put through to the hiring authority, don't leave your name and expect a return call. Instead, ask when there's a convenient time you might call back, or allow yourself to be put on hold. You can read job-search literature or compose cover letters while you wait. Be sure and keep your target's name and title and the purpose of your call on a card before you, however. You don't want to be at a loss for words when you're finally put through.

Other Tactics for Contacting Employers

Direct contact with the hiring authority—either through a third-party introduction (networking) or by calling for an appointment directly—is far and away the most effective job-hunting method. Your strategy and schedule should reflect that fact, and most of your energy should be devoted to direct contact. It's human nature, however, not to put all your eggs in one basket. You may want to explore other methods of contacting potential employers, but they should take up no more than a quarter of your job-hunting time.

Calling or writing to personnel offices may occasionally be productive, especially when you know that a company is looking for someone with your particular skills. But personnel people, by the nature of their responsibility, tend to screen out rather than welcome newcomers to the company fold. You're always better off going directly to the hiring authority.

Consider the case of a company that runs an ad in *The Wall Street Journal*. The ad may bring as many as 600 responses. The head of personnel asks one of the secretaries to separate the resumes into three piles according to educational level. The personnel chief automatically eliminates two of the three stacks. He or she then flips through the third and eliminates all but, say, eight resumes. The personnel specialist will call the eight applicants, screen them over the phone, and invite three for a preliminary interview. Of those three, two will be sent to the hiring authority for interviews. That means 598 applicants never even got a chance to make their case.

Statistically, fewer than one out of four job hunters succeed by going to personnel departments, responding to ads (either open or blind), or using various employment services. Some do find meaningful work this way, however. We repeat, if you decide to use a method other than networking or direct contact, don't spend more than 25 percent of your job-hunting time on it.

Fort Worth Post Office sheds light on blind ads

Often, ads ask a candidate to send a resume to a P.O. Box. If you decide to reply, you face several challenges. What company is involved? To whom should I address my cover letter? What is the company's position in the market?

The office of the Postmaster in Fort Worth states that if the holder of a post office box does business with the public, the post office must release the information it possesses on the holder. This information enables you to personalize your response and do some research to tailor your resume to a specific firm. It avoids a blind response.

Call the Post Office with the zip code indicated in the ad to get the facts—and get a competitive edge on other applicants.■

As you might expect, many books have been written on job-hunting strategy and techniques. Here is a list of selected resources.

SELECTED BOOKS ON JOB-HUNTING STRATEGY

Bolles, Richard N. *The Three Boxes of Life and How to Get Out of Them*. Berkeley, CA: Ten Speed Press, 1983.

Bolles, Richard N. *What Color Is Your Parachute?* Berkeley, CA: Ten Speed Press, annual updates.

Camden, Thomas M. *The Job Hunter's Final Exam*. Chicago: Surrey Books, 1990.

Cowle, Jerry. *How to Survive Getting Fired and Win*. New York: Warner Books, 1980.

Davidson, Jeffrey P. *Blow Your Own Horn: How to Market Yourself and Your Career*. New York: American Management Association, 1987.

Figler, Howard. *The Complete Job Search Handbook*. New York: H. Holt & Co., 1988.

Gerberg, Robert. *Robert Gerberg's Job Changing System*. Kansas City, MO: Andrews and McMeel, 1986.

Half, Robert. *How to Get a Better Job in This Crazy World*. New York: Crown, 1990.

Hart, Lois Borland. *Moving Up—Women and Leadership*. New York: AMACOM, 1980.

Higginson, Margaret V., and Thomas L. Quick. *The Ambitious Woman's Guide to a Successful Career*. Ann Arbor, MI: Books on Demand, UMI, 1991.

Krannich, Ronald, and Caryl, R. *Network Your Way to Job & Career Success: Your Complete Guide to Creating New Opportunities*. Manassas, VA: 1989.

Lott, Catherine, and Lott, Oscar. *How to Land a Better Job*. Lincolnwood, IL: National Textbook Co., 1989.

Moses, Bruce E. *How To Market Yourself...Yourself*. New York: Pro-Search, Inc., 1979.

Pettus, Theodore. *One On One—Win the Interview, Win the Job*. New York: Random House, 1981.

Rogers, Henry C. *Rogers' Rules for Businesswomen*. New York: St. Martin's Press, 1988.

Rust, H.L. *Job Search: The Complete Manual for Job Seekers.* New York: AMACOM, 1991.
Wallace, Phyllis Ann. *MBAs on the Fast Track.* New York: Ballinger, 1989.

There follows a selected list of organized groups ready-made for networking. Pick those that fit best into your career game plan, and work through them to land the job you want.

SELECTED DALLAS/FORT WORTH PROFESSIONAL ORGANIZATIONS, TRADE GROUPS, NETWORKS, CLUBS, AND SOCIETIES

Administrative Management Society
Dallas Chapter
8150 Brookriver Dr., Apt. 400
Dallas, TX 75247
(214) 631-3144
President: Barbara Patterson
Professional society for office managers, personnel professionals, and field operations managers. Publishes a newsletter and conducts monthly meetings.

Administrative Management Society
Fort Worth Chapter
1320 S. University Dr., Suite 400
Fort Worth, TX 76107
(817) 336-2565
President: Ronald B. Woods
Parallels Dallas chapter.

Advertising Club of Fort Worth
P.O. Box 820376
Fort Worth, TX 76182
(817) 283-3615
Contact: Grace Collins, Executive Director
Organization for professionals in the advertising business. Meets weekly and publishes a monthly newsletter with job openings.

American Apparel Manufacturing Association Southwest Division
P.O. Box 585931
Dallas, TX 75258
(214) 631-0622
Contact: Cindrie Drieth
Trade association that meets before each market. Has a job bank for the fashion industry and keeps a resume file.

American Association for Respiratory Care
11030 Ables Lane
Dallas, TX 75229
(214) 243-2272
Executive Director: Sam Giordano

National headquarters for respiratory therapists. Publishes two magazines with job listings and provides a job hotline for members only.

American Association of Medical Assistants
Garland Chapter
726 Twilight Dr.
Garland, TX 75040
(214) 272-2052
Contact: Linda Coena
Offers aid to people who want to be certified and provides continuing education programs.

Dallas Chapter
2510 Moreland
Mesquite, TX 75150
(214) 270-5226

Fort Worth Chapter
4100 Frawley Dr.
Fort Worth, TX 76180
(817) 284-2204

American Association of Medical Transcription
Fort Worth Chapter
3628 Oakwood
Fort Worth, TX 76104
(817) 336-0551
Membership: Joan Johns, President
National organization for medical transcribers. Conducts continuing education workshops and publishes a newsletter with job information.

American Association of Petroleum Landmen
4100 Fossil Creek Blvd.
Fort Worth, TX 76137
(817) 847-7700
Contact: Lee J. Molesworth, President
Conducts monthly meetings.

American Fashion Association
P.O. Box 586454
Dallas, TX 75258
(214) 631-0821
Contact: Bette Hamilton
Organization of sales representatives, apparel, and accessory manufacturers. List of manufacturers seeking sales representatives available to AFA members only.

American Guild of Organists
Dallas Chapter
7159 Wildgrove Ave.
Dallas, TX 75214

(214) 327-2742
Contact: Richard DeLong
National and local placement for members; publishes a newsletter.

American Institute of Architects
Dallas Chapter
2811 McKinney Ave., LB104, #20
Dallas, TX 75204
(214) 871-2788
Contact: Gloria Wise
Professional organization of licensed architects, affiliates, and associates in related fields. Conducts monthly meetings and publishes a newsletter. Keeps resumes on file, has job referral service, offers state and national networking opportunities.

American Institute of Architects
Fort Worth Chapter
4388 W. Vickery Blvd., Suite 101
Fort Worth, TX 76107
(817) 763-0242
Executive Director: Suzie Adams
Same membership requirements as Dallas Chapter. Conducts monthly meetings and publishes a newsletter. Local distributor for AIA documents.

American Institute of Chemical Engineers
Dallas Section
P.O. Box 830936
Richardson, TX 75083
(214) 470-1218
Chairman: Ken Konvicks
Monthly educational meetings, national job fairs, job ads in newsletter, informal referral service, and support groups.

American Marketing Association
Dallas/Fort Worth Chapter
P.O. Box 515144
Dallas, TX 75251
Schedules monthly educational programs; publishes a newsletter, provides a job bank, and conducts seminars. Contact by mail.

American Medical Women's Association
8226 Douglas Ave., Suite 709
Dallas, TX 75225
(214) 696-8227
Contact: Dr. Gretchen Megowan
Informal networking opportunities available at bi-monthly social functions.

American Planning Association
North Central Texas Section
P.O. Box 803309

Richardson, TX 75083
(214) 238-4240
President: Monica Willard
Organization of city planners. Publishes a bimonthly newsletter with
job openings; national journal lists job opportunities.

American Society for Training and Development
P.O. Box 541193
Dallas, TX 75354
(214) 242-3991
Contact: Ronnie Norvell
National association for trainers, developers, and human resource
managers. Networking opportunities at monthly meetings. Publishes
a monthly newsletter and offers job referrals to members.

American Society of Civil Engineers
Dallas Branch
2209 Wisconsin St., Suite 100
Dallas, TX 75229
(214) 620-8911
Contact: John Hillhouse
Publishes monthly newsletter with job listings. Informal networking
opportunities at monthly meetings.

American Society of Heating, Refrigeration, and Air-Conditioning Engineers
P.O. Box 660268
Dallas, TX 75266
(214) 954-5426
President: Leo Stambaugh
International organization of consulting engineers, mechanical
contractors, and vendors. Monthly meetings and informal job
referrals. National organization publishes newsletter, yearly
handbook, and other publications.

American Society of Interior Designers
Texas Chapter
1909-C Hi Line Dr.
Dallas, TX 75207
(214) 748-1541
State Administrator: Sherri Hendrix
Meets monthly and publishes a newsletter. Job openings are posted
on bulletin board at World Trade Center and resumes are kept on file.

American Society of Landscape Architects
12650 Schroeder
Dallas, TX 75243
(214) 231-5151
State Treasurer: Ricky D. Petty
Conducts monthly meetings and publishes a newsletter. National
association's newsletter advertises job openings.

American Society of Magazine Photographers
3630 Harry Hines
Dallas, TX 75219
(214) 520-7836
President: Ron St. Angelo
Conducts monthly meetings, publishes a newsletter, and provides informal job referrals. Helps graduates make transition from school to full-time work.

American Society of Mechanical Engineers
Southern Regional Office
1950 Stemmons Frwy., Suite 5037C
Dallas, TX 75207
(214) 746-4900
Regional Director: David Cook
Professional organization with more than 1,500 members in North and West Texas sections, including Dallas and Tarrant counties. Each section has monthly meetings and publishes a newsletter. Provides informal job referrals.

American Society of Safety Engineers
Southwest Chapter
1310 Deer Ridge Dr.
Duncanville, TX 75137
(214) 934-9750
Contact: Jennings Vaughn
Placement coordinator assists job hunters. Conducts monthly meetings and publishes a newsletter.

American Subcontractors Association
North Texas Chapter
9330 Amberton Pkwy., Suite 202
Dallas, TX 75243
(214) 669-1495
Executive Director: Linda Ramirez
Professional association of building subcontractors. Meets monthly and publishes a newsletter.

American Women in Radio & Television
Dallas Chapter
7700 John Carpenter Frwy.
Dallas, TX 75247
President: Sherry Gardner
Meets monthly and publishes a newsletter with some job listings. Provides networking opportunities. Contact by mail.

American Women in Radio & Television
Fort Worth Chapter
1148 W. Pioneer Pkwy., Suite C
Arlington, TX 76103
(817) 261-3344

President: Wanda Shantz
Same as Dallas chapter. Has a nationwide job bank.

Analytical Psychology Association of Dallas
10118 Medlock Dr.
Dallas, TX 75218
(214) 348-7284
Secretary: Shirley McElya
Monthly meetings and lectures open to the public. Publishes a
newsletter. Educational meetings and seminars scheduled twice a
year.

Apartment Association of Greater Dallas
9221 LBJ Frwy., Suite 214
Dallas, TX 75243
(214) 437-0177
Contact: Donna Derden
Organization for apartment managers. Conducts monthly educational
meetings, keeps resumes on file for six months, publishes a
newsletter, and has a job bank.

Appraisal Institute
1509 Main St., Suite 1206B
Dallas, TX 75201
(214) 742-3404
Executive Director: Norah Crow
Job-wanted notices published in local newsletter. Conducts monthly
professional development meetings.

Associated General Contractors
Dallas Chapter
11111 Stemmons Frwy.
Dallas, TX 75229
(214) 247-9962
Education Director: Raleigh Roussell
Schedules regular meetings, maintains a resume file, and publishes a
newsletter.

Association for Information and Image Management
Dallas/Fort Worth Chapter
5429 LBJ Fwy., #900
Dallas, TX 75240
(214) 851-7832
President: Robert Reidler
Professional association for micrographics and records management.
Conducts monthly meetings, publishes a newsletter with job
openings, and makes informal job referrals.

Association of Human Resource Systems Professionals
P.O. Box 801646
Dallas, TX 75380
(214) 661-3727

Contact: James Stroop
Association of human resource department professionals who schedule annual conference and spring and fall professional development courses.

Association of Information Systems Professionals
Dallas Chapter
P.O. Box 2652
Dallas, TX 75221
(214) 931-3722
President: Patty Seals
Organization for people who design, manage, and use information systems. Conducts monthly meetings and publishes newsletter with job openings. Bi-monthly international magazine also lists employment opportunities.

Association of Investment Analysts
6500 West Frwy., Suite 709
Fort Worth, TX 76116
(214) 688-1705
Association of portfolio managers and security analysts. Conducts bi-monthly luncheon meetings. Has a placement committee that keeps a resume file and assists job hunters.

Association of Records Managers and Administrators
Dallas Chapter
1258 Titan
Dallas, TX 75247
(214) 630-9221
Contact: Al Laird
Conducts monthly meetings and publishes a newsletter. Coordinates local job clearinghouse with resume file and employment openings.

Association of Women Entrepreneurs of Dallas
P.O. Box 835232
Richardson, TX 75083
(214) 235-2716
Membership Chairman: Sue Fowler
Provides education and support for women business owners. Holds monthly meetings and publishes a newsletter.

Beau Monde League
2670 Belknap Ave.
Dallas, TX 75216
(214) 376-5613
Contact: Louise Richardson
Association of cosmetologists. Awards scholarships and keeps a resume file.

Builders Association of Fort Worth-Tarrant County
P.O. Box 8644
Fort Worth, TX 76124

(817) 457-2864
Contact: Mike Sandlin
Trade organization for builders and associated personnel. Meets
monthly, sponsors seminars and workshops, and publishes a
newsletter.

Building Owners and Managers Association of Dallas
1717 Main, #LB19
Dallas, TX 75201
(214) 953-1170
Executive Director: Joe Morchart
Trade association for commercial property managers. Job referrals for
members only.

Building Owners and Managers Association of Fort Worth
777 Main St., Suite 890
Fort Worth, TX 76102
(817) 834-5251
President: Larry Taylor
Surveys changes in commercial building industry, publishes a
newsletter, conducts monthly meetings, and provides informal job
referrals.

Business and Professional Women of Fort Worth
P.O. Box 125
Dallas, TX 75221
(214) 361-8841
President: Patty Kelly
Regular meetings and networking opportunities scheduled by Fort
Worth and other area organizations.

Certified Public Accountants
Dallas Chapter
12222 Merit Dr., Suite 300
Dallas, TX 75251
(214) 960-8311
Executive Director: Margaret Cartwright
Promotes professional education and publishes a newsletter with job
advertisements. Keeps resumes on file.

Certified Public Accountants
Fort Worth Chapter
1701 River Run, Suite 607
Fort Worth, TX 76107
(817) 335-5055
Executive Director: Christi Stinson
Parallels Dallas Chapter.

Christian Medical and Dental Society
National Administrative Office
P.O. Box 830689
Richardson, TX 75083

(214) 783-8384
Contact: Don Kencke
Organization for Christian medical students, physicians, and dentists.
Promotes spiritual growth and evangelism.

Credit Management Association of Dallas
P.O. Box 64728
Dallas, TX 75243
(214) 699-6169
Contact: Scott Chilton or Keith Blue, (214) 699-6168
Non-profit organization for credit bureau members. Hosts quarterly
meetings.

Dallas Advertising League
P.O. Box 561152
Dallas, TX 75356
(214) 688-1705
Trade association for professionals in the advertising business. Holds
monthly meetings. Publishes a newsletter with a want-ad section.

Dallas Association for the Education of Young Children
P.O. Box 12854
Dallas, TX 75225
(214) 638-1703
Contact: Donna Cooper
Organizes training sessions for directors of children's centers.

Dallas Association of Black Women Attorneys
P.O. Box 50633
Dallas, TX 75250
(214) 767-3465
President: Joyce Shalten
Has job bank and makes informal employment referrals. Participates
in community projects.

Dallas Association of Educational and Office Personnel
P.O. Box 123
Dallas, TX 75204
(214) 557-6213
President: Barbara Riley
Organization of secretaries, clerks, and data processors who work for
the Dallas Independent School District.

Dallas Association of Law Librarians
P.O. Box 50183
Dallas, TX 75250
(214) 604-2867
President: Elena Carvojal
Coordinates job bank, holds monthly meetings, and conducts one
workshop each year. Monthly newsletter with occasional job listings.

Dallas Association of Legal Secretaries
3425 Lindhurst
Garland, TX 75044
(214) 969-1152
Contact: Sharon Lee
Professional organization of paralegals. Has a job bank and newsletter
with employment notices.

Dallas Association of Life Underwriters
12655 N. Central Expwy., Suite 808
Dallas, TX 75243
(214) 991-2364
Executive Director: Karen True
Conducts monthly educational programs and publishes a monthly
magazine.

Dallas Association of Speech Pathology and Audiology
P.O. Box 741974
Dallas, TX 75374
(214) 660-3784
President: Denise Gage
Provides informal job referrals, conducts educational bi-monthly
meetings, and publishes a newsletter.

Dallas Association of Texas Professional Educators
5446 Druid Ln.
Dallas, TX 75209
(214) 944-3640
President: Pat Jacobs
Professional organization for administrators, counselors, librarians,
teachers, and clerks. State organization publishes magazine with
employment information.

Dallas Association of Young Lawyers
2101 Ross Ave.
Dallas, TX 75201
(214) 969-7675
President: Cheryl Garbrick
Organization for lawyers under the age of 36.

Dallas Bankers Association
1999 Bryan St.
Dallas, TX 75201
(214) 954-0585
Hosts quarterly meetings and considers funding for charitable
organizations.

Dallas Bar Association
2101 Ross Ave.
Dallas, TX 75201
(214) 969-7066
Executive Director: Georgia Franklin

Organization for attorneys. Provides continuing education and publishes a newsletter.

Dallas Beauticians Association
2617 Martin Luther King Blvd.
Dallas, TX 75215
(214) 946-8947
Executive Director: J.L. Boykin
Organization of beauticians who meet monthly.

Dallas Business League
5980 Arapaho Rd., Suite 32E
Dallas, TX 75248
(214) 980-4294
Contact: Virginia Altman
Association of business workers, primarily in banking, law, and sales. Conducts monthly luncheon meetings.

Dallas Communications Council
6311 N. O'Connor Rd., #29
Irving, TX 75039
(214) 869-7674
Executive Director: Lee Duncan
Association of professionals in film, tape, talent, recording, and other communications industries. Promotes the local communications industry, schedules monthly meetings, raises funds, and publishes a monthly newsletter.

Dallas County Chiropractic Society
433 W. 12th St.
Dallas, TX 75211
(214) 948-9841
Contact: Dr. John Freeman
Sponsors educational programs and keeps a resume file.

Dallas County Dental Society
4100 McEwen Rd., #141
Dallas, TX 75244
(214) 386-5741
Contact: Linda Hill
Professional organization to educate dentists and to educate and serve the public.

Dallas County Funeral Directors Association
P.O. Box 3100
Dallas, TX 75231
(214) 238-7111
President: Cecil Williams
Provides informal job referrals.

Dallas County Library Association
1125 S. Buckner Blvd.

Grand Prairie, TX 75217
(214) 398-5595
President: Lee Shuey
Association for librarians or those interested in the field. Publishes a quarterly newsletter with job listings and makes informal referrals.

Turning volunteer work into a job

After spending many years working as a volunteer for various organizations, Marion Simon's daughters advised her to "stop giving it away." She decided to look for paid employment. But because she had never held a paid job, Marion was not sure how to begin her job search.

"As a woman in my middle years, I wondered where in the world I would go," says Marion. "I had a good education and a great deal of volunteer experience. I had planned and orchestrated large benefits and had done an inordinate amount of fund-raising over the years. I also had done community work in the inner city.

"I talked to some people at a local college. They told me I was well qualified and that I should just go out and look for a job. But I didn't know where 'out' was. Later, career counselors at another local college helped me put together a resume. Then I began to talk to people I knew. I was offered various jobs, none of which thrilled me.

"Then I happened to mention my job search to the president of a hospital where I had done a great deal of volunteer work," says Marion. "He asked me not to take a job until I had talked to him. Later, he hired me as his special assistant, with the charge to 'humanize the hospital.' Over a period of time, I developed a patient representative department.

"When I began the job 11 years ago, I was a one-person operation. As time went on, I added staff. I currently supervise a staff of 9, plus about 25 volunteers. The job of patient representative is now a full-fledged profession. Many women in the field began as volunteers. They knew a lot about the hospital where they were volunteering and thus made the transition into a paid position more easily."

We asked Marion what advice she has for volunteers who want to move into the paid work force. "Go to the career counseling departments of some of the small colleges. Ask them to review your background and tell you what kinds of jobs you may be qualified for. If they suggest that you need additional training, get it. But before you go back to school, investigate the kinds of jobs available in your chosen field. Think about how you can use your volunteer experience in a paid position. Take what you've done and build from it."

In job search lingo, Marion analyzed her volunteer work and identified her functional skills. If you can sell Girl Scout cookies, you can sell other products and services. If you coordinated the fund-raising project for the church building fund, you can coordinate projects for a salary. You just have to convince the hiring authority that your skills are transferable.■

Dallas County Rental Association
930 N. Belt Line
Mesquite, TX 75149
(214) 285-1863
President: Cliff Kellogg
Organization of general rental store managers. Schedules monthly meetings and has local and national newsletters.

Dallas County Veterinary Medical Association
P.O. Box 210675
Dallas, TX 75211
(214) 339-8756
Professional association of veterinarians. Promotes continuing education and publishes a monthly newsletter with employment notices.

Dallas Dietetic Association
1414 James Dr.
Cedar Hill, TX 75104
(214) 291-9484
President: Ann John
Professional organization for registered/licensed dieticians and those in related fields. Career guidance committee assists job hunters.

Dallas/Fort Worth Association of Metroplex Personnel Consultants
6211 W. Northwest Hwy., Suite C261
Dallas, TX 75225
(214) 691-3485
President: Henry Wright
Trade association of account executives of personnel service companies. Assists people who are looking for help with the job search. Individuals should call for referrals to job fairs, employment seminars, and agencies that specialize in their field.

Dallas Geological Society
1 Energy Square, Suite 170
Dallas, TX 75206
(214) 373-8614
President: Dorothy Newsom
Conducts continuing education programs and has an employment committee that keeps a resume file.

Dallas Group Psychotherapy Society
2505 Wycliff Ave.
Dallas, TX 75219
(214) 528-9240
Dean of Training: Juanita Kirby
Professional organization that provides training for members and non-members.

Dallas Human Resource Management Association
P.O. Box 118335
Carrollton, TX 75011
(214) 420-8775
President: Cheryl Rashide
Meets regularly, has an annual conference, and maintains a resume file.

Dallas Metropolitan Black Nurses Association
P.O. Box 4104
Dallas, TX 75208
(214) 374-7438
President: Doris Foreman
International organization of black nurses who support racial equality. Newsletter lists job-wanted ads.

Dallas Music Teachers Association
1920 Gansett Dr.
Plano, TX 75075
(214) 374-7438
President: Karen Sexton
Organization of professional music teachers.

Dallas Producers Association
P.O. Box 190769

Dallas, TX 75219
(214) 696-9040
President: Chip Richie
Organization of corporate and commercial film/video producers. Holds
monthly meetings and publishes a newsletter.

Dallas Professional Photographers Association
2323 N. Belt Line Rd.
Mesquite, TX 75150
(214) 289-1851
President: Hulda Neve
Professional organization for photographers. Publishes a newsletter
with employment information.

Dallas Psychological Association
12900 Preston Rd.
Dallas, TX 75230
(214) 386-4362
Employment Chairperson: Sandy Cook
Organization of psychologists, psychological associates, and students.
Provides state-wide employment information.

Dallas Restaurant Association
12770 Coit Rd., Suite 419
Dallas, TX 75251
(214) 233-2733
President: Dawn Jantsch
Organization for the food and beverage industry. Provides
information about the restaurant industry during monthly meetings,
publishes a newsletter and magazine, and awards scholarships.

Dallas School Administrators Association
3031 Allen St., Suite 204
Dallas, TX 75204
(214) 871-7056
President: Robert Watkins
Supports professional development programs and sponsors seminars.

Dallas Society of Illustrators
4409 Maple Ave.
Dallas, TX 75219
(214) 521-2121
President: David Spurlock
Networking organization for graphic and commercial artists who meet
monthly.

Dallas Society of Visual Communications
4409 Maple Ave.
Dallas, TX 75219
(214) 241-2017

Executive Director: Sue Reynolds
Conducts monthly meetings and provides employment referral service.

Dallas Women Lawyers Association
2500 Tierra Dr.
Irving, TX 75038
(214) 255-7454
Contact: Kelly F. Robbins
Holds monthly meetings and publishes a newsletter.

Desk and Derrick Club of Dallas
717 N. Harwood, # 3430
Dallas, TX 75201
(214) 953-2763
President: Louise Faircloth
Organization of women employed in petroleum and allied industries. Has an employment committee that assists members only.

Desk and Derrick Club of Fort Worth
4100 Fossil Creek Blvd.
Fort Worth, TX 76137
(817) 847-7700
President: Shirley Meine
Parallels Dallas chapter.

Direct Marketing Association of North Texas
4020 McEwen Rd., Suite 105
Dallas, TX 75244-5019
(817) 640-7018
Contact: Jody Henry
Organization for list brokers, printers, catalogers, and others in direct marketing industry. Conducts monthly meetings.

Downtown Network of Career Women
8637 Turtle Creek Blvd.
Dallas, TX 75225
(214) 393-1080
President: Elaine Copeland
Provides networking opportunities for professional women from all fields. Meets during monthly luncheons.

Educational Secretaries Association of Grand Prairie
833 Tarrant Rd.
Grand Prairie, TX 75050
(214) 262-1934
President: Judy Siddall
Organization of para-professionals in Grand Prairie School District. Conducts monthly meetings.

Electrical Women's Round Table
North Texas Chapter

P.O. Box 896
Lewisville, TX 75067
(214) 317-5110
Contact: Pat Lucas
Professional organization that provides networking opportunities.

Engineers Club of Dallas
1401 Elm St., Suite 4800
Dallas, TX 75202
(214) 747-0090
Contact: Alan L. Boles
Private club.

Executive Women of Dallas
P.O. Box 515546
Dallas, TX 75251
President: Deanie Renouf
Organization of women executives and business owners. Contact by mail.

Meetings are for meeting people

Laid off during a real estate slump, one enterprising 32-year-old escrow officer decided he would build up his finances by doing something he enjoyed—carpentry. After a few phone calls to friends and former business associates, his newly formed Home Carpentry Service was launched.

At the same time, he attended every possible escrow association meeting, dinner, and other professional events. "I set a goal," he recalls, "to contact at least three escrow company owners at each meeting, to let them know I was looking and available. Afterward, I'd write a letter to give them my phone number in case they wanted to get in touch right away."

About four months after his first dinner meeting, an officer from one of the larger title companies called him for an interview. "He couldn't get me working on that desk fast enough," he remembers. "The $15 I'd spent on that dinner ticket was the best investment I ever made."■

Fashion Group International of Dallas
P.O. Box 586278
Dallas, TX 75258

(214) 630-7152
Contact: Alice Higgins
Professional organization for the fashion industry.

Federally Employed Women
Fort Worth Chapter
4135 Norway
Grand Prairie, TX 75052
(214) 988-3175
President: Deborah Erwin
Conducts monthly meetings, publishes a newsletter, hosts seminars,
and provides networking opportunities.

Fort Worth District Dental Society
3123 McCart Ave.
Fort Worth, TX 76110
(817) 923-9337
Contact: Charles Kendall III, D.D.S.
Professional organization to educate dentists and to educate and serve
the public.

Fort Worth Florist's Association
c/o Bridal Blooms
4717 Ivanhoe
Fort Worth, TX 76132
(817) 370-0719
Contact: Kelly Norvell
Organization for florists in the retail, wholesale, and wire-service
floral industry. Promotes industry, organizes civic projects, and design
seminars. Conducts monthly meetings and publishes a newsletter.

Fort Worth Legal Secretaries Association
PLS 220 First City Bank Tower
Fort Worth, TX 76102
(817) 336-9333
Contact: Michele E. Rayburn
Professional association for legal secretaries. Provides continuing
education, conducts monthly meetings, and publishes a newsletter.

Fort Worth Personnel Association
P.O. Box 15350
Fort Worth, TX 76119
(817) 478-5431
Contact: Sharon Mullarkey
Schedules monthly meetings.

Fort Worth Professional Women's Organization
3200 Team Bank Bldg.
Fort Worth, TX 76102
(817) 878-6378
President: Carol Davidson
Network for business women in managerial positions.

Fort Worth/Tarrant County Young Lawyers Association
2015 Texas Building
200 W. 7th St.
Fort Worth, TX 76102
(817) 338-4092
President: Lisa Jamieson
Professional organization for young lawyers under the age of 36.
Publishes a newsletter with job openings and has resume file and job
bank.

**Fort Worth, Texas Association of Occupational Health
Nurses**
2304 Ridgeview St.
Fort Worth, TX 76119
(817) 777-8188
President: Gloria J. Schuford, R.N.
Maintains standards of occupational nursing practices to preserve the
health and safety of employed workers.

**Home & Apartment Builders Association of Metropolitan
Dallas**
8730 King George Dr.
Dallas, TX 75235
(214) 631-4840
Executive Vice-President: Simon McHugh
Trade association for residential builders and developers. Publishes
newsletter with employment ads and keeps resumes on file.

Home Economists in Business
North Texas Chapter
2139 N. Stemmons, #896
Lewisville, TX 75067
(214) 317-5110
President: Gloria Roberts
Monthly meetings scheduled from September through May. Publishes
a newsletter.

Hotel & Motel Association of Greater Dallas
1201 Elm St.
Dallas, TX 75270
(214) 746-6782
Executive Vice-President: Les Tanaka
Sponsors continuing education programs and provides job referrals.

Independent Insurance Agents of Dallas
8140 Walnut Hill Lane, Suite 707
Dallas, TX 75231
(214) 360-0666
Executive Director: Debi Ryan-Johnson
Schedules seminars and educational meetings.

Institute of Business Designers
North Texas Chapter
1400 Turtle Creek Blvd., Suite LB30
Dallas, TX 75207
(214) 742-4250
Association for designers, architects, and facilities management
personnel. Conducts monthly meetings, has job bank, and publishes
newsletter and annual membership roster.

Insurance Women of Dallas
P.O. Box 12204
Dallas, TX 75225
(214) 258-6820
Contact: B.J. Ellis
Employment committee assists insurance professionals locate jobs.
Has monthly meetings and publishes a newsletter.

Insurance Women of Fort Worth
P.O. Box 13672
Arlington, TX 76094
(817) 860-3566
President: Jerry Sheeran
Keeps resumes on file.

International Association of Business Communicators
Dallas Chapter
P.O. Box 2681
Dallas, TX 75221
(214) 701-2732
President: Gale Porter
Meets regularly for continuing education programs. Co-sponsors
telephone job bank. Call (214) 978-8070 to hear recording of job
openings.

International Association of Business Communicators
Fort Worth Chapter
c/o Fort Worth Clean City
1000 Throckmorton St.
Fort Worth, TX 76102
(817) 878-3046
President: Susan Green
Parallels Dallas chapter.

International Customer Service Association
Dallas Chapter
P.O. Box 214238
Dallas, TX 75221
(214) 855-7676
Contact: Dawn Kale
Organization for managers and professionals engaged in customer
service. Conducts monthly meetings and publishes a newsletter.

International Furnishings and Design Association
Southwest Chapter
P.O. Box 58045
Dallas, TX 75258
(214) 747-2406
Contact: Pamela Donohow
Organization for home furnishing executives. Conducts monthly meetings with networking opportunities and publishes a newsletter with job openings.

Irving Association of Educational Office Personnel
3029 Lark St.
Irving, TX 75062
(214) 259-4575
President: Carol Rosenbaum
Organization for all Irving Independent School District office personnel. Conducts meetings from September through May.

Irving Womens' Network
1033 McCoy Dr.
Irving, TX 75062
(214) 254-7047
Contact: Katherine Welch-Burke
Professional women conduct monthly meetings and publish a newsletter with job listings.

Licensed Vocational Nurses Association of Texas
Division IV
P.O. Box 4963
Dallas, TX 75208
(214) 941-9813
President: Florence Taylor
Promotes continuing education and helps members find employment.

Division 82
2041 Glenco Ter.
Fort Worth, TX 76110
(817) 335-4752
President: Barbara McDonald-Wather
Parallels Division IV.

Mechanical Contractors Association of Dallas
2720 Stemmons Frwy., Suite 201 South
Dallas, TX 75207
(214) 630-8991
Director: Anne Copeland
Trade association that helps members find employment through informal referrals.

Mesquite Educational Paraprofessional Association
405 E. Davis St.
Mesquite, TX 75149

(214) 288-6411
Contact: Ella Mae Wilcox
Professional organization for secretaries in education field.

National Association for Female Executives
Women's Information Network
P.O. Box 516291
Dallas, TX 75251
(214) 601-1404
Contact: Cleo Holden
Conducts monthly meetings with networking opportunities and
publishes a newsletter.

National Association of Accountants
P.O. Box 214417
Dallas, TX 75221
(214) 444-2100
President: Joe Zimmerman
Provides employment service, conducts bi-weekly meetings, and
publishes a newsletter.

National Association of Bank Women
Dallas Chapter
Murray Federal Savings
5550 LBJ Frwy., Suite 675
Dallas, TX 75240
(214) 851-6314
President: Kay Collis
Professional organization for women executives in the banking
industry. Provides informal job referrals, schedules educational
programs, and awards scholarships.

National Association of Bank Women
Greater Fort Worth Chapter
1001 E. Berry St.
Fort Worth, TX 76111
(817) 926-5411
Parallels Dallas Chapter.

National Association of Black Social Workers
Dallas Chapter
P.O. Box 150243
Dallas, TX 75315
(214) 670-6359
Contact: Willie Hucks
Addresses needs of black community, including unemployment.
Schedules monthly meetings and sponsors educational projects.

National Association of Female Executives
P.O. Box 516291
Dallas, TX 75251
(214) 601-1404

Coordinator: Jill Boruck
Provides networking and support for women in business. Conducts monthly meetings and publishes a newsletter.

National Association of Social Workers
Dallas Unit
10645 Longmeadow Dr.
Dallas, TX 75238
(214) 739-1558
Contact: Sherin Kline
Conducts monthly meetings and publishes a bi-monthly newsletter with job openings. Keeps jobs listings on file.

National Association of Women in Construction
Dallas Chapter
1109 Windmill Lane
Irving, TX 75061
(214) 827-9260
President: Patty Batchelor
Organization conducts educational meetings, awards scholarships, and maintains a job bank through a referral committee.

National Association of Women in Construction
Fort Worth Chapter
327 S. Adams St.
Fort Worth, TX 76104
(817) 877-5551
President: Paula Clements-Zang
Parallels Dallas Chapter.

Network for Executive Women
P.O. Box 2612
Fort Worth, TX 76113
(817) 336-9333
Executive Secretary: Ann Dunkin
Career-oriented women meet twice weekly in Fort Worth, Arlington, and Mid-Cities area. Job openings are announced and employment-related topics are discussed at meetings.

Network of Hispanic Communicators
P.O. Box 222313
Dallas, TX 75222
(214) 977-8456
President: Mercedes Olivera
Organization for journalists, advertising, and public relations professionals. Schedules monthly meetings, publishes newsletter with ads, and awards scholarships.

New Car Dealers Association of Metropolitan Dallas
2777 N. Stemmons Frwy., Suite 841
Dallas, TX 75207
(214) 637-0531

President: Drew Campbell
Trade association, promoting new car dealers by sponsoring car shows.
Job referrals made.

Newspaper Advertising Sales Association
333 W. Campbell Rd., Suite 210
Richardson, TX 75080
(214) 699-0766
President: Robert Collins
National organization of advertising salespeople. Offers informal
employment network and schedules monthly meetings.

North Dallas Bar Association
P.O. Box 515432
Richardson, TX 75251
(214) 980-0472
President: Samantha Arthur
Professional association for attorneys.

North Dallas Network of Career Women
119 Heartz Rd.
Coppell, TX 75019
(214) 559-2048
Forum for professional women who meet bi-weekly.

North Texas Optometric Society
1334 E. Pioneer Pkwy.
Arlington, TX 76010
(817) 461-4453
President: Dr. Wiley Curtis
Organization of optometrists. Publishes a newsletter. State journal lists
job openings.

Don't overlook the watering holes

You can't beat weekday happy hours at local bars as an informal way of making contacts.

In Dallas, **journalists** divide their time between Louie's (1839 N. Henderson St.) and Joe Miller's (3531 McKinney Ave.). Both are great places to congregate and pick up leads for stories from lawyers, politicians, and public relations execs. Many downtown **professionals** opt for Dick's Last Resort (1701 N. Market St.) or The Mucky Duck (3102 Welborn St.) in Oak Lawn, which is a great place to relax. Studio C (6311 N. O'Connor) serves as an oasis in the middle of Las Colinas in Irving for **film, video, and audio** types.

In Fort Worth, **attorneys, legal secretaries, and bankers** tip oversize drinks during happy hour at Billy Miner's Saloon (150 W. 3rd St.). Others mix and mingle downtown at Winfield's '08 (301 Main St.) Creative types—**artists, writers, and musicians**—have adopted J&J Blues Bar (937 Woodward), with the unforgettable telephone number: 870-BEER. Although the White Elephant (101 E. Exchange Ave.) is popular with tourists, locals have adopted it as a favorite hangout.■

Pan-African Business Federation
P.O. Box 2815
Dallas, TX 75221
(214) 376-8392
Contact: E. Hosea-Minor
Educational and business training organization.

PBX Telecommunicators of Dallas
10106 Kirkhaven
Dallas, TX 75238
(214) 341-5106
Sponsors workshops and fund-raising projects.

PBX Telecommunicators of Fort Worth
2201 Primrose Ave.
Fort Worth, TX 76111
(817) 834-7901
President: Jana Johnson
Parallels Dallas Chapter.

Press Club of Dallas
400 S. Houston St.
Dallas, TX 75202
(214) 748-3329
Executive Director: Mary Jane Hewes
Sponsors the annual Dallas Gridiron Show, which raises scholarship money, hosts annual Katie Awards, schedules annual roasts, social functions, and professional development meetings. Publishes a newsletter and provides informal job referrals.

Printing Industries Association of Texas
910 W. Mockingbird Lane, Suite 200
Dallas, TX 75247
(214) 630-8871

Executive Director: Nolan Moore
Promotes continuing education at meetings. Employment service for
members and non-members.

Professional Secretaries International
Big D Chapter
607 Heather Trail, Apt. 1311
Arlington, TX 76011
(214) 269-2959
President: Virginia Palazzo
Provides job referrals for members. Meets monthly, conducts
seminars, and publishes a bulletin.

Professional Secretaries International
Fort Worth Chapter
201 Main St., Suite 2500
Fort Worth, TX 76102
(817) 332-2500, ext. 457
President: Linda Gerch
Parallels above chapter.

Professional Secretaries International
Garland Chapter
5800 Preston Oaks Rd., Suite 1072
Dallas, TX 75240
(214) 651-4000
President: Barbara Sumrall
Parallels above chapter.

Professional Services Marketing Asociation
c/o Brice & Mankoff
300 Crescent Court
Dallas, TX 75201
(214) 969-1300
Contact: Tori Mannes
Law and accounting firm members who meet monthly.

Pro-Musica
5820 Northmoor Dr.
Dallas, TX 75230
(214) 368-6882
President: Anna Fagan
Organization of professional women musicians. Schedules regular
meetings and awards scholarships.

Public Library Administrators of North Texas
P.O. Box 96
Cedar Hill, TX 75104
(214) 291-7323
Contact: Pat Bonds
Informal group of library directors who meet ten times a year.

Internships can lead to permanent relationships

Working as an intern for a Dallas TV station proved to be the most valuable experience for a senior at Southern Methodist University.

Eric said, "I was in the office five days a week working for a top-rated station. I learned how to focus my goals, manage my time, and work under pressure. When a full-time position opened up, I was first in line. When the producer realized that I had been doing a lot of the work anyway, knew the ropes, and knew the people, my internship ended with an offer for a permanent job."

Although Eric was not paid for his work as an intern, some interns do receive a small stipend. Keep in mind also that internship programs are not limited to students. For more information, check the *Directory of Internships*, available at the public library.■

Public Relations Society of America
Greater Fort Worth Chapter
4100 Fossil Creek Blvd.
Fort Worth, TX 76137
(817) 847-7700
President: Carolyn Stephens
Conducts monthly meetings and publishes a newsletter with job-wanted listings. Has a job bank and resume file.

Public Relations Society of America
North Texas Chapter
P.O. Box 12033
Dallas, TX 75225
(214) 350-3118
Chapter Administrator: Kris Gold
Organization for practicing public relations professionals in the Dallas/Fort Worth area. Conducts monthly professional development meetings and seminars. Publishes a newsletter. Co-sponsors telephone job bank. Dial (214) 978-8070 to hear recorded message about employment opportunities.

Richardson Music Teachers Association
728 Greenhaven
Richardson, TX 75080
(214) 231-0767
President: Linda Secor
Conducts monthly meetings and provides job referrals.

Sales and Marketing Executives of Dallas
4100 McEwen St., Suite 101
Dallas, TX 75244
(214) 991-0516
Conducts monthly meetings, publishes a newsletter, keeps resumes
on file, and awards scholarships.

Sales and Marketing Executives of Fort Worth
5600 Colleyville Blvd.
Colleyville, TX 76034
(817) 656-9111
Executive Director: Charnan Logan
Professional organization for sales and marketing professionals and
students.

Sheet Metal and Air Conditioning Contractors
North Texas Chapter
712 N. Collins St.
Arlington, TX 76011
(817) 461-2521
Contact: Sylvia McRae
Professional contractors' organization.

Society for Marketing Professional Services
4125 Centurion Way
Dallas, TX 75244
(214) 392-7800
President: David Joiner
Job hotline (214) 526-2151 for members only. Meets monthly and
distributes several publications.

Society for Theatrical Artists Guidance and Enhancement
P.O. Box 214820
Dallas, TX 75221
(214) 559-3917
Executive Director: Susan McMath
Support group that promotes the performing arts in the Dallas/Fort
Worth area. Maintains resume file. Conducts annual membership
meeting.

Society of Children's Book Writers
North Central Texas Chapter
1814 Marble Dr., #1061
Arlington, TX 76013
(817) 861-1333
Contact: Betty Stone
Organization for children's book writers.

Society of Diagnostic Medical Sonographers
12225 Greenville Ave., Suite 434
Dallas, TX 75243

(214) 235-7367
Executive Director: Gwen Grim
Organization of professionals who work with medical diagnostic ultrasound. Schedules two meetings each year, has national job listings, and publishes a newsletter.

Society of Hispanic Professional Engineers
P.O. Box 59614
Dallas, TX 75229
(214) 350-9976
President: Hector Bass
Human Resource Committee makes job referrals. Publishes a newsletter.

Society of Industrial and Office Realtors
North Texas Chapter
2001 Bryan Tower
Dallas, TX 75201
(214) 748-9171
President: Gary V. Lindsey
Provides educational courses for commercial/industrial real estate professionals.

Society of Petroleum Engineers
P.O. Box 833836
Richardson, TX 75083
(214) 669-3377
Executive Director: Dan Adamson
Publishes several publications with employment sections.

Society of Professional Journalists
Dallas Chapter
714 Woodlawn Ave.
Dallas, TX 75208
(214) 946-5468
Schedules monthly meetings, publishes a newsletter, awards scholarships, and provides informal job referrals.

Society of Professional Journalists
Fort Worth Chapter
5533 Wheaton Dr.
Fort Worth, TX 76113
(817) 292-0826
Contact: Phil Record
Parallels Dallas Chapter. Also awards scholarships from proceeds of annual Texas Gridiron Show.

Society of Real Estate Appraisers
1509 Main St., Suite 1206B
Dallas, TX 75201
(214) 742-3404

Contact: Norah Crowe
Professional association of appraisers. Schedules special events, seminars, and workshops.

Society of Women Engineers
Region C Dallas Section
128 W. Landowne Circle
Coppell, TX 75019
(214) 462-8604
President: Anna Marie Moran
Professional organization that encourages women to enter and excel in engineering. Meets monthly from September through May. Publishes job information in newsletter.

Southwest Homefurnishings Association
P.O. Box 581207
Dallas, TX 75258
(214) 741-7632
Contact: Al Stillman
Trade association for the retail home furnishings industry.

Southwestern Association of Advertising Agencies
8700 Stemmons Frwy., Suite 303
Dallas, TX 75247
(214) 637-4442
Executive Director: Robert Burke
Association of advertising agency owners and managers. Publishes membership directory and monthly newsletter. Sponsors professional workshops and educational seminars.

Southwestern Booksellers Association
3404 S. Ravinia Dr.
Dallas, TX 75233
(214) 330-9795
Contact: Pam Lang
Trade organization of booksellers, writers, librarians, publishers, and agents. Publishes newsletter with job advertisements.

Southwestern Meat Packers Association
1333 Corporate Dr., Suite 213
Irving, TX 75038
(214) 550-1838
Trade organization representing meat packers and suppliers in Texas and surrounding states. Occasional job openings published in newsletter.

Tarrant County Bar Association
7001 Grapevine Hwy., Suite 510
Fort Worth, TX 76180
(817) 589-0270
President: Tim Truman
Professional association of lawyers.

Tarrant County Home Economics Association
3820 London Lane
Fort Worth, TX 76118
(817) 921-7494
President: Kim Kamin
Meets three times a year and sponsors training programs.

Tarrant County Veterinary Medical Association
c/o Matlock Rd. Animal Clinic
3634 Matlock,Rd.
Arlington, TX 76015
(817) 468-8857
President: Kirk Weicht
Organization of veterinarians. Conducts continuing education
programs and publishes a newsletter with job listings.

Tarrant County Women's Bar Association
3500 City Center II
301 Commerce St.
Fort Worth, TX 76102
(817) 335-4417
President: Linda Todd
Professional organization for women lawyers. Maintains job bank.

Texas Association of Certified Registered Nurse Anesthetists
8408 Old Moss Rd.
Dallas, TX 75231
(214) 348-7599
Professional organization that promotes continuing education.
National group publishes two magazines with job ads.

Texas Association of Film & Tape Professionals
3101 N. Fitzhugh Ave., #420
Dallas, TX 75204
(214) 520-2600
Office Manager: Jane Sibley
Association of film and video freelancers who work in the motion
picture, video, and commercial production industry. Publishes the
annual *Texas Film/Tape Directory* and sponsors meetings and seminars.

Texas Association of Teachers of Dancing
402 Forest Park
Dallas, TX 75234
(214) 827-1934
Examination Chairman: Jackie Troup Miller
Organization of members from five-state area who pass an
examination to qualify for membership. Supplies informal job
referrals, sponsors meetings, and publishes a newsletter.

Texas Electronics Association
111 S. Garland Ave., Suite 308

Garland, TX 75040
(214) 352-6285
President: Ron Unrugh
Publishes a monthly newsletter.

Texas Environmental Health Association
North Texas Association
2561 Matlock
Arlington, TX 76015
(817) 792-7282
Executive Secretary: John Shaffer
Organization of sanitary engineers and inspectors. Six regional
chapters meet regularly. Employment opportunities listed in local
and state newsletters.

Texas Music Teachers Association
Denton Chapter
2422 Nottingham
Denton, TX 76201
(817) 387-3255
Contact: Gladys Lawhon
Professional organization for music teachers.

Texas Nurses Association
District 4
515 Texas American Bank Building
Dallas, TX 75235
(214) 357-6227
President: Lucy Norris
Professional organization for registered nurses. Holds monthly
meetings and publishes newsletter with occasional job listings.

Texas Recreation & Park Society
P.O. Box 905
Arlington, TX 76004
Metro (817) 261-0876
Executive Director: Dianne Darrell
Professional organization for municipal park and recreation
personnel.

Texas Society of Professional Engineers
Dallas Chapter
8333 Douglas Ave., Suite 820
Dallas, TX 75225
(214) 361-7900
Executive Secretary: John Burkhoff
Conducts monthly meetings. Involved in local, state, and national
legislative issues.

Texas Society of Professional Engineers
Fort Worth Chapter
P.O. Box 2973

Fort Worth, TX 76113
(817) 335-2611
President: Jeff Peterman
Professional organization for engineers in all fields.

Texas Society of Professional Surveyors
North Central Texas Chapter
P.O. Box 1034
Hurst, TX 76053
(817) 656-2130
President: David Myers
Conducts monthly meetings.

Urban Management Assistants of North Texas
c/o North Central Texas Council of Governments
P.O. Drawer C.O.G.
Arlington, TX 76005
(817) 640-3300
Contact: Mary Hartsell
Organization of individuals in entry-level and mid-management
positions in local governments. Conducts regular meetings and
publishes newsletter with job openings.

Women in Communications
Dallas Professional Chapter
6839 Gaston Ave.
Dallas, TX 75214
(214) 327-0068
President: Emily Mortin
Professional organization for men and women in all fields of
communication. Has a career advisory committee that keeps resume
file and solicits jobs for members. Schedules monthly meetings and
publishes a newsletter.

Women in Communications
Fort Worth Professional Chapter
P.O. Box 9858
Fort Worth, TX 76147
(817) 594-8031
President: Mary Ellen Guay
Parallels Dallas chapter. Also provides a job bank for members and
non-members.

Women in Computing
P.O. Box 741174
Dallas, TX 75374
(214) 954-8663
Contact: Cathy Benson
Professional organization for women in computing and data
processing. Awards scholarships, publishes a newsletter with job
advertisements, and sponsors regular professional development
meetings.

Women of the Motion Picture Industry
Paramount Pictures
12770 Merit, LB119, #702
Dallas, TX 75251
(214) 770-4220
Contact: Charlene Baggese
Service organization for women in the motion picture industry.

Women's Association of Allied Beverage Industries
1325 Cornell St.
Lancaster, TX 75134
(214) 944-9024
President: Sue Prather
Service-oriented organization of employees in the alcoholic beverage industry. Schedules monthly meetings, makes informal job referrals, and publishes a newsletter.

Women's Transportation Club of Dallas
P.O. Box 10691
Dallas, TX 75207
(214) 840-5304
President: Gwen Wetsel
Organization of women who work for transportation companies or in a transportation department. Sponsors monthly educational meetings and publishes a newsletter with job openings.

What professional organizations can do for you

"To begin networking with professional organizations, all it takes is a few phone calls to the president and a couple of other members," says Gary Gollhoffer, past president of the Dallas Chapter of the American Institute of Industrial Engineers.

"These people often have their fingers on the pulse of the job market," says Gollhofer, who adds that his organization has helped quite a few jobless people.

Because of the fluctuations in the job market, Gollhofer says, his organization has been sensitive to employment issues. The AIIE regularly schedules meetings on career change, job-hunting skills, and other topics that help people who are out of work.

During board meetings, members often discuss who's looking for work and what's available. Gollhofer recalls how an engineer sent him a very impressive resume. But Gollhofer had trouble convincing the manager of another industrial engineering company that he should talk to the engineer. The manager said he didn't have any openings. Gollhofer urged the manager to at least meet with the engineer, adding, "You shouldn't let this guy get away."

Sure enough, he didn't. Once the manager talked to the engineer, he created a job for him.■

6

Using Professional Employment Services

Finding a good job is hard work. So your first impulse may be to turn that job over to professional employment services. After all, don't the pros have all the job listings? Unfortunately, they don't.

Yes, it's smart to use every available resource to generate leads and interviews. But professional employment services vary, from agencies that specialize in temporary clerical help to executive recruiters who deal primarily with top-management types. Employment agencies, career consultants, and executive recruitment firms differ greatly in the kinds of services they offer and in how—and by whom—they get paid. You can save yourself a lot of time, effort, and possibly money if you're familiar with the different kinds of professional employment services. One handbook that might prove useful is the *Directory of Approved Counseling Services* (American

Association of Counseling Development, 5201 Leesburg Pike 400, Falls Church, VA 22041).

**Who's good?
Who's not?**

"It pays to check out an employment service," says Ron Berry, president of the Better Business Bureau of Metropolitan Dallas.

You can call the BBB at (214) 220-2000 in Dallas or (817) 332-7585 in Fort Worth to ask if any complaints have been filed against the company. If they have, summaries of reports are read over the telephone. Or, you can write and ask them to mail the information to you.

Berry advises talking to several people who have recently used the employment service to find out if they were satisfied. "If you don't know someone, ask the company for several references and call them," he suggests.

Also, carefully read the employment contract and find out if the employment service charges a fee or if the employee pays the fee, says BBB operations director Betsy McKinney. There are a lot of misunderstandings by people who don't find out in advance who has to pay a fee.

Ask if an employment agency is registered by the Texas Department of Labor and Standards. "Don't use one that isn't registered or one that claims to guarantee employment," McKinney adds.

"Be especially wary of the work-at-home schemes that request money in advance to set up the business. Most of these operations collect the money and provide nothing in return, or they advise people to recruit other people for work-at-home operations so the system perpetutates itself," McKinney says.

Once you think you have a good job prospect, call the Better Business Bureau to check on the company. The time to find out about customer complaints or law enforcement action is before you go to work there, not after you have accepted the position.■

Employment Agencies

Employment agencies act as intermediaries in the job market between buyers (companies with jobs open) and sellers (people who want jobs). Agencies are paid for placing people. The fee may be paid by the company, but in some cases it is paid by the worker. Agencies that specialize in restaurant and domestic help, for example, often charge the worker a fee. Usually the placement fee amounts to a certain percentage of the worker's annual salary. In many cases, it should not be necessary for you to pay a fee for placement. Keep searching for a firm that won't charge a fee.

Employment agencies seldom place a candidate in a job that pays more than $30,000 a year. Most employment agencies concentrate on support jobs. Supervisory openings may be listed, too, but employment agencies usually don't handle middle- or upper-management positions. In the computer field, for example, computer operators, programmers, and perhaps systems analysts could find work through an agency. But directors of data processing or MIS (management information systems) would go to an executive search firm, or they would job hunt on their own.

A company that's looking for a secretary gains certain advantages by going to a reputable agency. It doesn't have to advertise or screen the hundreds of resumes that would probably pour in from even a small want ad in the Sunday *Dallas Morning News*. A good employment agency will send over only qualified applicants for interviews. Referrals are made quickly, and there is no cost to the company until it hires the secretary. For many companies, it's worth it to pay an agency fee to avoid the hassle of prescreening dozens, if not hundreds, of applicants.

The advantage to the agency of a successful placement (besides the fee) is repeat business. After two or three referrals work out well, an employment agency can generally count on receiving future listings of company vacancies.

The value to the job seeker of using an employment agency depends on a number of factors, including the quality of the agency, the kind of work you're looking for, how much experience you have, and how broad your network of personal and business contacts is. In addition, employment agencies, especially those providing office personnel, will provide training to prospective employees. This training, which could be worth hundreds of dollars, can prepare the job hunter for a number of different positions.

In general, an agency's loyalty will be to its source of income. Agencies are more interested in finding you a job than in finding you job satisfaction. Agencies are likely to pressure you to accept a job you don't really want, just so they can collect their fee. With few exceptions, an agency probably can't do much more for you than you could do for yourself in an imaginative and energetic job search. (Of course, there's the rub—conducting an imaginative and energetic job search.) If a company has to pay a fee to hire you, you're at a disadvantage compared with applicants who are "free." Giving an employment agency your resume could also be a serious mistake if you're trying to conduct a confidential job search.

On the other hand, a good agency can help its candidates develop a strategy and prepare for employment interviews. This training can be most valuable to people who are inexperienced in job-hunting techniques. Of course, you can probably learn job-search strategy and skills more inexpensively by reading this book, plus some of those in our bibliographies. Agency pros should know the market, screen well, and provide sound advice. A secretary who tries to investigate the Dallas/Fort Worth market on his or her own will very likely take longer to get the "right" job than someone who uses a quality agency.

Historically, certain employment agencies engage in practices that can only be called questionable at best, and the field as a whole is trying to polish up a somewhat tarnished image. A few unscrupulous firms have charged outrageous up-front fees in exchange for an uninspired resume, a pep talk on job-search strategies, and a list of job openings that were public domain. There are, of course, a number of reputable, highly professional employment agencies. But, as in any profession, there are also crooks. It's still a practice in some agencies to advertise non-existent openings to attract applicants for other, less desirable positions.

So much for the pros and cons of employment agencies. If you decide to try one, be sure it's a reputable firm. Ask people in your field to recommend a quality agency, and consult the Better Business Bureau and other resources listed in Chapter 2 to see if there have been any complaints about the agency you're considering.

Most important, *be sure to read the contract thoroughly, including all the fine print, before you sign it.* If you have any questions, or if there's something you don't understand, don't be afraid to ask. It's your right. Make sure you know who is responsible for paying the fee and what the fee is. Remember that *in some cases, an agency's application form is also the contract.*

When you go to an employment agency, treat it the same way you'd treat a job interview. Don't misrepresent yourself, but you want them to think of you as highly marketable. If the agency sees you as very difficult to place, they won't consider you a cost-effective client. If you've paid up-front money, too bad. Even if you haven't, you may have just wasted time that could be better spent conducting your own effective job search.

Here, then, is a selective listing of Dallas/Fort Worth employment agencies, including their areas of specialty.

EMPLOYMENT AGENCIES

AccountAbilitie
5520 LBJ Frwy., Suite 150
Dallas, TX 75240
(214) 980-4184
Accounting and financial.

Accounting Action Personnel
3010 LBJ Frwy., Suite 710
Dallas, TX 75203
(214) 241-1543
Accounting.

ADIA Personnel Services
4100 Spring Valley Rd., Suite 103
Dallas, TX 75244
(214) 661-1356
Administrative, accounting, legal, light industrial, and word processing.

Aware Affiliates
3004 Lancaster Ave.
Fort Worth, TX 76107
(817) 870-2590
Office, clerical, professional, and semi-professional.

Babich & Associates
6060 N. Central Expwy., Suite 544
Dallas, TX 75206
(214) 361-5735
Sales, administrative, and technical.

Brown and Keene Personnel Consultants
5910 N. Central Expwy.
Dallas, TX 75206
(214) 987-5050
Administrative support.

Carrollton Employment Services
1925 Belt Line Rd., Suite 409
Carrollton, TX 75006
(214) 416-8708
Secretaries, word processing, and sales.

Datapro Personnel Consultants
13355 Noel Rd., Suite 200
Dallas, TX 75240
(214) 661-8600
Data processing.

Robert Half
1300 Summit Ave.
Fort Worth, TX 76102
Metro (817) 870-1200
Accounting, financial, and data processing.

Management Recruiters of Fort Worth-Arlington
1009 W. Randol Mill Rd.
Arlington, TX 76012
Metro (817) 469-6161
Technical sales, data processing, medical, insurance, electronics, engineering, technical, and manufacturing.

Marshall Career Service
6500 W. Frwy., Suite 300
Fort Worth, TX 76116
(817) 737-2645
Executive and mid-management placements, specializing in accounting, financial, and operations postions.

Peggy Miller Personnel Consultants
15770 Dallas Pkwy., Suite 600
Dallas, TX 75248
(214) 357-0541
Administrative support.

Opportunity Unlimited Professional Placement
2720 W. Mockingbird Lane
Dallas, TX 75235
(214) 357-9196
Engineering and computer science, mainly working with aerospace, electronics, and telecommunications.

The Personnel Connection
14951 N. Dallas Pkwy., Suite 110
Dallas, TX 75240
(214) 934-1200
Clerical.

Salesworld
6600 LBJ Frwy., Suite 4184
Dallas, TX 75240
(214) 458-0920
Executive sales and marketing.

Secretaries of Dallas
350 Providence Tower West
5001 Spring Valley Rd., L.B. 5
Dallas, TX 75244
(214) 661-3733
Administrative support, secretaries, and word processors.

Snelling & Snelling
8350 N. Central Expwy.
Dallas, TX 75206
(214) 363-8800
Clerical and administrative.

Technology Recruitment
1701 N. Greenville Ave.
Dallas, TX 75206
(214) 669-8170
Engineering, electronics, and software.

Be firm with an agency

A friend of ours had this to say about her experience with employment agencies during her recent job search.

"I've been working as a secretary for 25 years," says Marietta. "When I decided to change jobs, I knew my qualifications supported my desire to work for someone at the level of president or chief executive officer. Unfortunately, I went on a lot of job interviews that I knew were not right for me. The salaries, job descriptions, and locations were all wrong. But I went because the agency suggested I do so.

"Now that I've found a job as administrative assistant to the president of an internationally based manufacturing firm, I'd like to offer this advice to fellow job searchers. Don't hesitate to be assertive with an agency. Demand that they arrange interviews that suit your qualifications and needs. If they can't, take your business elsewhere. Your time is valuable and should not be wasted on mismatched job interviews."■

Career Consultants

If you open the employment section of the **Sunday** *Dallas Morning News, Fort Worth Star-Telegram* or **the** Southwest edition of *The Wall Street Journal*, you'll see several ads for career consultants (also known as career counselors or private outplacement consultants). The ads are generally directed to "executives" earning yearly salaries of anywhere between $20,000 and $300,000. Some ads suggest that the consultants have access to jobs that are not listed elsewhere. Others claim, "We do all the work." Most have branch offices throughout the country.

Career consultants vary greatly in the kind and quality of the services they provide. Some may offer a single service, such as vocational testing or preparing resumes. Others coach every aspect of the job search and stay with you until you accept an offer. The fees vary just as broadly and range from $100 to several thousand dollars. You, not your potential employer, pay the fee.

There are many reputable consulting firms in the Dallas/Fort Worth area. But as is true of employment agencies, some career consultants have been unethical.

A qualified career consultant can be a real asset to your job search. But *no consultant can get you a job*. Only you can do that. You are the one who will participate in the interview, and you are the one who must convince an employer to hire you. A consultant can help you focus on an objective, develop a resume, research the job market, decide on a strategy, and/or train you in interviewing techniques. But you can't send a consultant to interview in your place. It just doesn't work that way.

Don't retain a career consultant if you think that the fee will buy you a job. The only reason you should consider a consultant is that you've exhausted all the other resources we've suggested here and still feel you need expert and personalized help with one or more aspects of the job search. The key to choosing a career consultant is knowing what you need and verifying that the consultant can provide it.

Check references. A reputable firm will gladly provide them. Check the Better Business Bureau and other resources listed in this book. Has anyone lodged a complaint against the firm you're considering? Before you sign anything, ask to meet the consultant who will actually provide the services you want. What are his or her credentials? How long has the consultant been practicing? Who are the firm's corporate clients?

Read the contract carefully before you sign it. Does the contract put the consultant's promises in writing? Has the consultant told you about providing services that are not specified in the contract? What does the firm promise? What do *you* have to promise? Are all fees and costs spelled out? What provisions are made for refunds? For how long a time can you use the firm's or consultant's services?

Be sure to do some comparison shopping before you select a consultant. A listing of area career counselors and consultants appears in Chapter 2.

Executive Search Firms

An executive search firm is paid by a company to locate a person with specific qualifications that meet a precisely defined employment need. Most reputable executive search firms belong to an organization called the Association of Executive Recruiting Consultants (AERC). The association publishes a code of ethics for its membership.

A search firm never works on a contingency basis. Only employment agencies do that. The usual fee for a search assignment is 30 percent of the first year's salary of the person to be hired, plus out-of-pocket expenses. These are billed on a monthly basis. During hard times, most companies forgo retaining search firms because it's so expensive.

It's difficult to get an appointment to see a search specialist. The best time to contact them is when you're employed. Executive search consultants have only their time to sell. If a specialist spends time with you, he or she can't bill that time to a client. If you can use your personal contacts to meet a search professional, however, by all means do so. Executive specialists know the market and can be very helpful in providing advice and leads.

Search firms receive dozens of unsolicited resumes every day. They seldom acknowledge receipt. They keep only a few for future search needs or business development. They really can't afford to file and store them all. Sending your resume to every search firm in the Dallas/Fort Worth area will be useful only if one firm coincidentally has a search assignment to find someone with *exactly* your background and qualifications. It's a long shot, similar to answering blind want ads.

EXECUTIVE SEARCH FIRMS

R.J. Dishaw and Associates
5440 Harvest Hill Rd., Suite 125
Dallas, TX 75230
(214) 788-1740

Ernst & Whinney Executive Search
2001 Ross Ave., Suite 2800
Dallas, TX 75201
(214) 979-1700

Hayman & Co.
400 N. Olive St., Suite 201
Dallas, TX 75201
(214) 953-1900

Heidrick and Struggles
1999 Bryan St., Suite 1919
Dallas, TX 75201
(214) 220-2130

Henard Associates
15303 Dallas Pkwy., Suite 970
Dallas, TX 75248
(214) 991-7151

Ward Howell International
1601 Elm St., Suite 900
Dallas, TX 75201
(214) 749-0099

Hyde Danforth & Co.
5950 Berkshire Lane, Suite 1600
Dallas, TX 75225
(214) 691-5966

Michael James & Associates
4340 Spring Valley Rd.
Dallas, TX 75244
(214) 386-0547

Korn/Ferry International
3950 Lincoln Plaza
500 N. Akard St.
Dallas, TX 75201
(214) 954-1834

Lamalie Associates
1601 Elm St., Suite 4246
Dallas, TX 75201
(214) 754-0019

Management Recruiters of Plano
101 E. Park Blvd., Suite 355
Plano, TX 75074
(214) 424-3339

Meador Wright Associates
6211 W. Northwest Hwy., Suite C261
Dallas, TX 75225
(214) 691-3485

Odell & Associates
12700 Park Central Place, Suite 1800
Dallas, TX 75251
(214) 458-7900

Page-Wheatcroft & Co.
Preston Commons East
18333 Preston Rd.
Dallas, TX 75225
(214) 742-5656

Peat Marwick Main & Co.
1601 Elm St., Suite 1400
Dallas, TX 75201
(214) 754-2000

Paul R. Ray & Carre Orban International
301 Commerce St., Suite 2300
Fort Worth, TX 76102
(817) 334-0500

Roth Young
5344 Alpha Rd.
Dallas, TX 75240
(214) 233-5000

Spencer Stuart
1200 First City Center
1717 Main St., Suite 5300
Dallas, TX 75201
(214) 658-1777

Social Service Agencies

Unlike professional employment agencies, career consultants, and executive search firms, social service agencies are not-for-profit. Many concentrate on aiding the indigent, handicapped people, and those with minimal financial resources. Social service agencies offer a wide range of services, from counseling and vocational training to job placement and follow-up—and their services, in general, are free.

DALLAS/FORT WORTH SOCIAL SERVICE AGENCIES

The Bethlehem Foundation
2603-A Idaho St.
Dallas, TX 75376
(214) 371-3407
Job referral and counseling for the economically disadvantaged.

Better Influence Association
4616 E. Lancaster Ave.
Fort Worth, TX 76103
Metro (817) 429-9462
Fees: Sliding scale
Career development and employment services for residents of the Southside, Poly, Stop Six, Eastwood, Forest Hill, and Highland Hill neighborhoods.

Citizen's Development Center
8800 Ambassador Row
Dallas, TX 75247
(214) 637-2911
Vocational evaluations, work adjustment training, job placement, and follow-up for disabled persons who are at least 16 years old.

Dallas Center for Independent Living
8625 King George Dr., Suite 210
Dallas, TX 75235
(214) 631-6900
Employment assistance referrals made for physically and mentally disabled individuals. Provides independent living classes.

Dallas Inter-Tribal Center
209 E. Jefferson Blvd.
Dallas, TX 75203
(214) 941-1050
Job training, counseling, and placement through job bank for American Indians and others in Dallas and Tarrant County.
Offers nutrition, food, medical, and dental services. Also has Job Training Partnership Administration programs and drug and alcohol abuse counseling.

Dallas Urban League
2121 Main St., Suite 410
Dallas, TX 75201
(214) 747-4734
Assists minority groups and economically disadvantaged in vocational counseling and employment. Sponsors Seniors in Community Service Employment Program for older workers.

EXPANCO
3005 Wichita Court
Fort Worth, TX 76140
(817) 293-9486
Provides a controlled work environment for people who are at least 16 years old and not employable in other industries.

Family Service of Tarrant County
Central Office
1424 Hemphill St.
Fort Worth, TX 76104
(817) 927-8884
One of seven area offices offering counseling and an employee assistance program.

Girls Incorporated of Metropolitan Dallas
2900 Turtle Creek Plaza, Suite 530
Dallas, TX 75219
(214) 526-1676
Provides education and counseling for girls 6-18. Pre-employment programs and job placement for girls up to 18 years old.

Goodwill Industries of Dallas
2800 N. Hampton Rd.
Dallas, TX 75112
(214) 638-2800
Vocational counseling, training, and job placement for multi-handicapped adults through the Job Training Partnership Administration.

Jewish Family Service
7800 Northaven Rd., Suite B
Dallas, TX 75230
(214) 696-6400
Assistance provided to Jewish people in job assessment, guidance, work readiness, and job search. Help provided for vocationally handicapped adults, elderly, new residents, displaced homemakers, or workers displaced by industrial or technological changes. Also runs a food bank.

Liberation Community
3540 E. Rosedale Ave.
Fort Worth, TX 76105
(817) 534-7186

Employment services through Job Training Partnership
Administration, job club, and adult education for G.E.D. preparation,
English as a Second Language, and basic skills for low-income people.

Loaves and Fishes
1709 E. Hattie St.
Fort Worth, TX 76104
(817) 536-9100
Day labor service. Provides daily lunch and serves as distributor of
food bank collections.

Metrocrest Service Center
1002 S. Broadway St.
Carrollton, TX 75006
(214) 446-2100
Job search and assistance program for residents of Addison, Carrollton,
Coppell, and Farmers Branch. Emergency assistance provided when
funds are available.

M.O.V.E. Employment Resources
13749 Neutron, Suite 100
Farmer's Branch, TX 75244
(214) 991-2245
Employment assistance for people "labeled" mentally retarded.
Includes job development, placement, on-the-job training, and post-
training support in full- and part-time jobs.

Multicultural Community Center
1314 N. Munger Blvd., 3rd Floor
Dallas, TX 75206
(214) 828-9891
Administers the Texan Training and Employment Center programs for
refugee women and youths and the U.S. Catholic Conference
Refugee Job Placement program.

Project Link/Mainstream
717 N. Harwood, Suite 890
Dallas, TX 75201
(214) 969-0118
Job placement services for disabled persons who are at least 16 years
old and have marketable job skills.

Restart Corporation
P.O. Box 191294
Dallas, TX 75219
(214) 521-9704
Provides job-search and life-management skills training classes for the
homeless who are at least 18 years old. Clients reside on the premises
during the 5 1/2-week program. Couples are accepted. Participants
receive free meals, child care, and transportation. Must read at a
minimum of 7th-grade level and be drug and alcohol free.

Tarrant County Employment and Training Administration
100 E. Weatherford, Rm. 302
Fort Worth, TX 76196
(817) 884-1464
Provides employment assistance, training, and placement for those meeting low-income requirements.

Washington Street Presbyterian Mission
3525 State St.
Dallas, TX 75204
(214) 824-6801
Employment and job training for homeless and needy.

Woman's Center
515 Custer Rd.
Richardson, TX 75080
(214) 238-9516
Variety of programs, including Pathways to Achievement sessions on finding potential, considering lifework planning, and preparing for the job hunt. Three-part program includes doing a vocational self-assessment, learning job-search skills, and exploring crossroads. Women-in-Transition program helps individuals reenter the job market after losing spouse through death, divorce, or separation. Befrienders program offers immediate job-search assistance. Resource center and informal network help women locate employment.

Women's Center of Tarrant County
1723 Hemphill St.
Fort Worth, TX 76110
(817) 927-4050
Employment assistance through Job Search Club that starts every two weeks. Participants can use a job bank that contains an average of 1,700 job openings. Extra help provided through Mentors Network. Many other programs are offered, including one for assisting low-income single parents with young children.

Women's Resource Center
Young Women's Christian Association
4621 Ross Ave., 3rd Floor
Dallas, TX 75204
(214) 821-9595
Employment service available at YWCA's headquarters at 4621 Ross Ave. and at nine Dallas County branches. Offers individual career counseling, testing, support groups, quarterly YWCA breakfasts, and bi-monthly lunches with networking opportunities. Explore course is offered in the spring and fall. The self-discovery program includes eight sessions at several Dallas County locations.

The Working Connection
440 S. Main
Fort Worth, TX 76104

(817) 871-8790
Provides assessment, training, and placement assistance for applicants who meet economically disadvantaged criteria.

Help for vets

The work of the **Vietnam Veterans of America** in establishing memorials to Vietnam veterans is well-known. But many people do not realize that the group also has established more than 100 outreach centers nationwide. The main objective of these centers is to help men and women veterans of the Vietnam War readjust to civilian life.

The centers offer a variety of services. They solicit job listings from both the public and private sectors. Veterans who need additional help are referred to appropriate counseling groups, health agencies, and other organizations.

For more information, contact the Vet Center in Dallas at (214) 361-5896 or the Vietnam Veterans Counseling Center of Fort Worth at (817) 921-3733.■

Government Agencies

Many job seekers do not take advantage of the employment listings available through local, state, and federal government agencies because they assume most of the positions will be for lower-paying, unskilled jobs. Actually, that's not always the case. Most of these services are free, so you may as well stop by one or more of the following offices and see what is available.

American G.I. Forum/Veteran's Outreach Program
Veterans Outreach Program
801 W. Magnolia Ave.
Fort Worth, TX 76104
(817) 926-6873
Assistance service, including job placement for Vietnam-era veterans.

Dallas County Community Action Committee
2121 Main St.
Dallas, TX 75201
(214) 939-0588
Provides programs that include the Senior Worker Program for low-income individuals who are at least 55 years old. Also provides some financial assistance for utilities.

**Dallas County Department of Human Services
Employment and Training Division**
3625 N. Hall St., Suite 900
Dallas, TX 75219
(214) 522-7291
Employment and training program through the Job Training
Partnership Act for low-income Dallas County residents who live
outside Dallas city limits. Programs include in-school youth
employment, classroom vocational training, job placement, and on-
the-job training with private sector employers. Five area offices in
Garland, Grand Prairie, Irving, Lancaster, and Mesquite.

Dallas Opportunities Industrialization Center
4460 S. Marsalis Dr.
Dallas, TX 75216
(214) 375-5064
Job training and placement program for economically disadvantaged.

Dallas SER
Jobs for Progress
4501 Lemmon Ave.
Dallas, TX 75219
(214) 520-6573
Offers English classes, summer youth programs, clerical skills, job-
search assistance, on-the-job training, and counseling for Spanish-
speaking Dallas/Fort Worth-area residents. One of four branch offices.

Deaf Action Center
3115 Crestview Dr.
Dallas, TX 75235
(214) 521-0407
Career Center, with assistance in job placement for deaf and multi-
disabled adults. Sponsors summer youth program and sign-language
classes.

Garland Neighborhood Service Center
210 Corver St.
Garland, TX 75040
(214) 205-3310
Employment referral and placement. G.E.D and E.S.L classes.

Private Industry Council of Dallas
3625 N. Hall St, Suite 900
Dallas, TX 75219
(214) 522-7191
Provides job training for disadvantaged Dallas youths and adults
through the Job Training Partnership Act. Offers vocational classroom
instruction, on-the-job training, English instruction, and recruitment.

Rehabilitation Hospital of North Texas
3200 Matlock Rd.
Fort Worth, TX 76015

(817) 468-4000
Work adjustment training for physically and mentally disabled adults through on-the-job training, vocational evaluation, and follow-up.

Senior Community Service Employment Program
2727 Inwood Rd., Suite 100
Dallas, TX 75235
(214) 520-6380
On-the-job training in community service and non-profit agency leads to permanent jobs in the public or private sector. Promotes meaningful, part-time work for persons 55 years and older whose income doesn't exceed U.S. Department of Labor guidelines.

Tarrant County Employment and Training (JTPA)
100 E. Weatherford St., Suite 302
Fort Worth, TX 76196
(817) 334-1464
Provides training, placement, and employment for economically disadvantaged Tarrant County residents who live outside of Fort Worth, Arlington, Euless, Haltom City, and White Settlement. Helps economically disadvantaged youths who are at least 18 years old and dislocated workers. Also provides summer youth training for 14 to 21-year-olds and an in-school youth program providing after-school jobs.

Texas Commission for the Blind
3628 McCorh Ave.
Fort Worth, TX 76110
(817) 926-4646 (TDD & VOICE)
Job guidance, training, and placement services for blind and visually impaired individuals in an 11-county area.

Texas Employment Commission
Dallas District Office
8300 John Carpenter Frwy.
Dallas, TX 75356
(214) 631-6050
Provides counseling, job bank, unemployment insurance, and special assistance at nine area centers. Special help provided for veterans, disabled workers, and ex-offenders.

Texas Employment Commission
Fort Worth District Office
301 W. 13th St.
Fort Worth, TX 76101
(817) 335-5111
Parallels Dallas office. Has two other area centers.

Texas Rehabilitation Commission
3636 Lemmon Ave., Suite 100
Dallas, TX 75219

(214) 341-0569
One of four offices in Dallas that provides job training, evaluation, placement, and follow-up to help disabled individuals return to the workplace.

U.S. Department of Labor
Employment and Training Administration
525 Griffin Square, Suite 502
Dallas, TX 75202
(214) 767-4993
Offers job referrals through apprenticeship program.

U.S. Department of Labor
Women's Bureau
525 Griffin St., Suite 731
Dallas, TX 75202
(214) 767-6985
Employment referrals made to other Labor Department services.

U.S. Office of Personnel Management
Federal Job Information Center
Dallas Area Office
1100 Commerce St.
Dallas, TX 75242
(214) 767-8035
Conducts recruiting and examining for federal employment. Provides information on how to apply for federal jobs and advertises job openings in the Dallas/Fort Worth area.

Veterans Administration
1100 Commerce St., Room 1B29
Dallas, TX 75242
(214) 824-5440
Job assistance program to link veterans with employment and training opportunities. Provides special help for educationally disadvanged and service-disabled veterans.

Working Connection
440 S. Main St.
Fort Worth, TX 76104
(817) 870-8790
Provides assessment, on-the-job training, job club, and job placement. Skill training for auto mechanics, account clerks, machinists, clerk/typists, electronics assemblers, food service workers, stenographers, and welders.

How To Succeed In an Interview

If you've read straight through this book, you already know that networking (see Chapter 5) is one of the most important and useful job-hunting techniques around. Networking is nothing more or less than using personal contacts to research the job market and to generate both exploratory and formal job interviews.

Networking and interviewing go hand in hand; all the contacts in the world won't do you any good if you don't handle yourself well in an interview. No two interviews are ever identical, except that you always have the same goal in mind: to convince the person to whom you're talking that he or she should help you find a job or hire you personally. An interview is also an exchange of information. But you should never treat it as you would a casual conversation, even if the "interviewer" is an old friend.

Preparing for the Interview: The 5-Minute Resume

Whether you're talking to the housewife next door about her brother-in-law who knows someone you want to meet or going through a final, formal interview with a multinational corporation, you are essentially making a sales presentation—in this case, selling yourself. Your goal is to convince the interviewer that you have the ability, experience, personality, maturity, and other characteristics required to do a good job and to enlist the interviewer's help in getting you that job.

In an informal interview you'll be talking first to friends and acquaintances. Most of the people you'll be talking to will want to help you. But they need to know who you are, what you've done, what you want to do, and most important, *how they can help you.*

To prepare for any interview, first perfect what we like to call the five-minute resume. Start by giving a rough description, not too detailed, of what you're doing now (or did on your last job) so that when you're telling your story, the listener isn't distracted by wondering how it's going to end.

Then go all the way back to the beginning—not of your career, but of your life. Talk about where you were born, where you grew up, what your folks did, whether or not they're still living, what your brothers and sisters do, and so on. Then trace your educational background briefly and, finally, outline your work history from your first job to your latest.

"What!" say many of our clients. "Drag my PARENTS into this? Talk about my crazy BROTHER and the neighborhood where we grew up?"

Yes, indeed. You want to draw the listener into your story, to make him or her interested enough in you to work for you in your search. You want the interviewer to know not only who you are and what you have achieved but also what you are capable of. You also want to establish things in common with the listener. The more you have in common, the harder your listener will work for you.

Co-author Tom Camden, we are not ashamed to admit, is a master of the five-minute resume. Here's how he would begin a presentation to someone whom he thought could help him.

"Would it be all right with you if I gave you a broad-brush review of my background? Let you know what I've done, what I'd like to do? That'll give us some time to talk about how I should go about this job search. Maybe I could pick your brain a little about how you can help me. OK?

"Currently, I'm president of Camden Associates, an out-placement personnel agency.

"Originally, I'm from the Southwest Side of Chicago, near Midway Airport. I'm 54 years old, married with five grown children.

"My father was a security guard at IIT Research Institute; my mother is retired. She used to work for Walgreens—made aspirins, vitamins, and other pills. I'm the oldest of four children. My brother John does the traffic 'copter reports for a Chicago radio station. My sister Connie is a consultant for an industrial relations firm.

"I went to parochial schools. When I was 14, I left home and went into a monastery. I stayed there until I was 19. Then I went to Loyola University, studied psychology, got my degree in '59. I was also commissioned in the infantry.

"I started my graduate work in Gestalt psychology. In 1960 Kennedy called up troops for the Berlin crisis. That included me, so I spent a year on active duty. Following that, I came back and continued my graduate work in industrial relations..."

Tom took exactly a minute and a half to make this part of his presentation, and he's already given his neighbor several areas in which they may have something in common. He's volunteered enough information not only to get the neighbor interested in his story but to let the neighbor form judgments about him. People don't like to play God, says Tom. Yet it's a fact of life that we constantly form judgments about each other. In an interview—even an exploratory, informal one—you may as well provide enough information to be judged on who you are rather than on what someone has to guess about your background. What does it mean to be the oldest of four kids? What can you deduce from Tom's middle-class background?

The typical personnel professional will tell you that the number of brothers and sisters you have has nothing to do with getting a job. Technically, that's true. The law says that an employer can't ask you how old you are, your marital status, and similar questions. Yet anyone who's considering hiring you will want to know those things about you.

The typical applicant begins a presentation with something like, "I graduated from school in June, nineteen-whatever, and went to work for so-and-so." Our task in this book is to teach you how *not* to be typical. Our experience has convinced us that the way to get a job offer is to be *different* from the rest of the applicants. You shouldn't eliminate the first 20 years of your life when someone asks you about your background! That's the period that shaped your basic values and personality.

Neither should you spend too much time on your personal history. A minute or two is just about right. That gives you from three to eight minutes to narrate your work history. Most exploratory interviews, and many initial employment interviews, are limited to half an hour. If you can give an oral resume in 5 to 10 minutes, you have roughly 20 minutes left to find out what you want to know (more on that shortly).

The five-minute resume revisited

Psychologist and career expert Gayle Roberts has her own slant on the five-minute resume. She believes that "while nothing works every time, you should try to emphasize those aspects of your personal history that have a bearing on your current qualifications for the job you're seeking.

"For example, I am one of those rare creatures who always liked school. I got along fine with the teachers. I even liked studying and taking tests. I liked to learn, and I still do. That's part of why I choose to work in an academic setting. I think it's helpful to mention my long history as a book worm any time I'm applying for a position that requires research, writing, or critical thinking skills. I don't think I'd mention it if I were going for a sales position.

"I personally wouldn't recommend saying too much about your past unless you can connect it to the present in a way that makes you look like a better job candidate. Everybody has a number of revealing personal anecdotes. The trick is to pick the right ones." ■

A word about your work history. If you've done the exercises in Chapter 2, or written your own resume, you ought to be able to rattle off every job you've had, from the first to the latest, pretty easily. In the oral resume you want especially to *emphasize your successes and accomplishments* in each job. This will take some practice. We are not accustomed to talking about ourselves positively. From childhood we're conditioned that it's not nice to brag. Well, we are here to tell you that if you *don't* do it in the interview, you *won't* get the offer.

We repeat: *the interview is a sales presentation.* It's the heart of your job search, your effort to market yourself. In an exploratory interview, the listener will be asking, "Should I help this person?" In a formal interview, the employer will be asking, "Should I hire this person?" In either case, the answer will be "yes" only if you make a successful presentation, only if you convince the interviewer that you're worth the effort.

So, the first step in preparing for any interview, formal or informal, is to *practice your five-minute resume.* Go through it out loud enough times so that you're comfortable delivering it. Then work with a tape recorder and critique yourself. Try it out on a couple of friends.

When you're preparing for a formal employment interview, *do your homework* on the company. This advice is merely common sense. But it's surprising how many candidates will ask an interviewer, "What does this company do?" Don't be one of them. Before you go in for an employment interview, find out everything you can about the company—its history, organization, products and services, and growth expectations. Get hold of the company's annual report, catalogs, and brochures. Consult your networking contacts, and use the resources in Chapter 4.

Steps to a Successful Interview

Before the Interview

- Self-assessment: identify strengths, goals, skills, etc.
- Research the company.
- Rehearse what you plan to say. Practice answers to common questions.
- Prepare questions to ask employer.

During the Interview

- Make sure you arrive a few minutes early.
- Greet the interviewer by his/her last name; offer a firm handshake and a warm smile.
- Be aware of non-verbal communication. Wait to sit until you are offered a chair. Sit up straight, look alert, speak clearly and forcefully but stay relaxed. Make good eye contact, avoid nervous mannerisms, and try to be a good listener as well as a good talker. Smile.
- Follow the interviewer's lead, but try to get the interviewer to describe the position and duties to you fairly early in the interview so you can then relate your background and skills in context.
- Be specific, concrete, and detailed in your answers. The more information you volunteer, the better the employer gets to know you.

- Offer examples of your work that document your best qualities.
- Answer questions as truthfully and as frankly as you can. Do not appear to be "glossing over" anything. On the other hand, stick to the point and do not over-answer questions. The interviewer may steer the interview into ticklish political or social questions. Answer honestly, trying not to say more than is necessary.

Closing the Interview

- Don't be discouraged if no definite offer is made or specific salary discussed.
- If you get the impression that the interview is not going well and that you have already been rejected, do not let your discouragement show. Once in a while, an interviewer who is genuinely interested in you may seem to discourage you to test your reaction.
- A typical interviewer comment toward the close of an interview is to ask if you have any questions. Prepare several questions in advance, and ask those that weren't covered during the interview.
- At the conclusion of your interview, ask when a hiring decision will be made. Also thank your interviewer for his or her time and express your interest in the position.

After the Interview

- Take notes on what you feel you could improve upon for your next interview.
- If you are interested in the position, type a brief thank-you letter to the interviewer, indicating your interest.
- If offered the position, one to two weeks is a reasonable amount of time to make a decision. All employment offers deserve a written reply whether or not you accept them.

How to dress

A young friend of ours who wanted to break into real estate finally landed her first big interview—with Coldwell Banker. It was fairly easy for her to do her homework on a company of that size. Two days before the interview, however, it suddenly dawned on her that she had no idea how to dress. How did she solve her problem?

"It was pretty easy, actually, and fun, too," says Susan. "All I did was go and hang around outside the office for 15 minutes at lunchtime to see what everyone else was wearing."

However, we recommend that even if the office attire is casual, one should still dress professionally. One career counselor recommends that one should "always dress one step above the attire of those in the office where you are interviewing." ∎

What Interviewers are Looking For

∎ **General Personality:** Ambition, poise, sincerity, trustworthiness, articulateness, analytical ability, initiative, interest in the firm. (General intelligence is assumed.) Different firms look for different kinds of people—personalities, style, appearance, abilities, and technical skills. Always check the job specifications. Don't waste time talking about a job you can't do or for which you do not have the minimum qualifications.

∎ **Personal Appearance:** A neat, attractive appearance makes a good impression and demonstrates professionalism.

∎ **Work Experience:** Again, this varies from job to job, so check job specifications. If you've had work experience, be able to articulate the importance of what you did in terms of the job for which you are interviewing and in terms of your own growth or learning. Even if the work experience is unrelated to your field, employers look upon knowledge of the work environment as an asset.

∎ **Verbal Communication Skills:** The ability to express yourself articulately is very important to most interviewers. This includes the ability to listen effectively, verbalize thoughts clearly, and express yourself confidently.

∎ **Skills:** The interviewer will evaluate your skills for the job, such as organization, analysis, and research. It is important to emphasize the skills that you feel the employer is seeking and to give specific examples of how you developed them. This is the main reason why it is important to engage in self-assessment prior to the interview.

∎ **Goals/Motivation:** Employers will assess your ability to articulate your short-term and long-term goals. You should seem ambitious, yet realistic about the training and qualifications needed to advance. You should demonstrate interest in the functional area or industry and a desire to succeed and work hard.

█ Knowledge of the Interviewer's Company and Industry: At a minimum, you really are expected to have done some homework on the company. Don't waste interview time asking questions you could have found answers to in printed material. Know the firm's position and character relative to others in the same industry. General awareness of media coverage of a firm and its industry is usually expected.

Handling the Interview

In an exploratory, or informal, interview most of the people you'll talk with will want to help you. But they need to know *how*. After you've outlined your personal and work history, ask your contact how he or she thinks your experience fits into today's market. What companies should you visit? Specifically, what people should you contact?

When someone gives you advice or a recommendation to call someone else, do it! Few things can be more irritating than to provide free counsel to someone who then ignores it. If your contact suggests that you call Helen Smith, call her!

In a formal employment interview, there are several typical questions you can expect to encounter, though not necessarily in this order:

> Tell me about yourself. (This is your cue for the five-minute resume.)
>
> Why do you want to change jobs?
>
> What kind of job are you looking for now?
>
> What are your long-range objectives?
>
> What are your salary requirements?
>
> When could you be available to start here?
>
> Tell me about your present company.
>
> What kind of manager are you?
>
> How would you describe yourself?
>
> What are your strengths and weaknesses?

(In the course of his career, Tom Camden has posed this last question to untold numbers of applicants. "They'll list two or three strengths," he says, "and then can't wait to tell me about their weaknesses." Don't be one of those people! Accentuate the positive. Remember, this is a competitive interview.)

Describe your present boss.

To whom can I talk about your performance?

Are you open to relocation?

How long have you been looking for a new job?

Why are you interested in this company? (This is your golden opportunity to show the interviewer that you've done your homework on the company.)

Practice your answers to these questions *before* you go in for the interview. Anticipate other questions you might be asked, and develop answers for them. In general, keep your responses positive. Never volunteer a negative about yourself, another company, or a former employer. Even if you hate your present boss, describe your areas of disagreement in a calm, professional manner. You are selling *yourself,* not downgrading others. Even if you're not particularly interested in the company, always conduct the interview as if you were dead set on getting the job.

The interviewer will apply your responses to the questions he or she *really* wants answered:

Does the applicant have the ability to do the job?

Can he or she manage people?

How does he or she relate to people?

What kind of person is this? A leader? A follower?

What strengths does he or she have that we need?

Why the number of job changes so far?

Where is he or she weak?

How did the applicant contribute to present and past companies?

What are his or her ambitions? Are they realistic?

Is he or she too soft or too tough on subordinates?

What is this person's standard of values?

Does he or she have growth potential?

Is there a health problem anywhere?

What is the nature of the "chemistry" between us?

What will the department manager think of this applicant as opposed to the others?

Should this person get an offer?

The interview should not be a one-sided affair, however. Questions that you should ask the interviewer are equally important in this exchange of information. For example, you have to know about the job, the company, and the people in your future employment situation. It's necessary to use your judgment to determine how and when to ask questions in an interview. But without the answers, it will be next to impossible for you to make a sound decision if you receive an offer. Some of the questions you want answered are:

> What are the job's responsibilities?
>
> What is the company's recent history? Its current objectives? Its market position?
>
> Where are its plants located? What distribution systems does it use?
>
> To whom will I report? What's his or her background?
>
> How much autonomy will I have to get the job done?
>
> Why is the job available?
>
> Where does the job lead?
>
> What about travel requirements?
>
> Where is the job located?
>
> Are there any housing, school, or community problems that will develop as a result of this job?
>
> What is the salary range? (Do not raise the question of explicit salary at this point.)
>
> What is the detailed benefit picture?
>
> What is the company's relocation policy?
>
> When will an offer decision be made?
>
> What references will be required?
>
> When would I have to start?
>
> What is the personality of the company?
>
> Do the job and company fit my plan for what I want to do now?
>
> What's the next step?

Following the Interview

Many job seekers experience a kind of euphoria after a good interview. Under the impression that a job offer is imminent, a candidate may discontinue the search. This is a serious mistake. The decision may take weeks, or may not be made at all. On the average, about six weeks elapse between the time a person makes initial contact with a company and when he receives a final answer. If you let up on the search, you will prolong it. Maintain a constant sense of urgency. Get on with the next interview. Your search isn't over until an offer is accepted and you actually begin the new job.

Always follow up an interview with correspondence. The purpose of the letter is to supplement the sales presentation you made. Thank the interviewer for his or her time and hospitality. Express interest in the position (ask for the order). Then mention three additional points to sell yourself further. Highlight how your specific experience or knowledge is directly applicable to the company's immediate needs. Try to establish a date by which a decision will be made.

If you think you could benefit from professional counseling in interviewing skills, consider the resources suggested in Chapter 2 and in Chapter 6. You may also find it helpful to refer to some of the following books.

BOOKS ON INTERVIEWING

Allen, Jeffrey. *How to Turn an Interview Into a Job.* New York: Simon & Schuster, 1988.

Biegeleisen, J.I. *Make Your Job Interview a Success: A Guide for the Career-Minded Job Seeker.* New York: Arco, 1991.

Fear, Richard A. *The Evaluation Interview.* 4th ed. New York: McGraw-Hill, 1990.

Goodale, James G. *The Fine Art of Interviewing.* Englewood Cliffs, NJ: Prentice-Hall, 1982.

King, Norman. *The First Five Minutes: The Successful Opening Moves in Business, Sales and Interviews.* New York: Prentice Hall, 1987.

Kohlmann, James D. *Make Them Choose You: The Executive Selection Process.* Englewood Cliffs, NJ: Prentice Hall, 1987.

Krannich, Caryl R. *Interview for Success.* San Luis Obispo, CA: Impact, 1982.

Marcus, John J. *The Complete Job Interview Handbook.* 2nd ed. New York: Harper & Row, 1988.

Medley, H. Anthony. *Sweaty Palms: The Neglected Art of Being Interviewed.* Berkeley: Ten Speed Press, 1991.

Smart, Bradford D. *The Smart Interviewer.* New York: John Wiley & Sons, 1989.

Yate, Martin. *Knock 'em Dead with Great Answers to Tough Questions'.* Holbrook, MA: Bob Adams, 1991.

How to get the most from your references

References should be kept confidential and never revealed until a company is close to making you an offer, and you want to receive one.

Always brief your references before you supply an interviewer with their names and numbers. Tell the references what company you're interviewing with and what the job is. Give them some background on the company and the responsibilities you'll be asked to handle.

Your references will then be in a position to help sell your abilities. Finally, don't abuse your references. If you give their names too often, they may lose enthusiasm for your cause.∎

What To Do If Money Gets Tight

ny job search takes time. One particularly pessimistic career counselor we know suggests you plan to spend about two weeks of search time for every thousand dollars you want to earn per year. (Pity the poor soul who wants to make $60,000!) A more optimistic estimate for a job search is around three months, provided the search is conducted full time.

If you already have a full-time job, it will take you longer to find a new one. But at least you will be receiving a paycheck while you're looking. This chapter is intended for those who are unemployed and facing the prospect of little or no income during the search.

When the financial squeeze is on, the first thing to do is make a thorough review of your liquid assets and short-term liabilities. Ask yourself how much cash you can expect to receive during the next three months from the following sources, plus any others you might come up with:

Savings
Securities
Silver and gold
Insurance loan possibilities
Second mortgage possibilities
Unemployment compensation
Severance pay
Accrued vacation pay
Personal loan sources (relatives, friends)
Sale of personal property (car, boat, stamp collections, etc.)

Then you should consider exactly what bills absolutely *must* be paid. Don't worry about your total outstanding debt. Many creditors might be willing to make arrangements to forgo principal as long as interest payments are made. It is vitally important to talk to your creditors as soon as possible to avoid being hounded and to assure them that you are working with them.

The final step is easy—if sometimes painful. You compare the amount of money you have on hand or expect to receive with the amount you know you'll have to spend. The difference tells you exactly what kind of financial shape you're in.

The old adage has it that it's better to be unemployed than underemployed. If you can afford it, it's wise not to take a part-time or temporary job. The more time you spend looking for a good full-time position, the sooner you're likely to succeed. But if the cupboard looks pretty bare, it may be necessary to supplement your income any way legally possible in order to eat during the search.

Fast talk nets big part-time $$$

People who need to earn money while job hunting might consider the telemarketing, or telephone sales, industry. Debra Schwartz, who has worked as a telemarketing manager, feels that the field offers a variety of challenges and rewards.

"Being a telemarketer is almost like being an actor in a radio play," says Debbie. "Your success depends on how well you control your voice. You also have to be able to receive feedback from people without the benefit of eye contact or body language."

We asked Debbie what telemarketing managers look for in the people they hire. "The crucial element is the person's voice. Telemarketers must speak clearly and have pleasing voices. They also must use standard English grammar. Previous sales experience is a plus, although it's not necessary. Managers also look for people who can handle rejection. A person might get rejected 25 or 30 times before making a sale."

According to Debbie, most telemarketers work in four-hour shifts. "You can't work on the phone for more than four hours without becoming ineffective. Also, many firms operate only in the afternoons and evenings. But some firms do have morning hours—those involved in corporate sales, for example."

How much can a telemarketer expect to make?

"Top people can make over $10 per hour," says Debbie. "The average telemarketer makes about $4-$8 per hour. The pay varies depending on whether you are working on a straight commission basis or are being paid a base hourly wage plus commissions."

Debbie suggests investigating a telemarketing firm carefully before accepting a job since there are quite a few fly-by-night operations. But she emphasizes the many benefits of working for a reputable firm: "Telemarketing is a great experience for job hunters. Many of the basic sales techniques that you learn are usable when promoting yourself to a potential employer."

Getting a part-time job in telemarketing requires persistence since managers receive hundreds of calls and applications. "Don't give up," advises Debbie. "Have your sales pitch ready when you call. Sell yourself on the phone in the

> same way that you would sell a product once you're hired." ■

Try to find part-time or temporary work that leaves you as free as possible to interview during the day. For this reason, many people choose to drive a cab at night or work in a bar or restaurant during the evenings. This kind of job gives you the advantage of flexible hours, but the pay is not always desirable. Commissioned sales positions abound in almost every industry. But if your personality isn't suited to sales work, don't pursue it. You'll find it very frustrating.

It's best if you can locate part-time work in your chosen field. The pay is usually more attractive, and you can continue to develop your network of contacts. Many professionals can freelance. An administrative assistant, for example, might be able to find part-time work at a law firm. An accountant might be able to do taxes on a part-time basis and still gain access to new referrals.

Another option for those of you with an entrepreneurial flair is to hire out on a contractual basis to employers when you interview with them. Say you're a computer programmer. A company might not have enough computer work to justify hiring someone to fill a full-time position. So you suggest they hire you on a temporary basis until the project is complete. Or suggest one day a week, because that's all the time it will take, or on an as needed basis. The advantage to a company is that they don't have to pay you any benefits (except those you're able to negotiate). The advantage to you is income in your chosen field.

People with technical skills can work themselves into becoming a full-time freelancer in just this way. They might even talk an employer OUT of hiring them full time and negotiate contract work in order to maintain the freedom of their self-employed status.

Here are some additional sources to consider when the money is really tight and you need part-time or temporary work.

SELECTED SOURCES FOR PART-TIME AND TEMPORARY WORK

Accountants on Call
300 Crescent Court
Dallas, TX 75201
(214) 979-9001
Accounting clerks, office managers, controllers, tax specialists, and credit managers.

Accountemps
Three NorthPark East, Suite 200
Dallas, TX 75231
(214) 363-3300
Accountants, bookkeepers, and data processors.

Adia
600 N. Pearl St.
Dallas, TX 75200
(214) 953-1430
Clerical, secretarial, communications, legal, marketing, and
accounting.

ASA Services
2310 Ridge Rd., Suite C
Dallas, TX 75087
(214) 771-5656
Legal secretaries, word processors, receptionists, paralegals, court
runners, and file clerks.

Availability Temporary Services
400 N. St. Paul St.
Dallas, TX 75201
(214) 979-0097
Office, light industrial, and bookkeeping.

Burns International Security Services
8150 Brookriver Dr., Suite 103A
Dallas, TX 75247
Metro (214) 638-1666
Security guard service.

CDI Temporary Services
3030 LBJ Frwy., Suite 240
Dallas, TX 75234
(214) 241-6111
Data processing, word processing, and clerical.

Continental Personnel Service
6060 N. Central Expwy., Suite 630
Dallas, TX 75200
(214) 363-5296
Sales, management, accounting, insurance, and medicine.

Durham Temporaries
1555 W. Mockingbird Lane.
Dallas, TX 75235
(214) 630-9364
Industrial and clerical.

Firstword Temporaries
14785 Preston Rd., Suite 890

Dallas, TX 75240
(214) 788-4900
General office, legal secretaries, and data processors.

Global Technical Services
P.O. Box 161127
Fort Worth, TX 76161
(817) 831-7765 FAX: (817) 831-6915
Contract labor services, specializing in engineers, designers, drafters, and aircraft personnel.

Help Unlimited
1475 Prudential Dr.
Dallas, TX 75235
(214) 630-3851
Light industrial and general labor.

Jess Temporaries
2800 S. Hulen, Suite 215
Fort Worth, TX 76109
(817) 926-1793
Clerical.

Kelly Services
6200 LBJ Frwy., Suite 180
Dallas, TX 75240
(214) 233-9093
Office, word processing, records management, and light industrial.

Kelly Services
6000 Western Place, Suite 115
Fort Worth, TX 76107
(817) 731-0785
Office, clerical, and general labor.

Labor Force
4248 Harry Hines Blvd.
Dallas, TX 75219
(214) 528-0186
General labor.

Manpower Temporary Services
12001 N. Central Expwy.
Dallas, TX 75243
(214) 490-0222
Office, light industrial, sales promotion, and data processing.

Manpower Temporary Services
2000 E. Lamar St., Suite 400
Arlington, TX 76006
(817) 277-7522
Same as Dallas office.

Norrell Temporary Services
8150 Brookriver Dr.
Dallas, TX 75247
(214) 631-0397

301 Commerce St., Suite 310
Fort Worth, TX 76102
(817) 870-1999
Word processing and clerical.

Olsten Word Processing Temps
9400 N. Central Expwy., Suite 112
Dallas, TX 75231
(214) 373-7400
Secretarial, word processing, technical, legal, marketing, light
industrial, and accounting.

Peakload Temporary Services
118 Hemphill St.
Fort Worth, TX 76102
Metro (817) 654-4409
Industrial help, contract payrolling services.

The Personnel Connection
8701 Bedford Euless Rd., Suite 530
Hurst, TX 76053
Metro (817) 589-1741
General labor.

Pinkertons
1150 Empire Central Place., Suite 108
Dallas, TX 75247
(214) 631-5934
Security guard service.

Prime Timers
312 Main St.
Fort Worth, TX 76102
(817) 338-1050
Temporary placement of people over 40 in accounting, word
processing, and general office work.

Southwest Temporaries
2710 Ave. E East
Arlington, TX 76011
(817) 649-7000
Secretarial, legal, data processing, and accounting.

Temporary Employment Associates
University Tower
6440 N. Central Expwy., Suite 603
Dallas, TX 75206

(214) 987-0047
Secretarial, keypunch, and payroll.

TempsAmerica West
1910 Pacific Ave., Suite 540
Dallas, TX 75201
(214) 922-9229
Word processors, accounting clerks, and bookkeepers.

Today's Temporary
2001 Bryan Tower
Dallas, TX 75201
(214) 969-7333

Today's Temporary
3840 Hulen, Suite 125
Fort Worth, TX 76107
(817) 735-1091
Word processing, secretarial, accounting, general office work.

Yellow Cab of Dallas
1610 S. Ervay St.
Dallas, TX 75215
(214) 565-9132
Taxicab leasing.

Yellow Checker Cab
2200 S. Riverside Dr.
Fort Worth, TX 76104
(817) 534-7777
Taxicab leasing.

Federal, State, and Local Government Assistance Programs

If you've exhausted all your resources and can't find part-time or temporary work, you might consider government or private assistance. Many people bridle at the mere mention of "charity" or "welfare." But the help you receive may be needed—and temporary. It's a way of bridging the gap until you land a job. More people take advantage of these sources of assistance than you might imagine. In the case of state and federal aid, your tax dollars have helped to provide the benefits. Your taxes have also paid for the salaries of the people distributing the benefits.

Don't pass judgment on the merits of the following sources until you talk with the professionals who administer their respective programs. Pros can advise you on eligibility and benefits and can also provide you with other ideas and resources.

The Texas Department of Human Services has offices in Dallas and Tarrant counties. It administers Medicaid, Food

Stamps, and Aid to Families with Dependent Children (welfare) programs. Some funds are available for limited emergency assistance. Check with the local office to see if you are eligible.

Dallas and Tarrant County Health Departments operate programs for child health, pre-natal and post-partum care, and family planning, as well as immunization, dental health, adult health, chronic disease, sexually transmitted diseases (STD), stroke and heart attack prevention, community care (elderly), and environmental health programs.

The following organizations represent some major sources of aid available in the Dallas/Fort Worth area:

GOVERNMENT AID SOURCES

City of Dallas Action Center
Dallas City Hall, 2/A
1500 Marilla St.
Dallas, TX 75201
(214) 744-3600
Central clearinghouse for residents seeking information about city services. Provides assistance in contacting county, state, and federal agencies.

City of Dallas Health and Human Services
City Hall, 7/A/North
1500 Marilla St.
Dallas, TX 75201
(214) 670-5216
Provides referrals to divisions or special programs provided by the city of Dallas.

Dallas County Community Action Committee
2121 Main St., Suite 100
Dallas, TX 75201
(214) 939-0588
Neighborhood centers offer limited emergency assistance, food, and clothing. Promotes self-sufficiency among low-income individuals and families in Dallas County through the senior work program and youth job search assistance programs. Has two other branches.

Dallas County Health Department
1936 Amelia Court
Dallas, TX 75235
(214) 920-7900
Public health services for Dallas County residents who live outside Dallas city limits.

Dallas County Public Welfare
4917 Harry Hines Blvd.

Dallas, TX 75235
(214) 920-7850
Financial assistance for individuals and families who have health
problems or meet other eligibility requirements. One-time-only
assistance provided to unemployed heads of households in paying
utilities. Also offers employment and training programs.

Martin Luther King Jr. Community Center

2922 Martin Luther King Jr. Blvd.
Dallas, TX 75215
(214) 670-8367
Multi-purpose center, offering counseling, health, employment, child
care, senior citizen, and other community services. A Dallas County
nutrition program offers noon meals. Employable individuals who
meet requirements receive some emergency assistance for paying
utilities. Also houses branch of the Texas Employment Commission.

Neighborhood Resources Development Program

City of Fort Worth
1000 Throckmorton St.
Fort Worth, TX 76102
(817) 870-7540
Information and referral service to local agencies. Energy crisis
program funds available to help individuals retain utility services.
Tarrant County Centers:
Como Office, 4900 Horne St., (817) 731-0521
Martin Luther King, Jr., 5565 Truman Dr., (817) 457-2076
Mansfield Office, 341 Debbie Lane, (817) 473-0253
North Tri-ethnic, 2950 Roosevelt St., (817) 625-8257
Riverside Office, 201 S. Sylvania Ave., (817) 831-0355
Sansom Park NRD Center, 5428 Cowden St., (817) 624-3139
Southside NRD Center, 959 E. Rosedale St., (817) 332-7786
Worth Heights Office, 3551 New York Ave., (817) 921-5321

Parkland Memorial Hospital

5201 Harry Hines Blvd.
Dallas, TX 75235
(214) 590-8000
Low-cost medical services for Dallas County residents, including
emergency, surgical, psychiatric, and outpatient care.

John Peter Smith Hospital

1500 S. Main St.
Fort Worth, TX 76104
(817) 429-5156
Low-cost outpatient and hospital care for Tarrant County residents
who meet federal guidelines.

Social Security Administration

Dallas Area Office
10910 N. Central Expwy.
Dallas, TX 75231

(800) 234-5772
Cash and health benefits through social security retirement and survivor's insurance, disability insurance, supplemental security income, and Medicare.

Social Security Administration
Fort Worth Area Office
Federal Building
819 Taylor St., Room 1A07
Fort Worth, TX 76102
(800) 234-5772
Parallel services to Dallas office.

Tarrant County Department of Human Services
208 E. Weatherford St.
Fort Worth, TX 76196
(817) 921-5511
Financial assistance through vouchers for food, rent, and utility payments. Referrals, counseling, and shelter for eligible homeless families with children.
Branch offices:
501 W. Main St., Arlington, (817) 459-6869
613 Brown Ter., Hurst, (817) 285-0044
3206 Miller Ave., Fort Worth, (817) 531-5620

Texas Department of Health
Public Health Region 5
2561 Matlock Rd.
Arlington, TX 76015
Metro (817) 261-2911
Provides information and referrals to inexpensive health service programs, including chronically ill and disabled children's services program, early childhood intervention program, and social work services.

Texas Department of Human Services
Region Five
631 106th St.
Arlington, TX 76011
(817) 640-5090
Food stamps, medical, and social services for adults and children who meet income guidelines.
Food Stamp program offered at the following Tarrant County sites:
308 E. 4th St., Fort Worth, (817) 335-5171
3128 S. Riverside Dr., Fort Worth, (817) 921-5511
2526 Jacksboro Hwy., Fort Worth, (817) 625-2161
1540 New York Ave., Arlington, (817) 460-6491

Texas Employment Commission
Dallas District Office
8300 John Carpenter Frwy.
Dallas, TX 75247

(214) 631-6050
Provides unemployment insurance for those who are eligible and cannot find employment through the commission's job bank.
Special help provided for elderly, youths, handicapped, ex-offenders, and women with dependent children.

Texas Employment Commission
Fort Worth District Office
310 W. 13th St.
Fort Worth, TX 76102
(817) 335-5111
Parallel services to Dallas District Office.

Filing for Unemployment Benefits

Here are three good reasons to check with the Texas Employment Commission (addresses above): 1) there's no charge for any of the services; 2) you'll probably find leads for better jobs than you expected; 3) and you may qualify for one of the programs assisting special groups.

An average of 2,000 available positions are listed in the TEC's computerized job bank. On weekdays, you can contact any one of the 13 area offices to check on what's available. At least 50 percent are professional, clerical, and sales jobs. And a majority are permanent, full-time positions.

The government-funded public employment agency also provides free employment testing and counseling and makes referrals to social agencies. Special assistance is provided to veterans.

Job Search Seminars are offered in the downtown Fort Worth office, downtown Dallas, and Richardson-Plano offices. Anyone who is receiving unemployment compensation is eligible to attend the five-day workshop. Participants prepare for the job search by watching a video job-hunting course developed by Karli and Associates. In addition, they learn to communicate more effectively with employers by having mock job interviews videotaped so they can see where they need to improve.

The TEC also helps people find seasonal employment. Several weeks before the State Fair of Texas opens in October, a TEC booth is set up on the Dallas fairgrounds to sign up as many as 1,000 people for temporary jobs. The TEC also assists storeowners in large shopping malls to find workers for the Christmas rush.

Anyone who is unemployed can register at the TEC for unemployment insurance. The amount of money individuals are eligible to receive depends on their former income and reasons for their last job separation. The TEC requires people to search actively for a job while they receive unemployment compensation. Checks are mailed twice a month for up to 26 weeks.

To sign up for benefits, bring personal identification, such as a driver's license or military identification, and source of work eligibility, such as a social security card. Also, bring the name and mailing address of your last employer to one of the 12 offices in the Dallas/Fort Worth area. If you were employed outside of Texas during the past 24 months, you will need the names and addresses of all the companies you worked for during that time.

For more information, call the Fort Worth office at (817) 335-5111 or the Dallas office at (214) 631-6050.

TEC Offices in the Dallas Area:

Garland, 217 N. 10th St., (214) 276-8361

Grand Prairie, 202 W. Hwy. 303, (214) 264-5881

Irving, 201 S. Rogers St., (214) 254-9135

Lancaster-Kiest Office, 408 Lancaster-Kiest Shopping Center, (214) 372-1471

Martin Luther King Jr. Community Center, 2922 Martin Luther King Jr. Blvd., (214) 421-2460

Northwest-Carrollton, 1718 Trinity Valley Dr., (214) 620-1351

Dallas East Office, 4625 Eastover Dr., Mesquite, (214) 388-5840

Richardson-Plano, 1222 E. Arapaho Rd., (214) 234-5391

Kessler Hills, 1050 N. Westmoreland Rd., (214) 330-5183

TEC Offices in Tarrant County:

Arlington, 979 N. Cooper St., (817) 265-8431

Downtown Fort Worth, 301 W. 13th St., (817) 335-5111

Bedford, 1809 Forest Ridge Dr., (817) 545-1809

Private Charitable Organizations

American Red Cross
2300 McKinney Ave.
Dallas, TX 75201
(214) 871-2175
Limited financial aid and shelter for families, service personnel, and others experiencing short-term crisis.

Arlington Charities
811 Secretary St.
Arlington, TX 76015

(817) 275-1511
Clothing, household items, and food provided on a short-term basis for Arlington residents.

Catholic Charities
Dallas Office
3845 Oak Lawn Ave.
Dallas, TX 75219
(214) 520-6590
Limited emergency financial aid to low-income families in East Dallas provided by Brady Social Service Center, 4009 Elm St., (214) 826-8330.

Catholic Charities
Fort Worth Office
1404 Hemphill St.
Fort Worth, TX 76104
(817) 921-5381
Food, clothing, furniture, and emergency financial assistance for travelers and Tarrant County residents.
Other sites:
813 Brown Ridge Ter., Bedford, (817) 282-6646
2024 N. Houston St., Fort Worth, (817) 626-3402
349 N.W. Renfro St., Burleson, (817) 295-6252

Community Council of Greater Dallas
Information and Referral Services
2121 Main St., Suite 500
Dallas, TX 75201
(214) 747-3711
24-hour emergency referral service to health, welfare, and social service agencies.

Consumer Credit Counseling Service of Greater Dallas
1949 Stemmons Frwy., Suite 200
Dallas, TX 75207
(214) 748-2227
Credit counseling for financially distressed individuals. No fee for counseling; small fee for debt liquidation.
Branch Offices:
201 E. Abram, Suite 730, Arlington, (817) 461-2227
1525 N. Interstate 35, Suite 206, Carrollton, (214) 242-6548
7125 Marvin D. Love Frwy., Suite 102, Duncanville, (214) 709-3000
100 N. Central Expwy., Suite 400, Richardson, (214) 437-6252

Jewish Family Service
7800 Northaven Rd., Suite B
Dallas, TX 75230
(214) 696-6400
Provides guidance counseling.

Salvation Army
6500 Harry Hines Blvd.
Dallas, TX 75235
(214) 353-2731
Meals, lodging, and casework service for transient men, women, and children. Temporary emergency assistance for families who do not meet public agencies' requirements.

SEARCH (Southeast Area Churches Association)
3301 E. Rosedale
Fort Worth, TX 76105
(817) 531-2211
Emergency food, clothing, shelter, transportation, medical, and utility assistance.

YWCA of Fort Worth and Tarrant County
512 W. 4th St.
Fort Worth, TX 76102
(817) 332-6191
Residence service for women available for $30-$55 per week. Low-cost meals served. Child care provided for a fee.

Where To Turn If Your Confidence Wilts

Recently a bank fired a loan officer who had worked there for more than 10 years. The employee was 58 years old, about five feet, six inches tall, weighed almost 300 pounds, and did not have a college degree. His written communication skills were negligible. His poor attitude and appearance, lack of enthusiasm, and dismal self-esteem suggested he would be unemployed a long time.

The bank decided to use Tom Camden and Associates' outplacement service to help the person get another job. "There wasn't much we could do about changing his age, education, size, or communication skills," Tom recalls. "But we certainly could—and did—work with him on improving his self-esteem and changing his attitude toward interviewing for new jobs."

After a four-month search, the loan officer succeeded in landing a position that exactly suited his needs. His new job even was located in the neighborhood where he lived. It seemed like a typical success story—until the bank informed Tom Camden about how dissatisfied that person was with the counsel he had received. The man told the bank that they would have been better off paying *him* the consulting fee instead of retaining outside help.

"He was really angry," Tom recalls. "And also full of stress, guilt, fear, anxiety, desire for vengeance, and a host of other emotions."

Such feelings, unfortunately, are not at all unusual. In fact, they're a normal part of any job search, particularly for those who have been laid off or fired. That's because rejection, unfortunately, is inevitable in any job search.

If you've read Chapter 5, you know that you may speak with up to 300 people on a formal or informal basis while you're looking for suitable work—and a healthy percentage of those people will be unable or unwilling to help you. Every job seeker must anticipate rejection—it comes with the territory. Being turned down in an interview is a painful experience, and it's normal to feel hurt. The trick is to keep those hurt and angry feelings from clouding your judgment or affecting your behavior.

What To Do If You Get Fired

Being fired ranks just after the death of someone you love or divorce when it comes to personal traumas. If it should happen to you, *take time to evaluate the bad news before accepting a settlement offer.* If you quickly accept what your employer has to offer, it will be much more difficult to change your situation later. Tell the boss you want some time to think about a settlement. Then go back in a day or two and negotiate.

Stay on the payroll as long as you can, even if your pride hurts. Find out if you are eligible for part-time work or consulting jobs to tide you over until you find your new job. You may be able to hang on to insurance and other benefits until you've found new employment.

Try to negotiate a generous severance payment. In the last five years, severance agreements have risen dramatically in some industries. What the company offers at first may not be their maximum. Negotiation doesn't always work, but you certainly ought to try to get the most for your years of service.

Check with your personnel office to make sure you're getting all the benefits to which you are entitled, such as vacation pay and profit sharing. Check your eligibility for unemployment compensation before you accept an offer to resign instead of being terminated.

Don't attack management during your termination interview. It may cost you good references and hurt your chances of finding a new job.

Take advantage of any placement assistance that is offered. Don't reject the company's offer to help even if your pride has been stung.

Dealing with Emotional Stress

If you're beginning to feel your confidence wilt, reread the tips in Chapter 5 for treating yourself well. Put yourself on a regular schedule. Make sure you're eating healthy foods and getting enough rest and exercise. Don't punish yourself for being unemployed or losing a job offer.

One of the worst things that can happen in any job search is to let rejection undermine your self-confidence. Like the little boy at the door who asks, "You don't want to buy a magazine, do you?" a person who doesn't feel good about himself will not easily convince an employer that he should be hired. Each new rejection further erodes self-esteem, and the job search stalls or takes a nose dive: "Maybe I *am* a loser. Perhaps I was lucky to have my old job as long as I did. Maybe my sights are set too high. I suppose I should look for something less responsible at a lower salary."

Thoughts such as these cross most people's minds at some time or other in the job search. As we've said, it's normal to feel hurt, angry, and depressed after a series of rejections. It's important, however, to recognize these feelings and learn to work them out in some non-destructive way. It is *not* normal to let such feelings sabotage your job search. Just because you're unemployed or looking for a new job doesn't mean you're a bad or worthless person. The only thing "wrong" with you is that you haven't found the offer that you want.

When your confidence starts to wilt, turn to a trusted friend or relative. Talk about your feelings frankly. Get mad or sad or vengeful. Then get back to work on your job search. Don't let fear of rejection keep you from making that next call. It may be just the lead you're looking for.

There are no hard and fast rules on when to seek professional counseling and support, but we can offer certain guidelines. If you seriously think you need professional help, you ought to investigate two or three sources. Besides the ones we've listed below, check with your minister, priest, or rabbi.

If you feel you have nowhere else to turn, or if you don't want to share your feelings with anyone you know, you should consider professional counseling. If you're not making calls, not preparing for interviews, or not doing what you know you have to do to get the job you want, you could probably use some counseling.

Everybody feels bad about being rejected. But if you allow those feelings to overwhelm you, or if they're interfering with finding a job, it's probably time to talk with a professional. Another sure sign is if you're waking up most mornings too sick or lethargic from overeating, overdrinking, or abusing some other substance to do what you have to do.

Where To Find Help for Emotional Problems

A listing in this book does not constitute an endorsement of any institution, therapist, or school of therapy. Therapy depends a great deal on the "chemistry" between therapist and patient—something only you can evaluate. A basic rule of thumb is that if you're not comfortable with or confident in a particular therapist, it may not be wise to continue seeing him or her.

Therapy is offered by quite a variety of people, from psychiatrists and psychologists with years of postgraduate training to those with considerably lower levels of education and experience. Before engaging a therapist, check his or her credentials. Where was the therapist trained? What degrees does the therapist hold? How long has the therapist been practicing? Does he or she belong to any professional associations?

Psychotherapist Mary Lee Palmer recommends that you interview several therapists before you enter therapy—even if you have to buy 15 minutes of their time. Ask about cost, credentials, whether your health insurance covers their fees, the type of therapy they practice, the length of time they anticipate would be required to deal with your concerns. The answers to all of these questions are important. But equally important is the sense of rapport you feel. It is vital that you feel comfortable confiding in this person.

There are a number of professions that practice counseling and therapy. The following rundown is arranged more or less in order of years of training, which in turn usually determines the fee charged. A psychiatrist is an M.D. and is able to prescribe medication. A psychologist usually has a Ph.D. and has gone through an internship. A clinical social worker has an M.S.W. and has conducted therapy under supervision while in training. There are also licensed professional counselors, psychiatric nurses, and pastoral counselors.

One of the best ways to find out who might be helpful for you is to ask your friends for recommendations. If someone you know well has been helped and swears by a therapist, that's a strong testimonial. There are, unfortunately, a bewildering variety of schools of therapy. Each one has its detractors and its supporters. What worked for your friend might not work for you. Ask your friend how the therapist worked, and try to envision yourself going through a similar process. Today many therapeutic interventions offer relatively rapid relief. Plan on about six to eight sessions to help you get back on your feet.

SELECTED CRISIS CENTERS AND INSTITUTIONS

Alcoholics Anonymous
Fort Worth Central Office
316 Bailey Ave.
Fort Worth, TX 76107
(817) 332-3533
Offers referrals to numerous AA groups in Tarrant County. Free.

Alcoholics Anonymous
Metropolitan Dallas
13500 Midway Rd., Suite 100
Dallas, TX 75244
(214) 239-4599
Provides information and referrals for alcoholics and their families. Offers counseling, support groups, and halfway houses. Free.

American Indian Center
818 E. Davis St.
Grand Prairie, TX 75050
(214) 262-1349
Crisis counseling for American Indians and a halfway house for alcohol rehabilitation. Free.

Azle Pastoral Counseling Center
229 S. Stewart St.
Azle, TX 76020
(817) 444-2929
Individual and group counseling for marriage, family, and personal life adjustment. Initial fee of $20, plus testing expenses, and then a sliding scale fee for other visits.

Catholic Charities
3845 Oak Lawn Ave.
Dallas, TX 75219
(214) 528-4870
A variety of programs provided, including emergency help for refugees and migrants. Counseling billed on sliding scale.

Center for Creative Living
2401 Oakland Blvd.
Fort Worth, TX 76103
Metro (817) 429-0521

Psychotherapy, personal counseling, vocational counseling, day care, pre-school, grade school, and crisis intervention. Sliding scale fees.

CONTACT—Dallas
Telephone Counseling
P.O. Box 742224
Dallas, TX 75374
Administration: (214) 233-0866
Counseling Line: (214) 233-2233
Teen Line: (214) 233-TEEN
Trained volunteers provide 24-hour telephone counseling and referrals for distressed individuals. Provides referrals to emergency aid, including food, shelter, and prescription medicine.

CONTACT—Tarrant County
P.O. Box 1431
800 W. Randol Mill Rd.
Arlington, TX 76012
Administration: (817) 277-0071
Counseling Line: (817) 277-2233
Parallels Dallas office.

Crisis Intervention
716 W. Magnolia St.
Fort Worth, TX 76104
Counseling Hotline: (817) 927-5544
Trained volunteers provide 24-hour telephone counseling and referrals.

Dallas Council on Alcoholism and Drug Abuse
4525 Lemmon Ave., Suite 300
Dallas, TX 75219
24-hour assistance line: (214) 522-8600
Provides public education, information and referrals, employee assistance program. Sliding scale fees.

F.A.C.T.S. (Family Assessment, Consultation and Therapy Service)
600 8th Ave.
Fort Worth, TX 76104
Metro (817) 654-FACT
Counseling for individuals, groups, and families concerning anger control, domestic violence, marital discord, substance abuse, and sexual abuse. Fees vary; limited sliding scale fees.

Family Guidance Center
2200 Main St.
Dallas, TX 75201
(214) 747-8331
Counseling for individuals, couples, and families. Psychiatric consultation and psychological testing. Outreach to minority and low-income neighborhoods. Sliding scale fees.

First United Methodist Church Counseling Service
800 W. 5th St.
Fort Worth, TX 76102
(817) 924-8521
Counseling for couples, individuals, codependency, adult children of alcoholics, and smoking. Alcohol and drug use assessments available. Workshops in assertiveness, marriage enrichment, divorce adjustment, stress management, retirement, communications, and listening skills. Fees vary from $45 for individual counseling to sliding scale.

Church groups offer support

Churches are taking a more active role in helping the unemployed. One of the largest organizations is the Inter-Faith Job Search Council that meets in different churches every Saturday morning except on holidays. This is a non-denominational organization of volunteers. Churches provide the space.

Most meetings include a motivational speaker to help boost morale. Other sessions are provided on a variety of topics that rotate each week. Among the most frequently discussed subjects are resume writing, marketing yourself, interviewing, networking, managing your finances, and how to cope emotionally if you lose your job.

An important part of the session is networking, which gives people an opportunity to pass out resumes and to exchange job leads. The atmosphere is friendly and casual, with free donuts and coffee served at the half-day sessions.

Many of the larger churches provide reference books and job-hunting material in their libaries that also can be helpful.

Notices of the meetings are run in church calendars. For more information, call David Lajoi at (214) 644-1491, Bob Mahoney at (214) 988-0104, or Joe Lang at (214) 526-3997.■

Iatreia Institute
1152 Country Club Lane
Fort Worth, TX 76112

(817) 654-9600
Multidisciplinary mental health clinic, providing individual, relationship, and family counseling as well as specializations in career development.

Interfaith Job Search Council of Tarrant County
(817) 731-9876
Contact: Dianne Stewart

Jewish Family Service
7800 Northaven Rd.
Dallas, TX 75230
(214) 696-6400
Individual and family counseling. Assessment, guidance, and vocational counseling services. Sliding scale fees.

Mental Health Association of Dallas County
2929 Carlisle St.
Dallas, TX 75204
(214) 871-2420
Referrals and information for counseling and self-help groups that deal with a variety of mutual concerns.

Metroplex Psychotherapy Services
9304 Forrest Lane, Suite 107
Dallas, TX 75243
(214) 238-1267
Counseling for problems of depression, stress, single living, parenting, and work. Evaluation, diagnosis for treatment, and psychiatric consultations for individuals, couples, and families. No services for children. Sliding scale fees.

Nexus
8733 La Prada Dr.
Dallas, TX 75228
(214) 321-0156
Residential and day programs for adolescents and women who are dealing with alcohol and drug-abuse problems. In and outpatient services available. Individual and employment counseling available. Sliding scale fees.

Oak Lawn Community Services
3434 Fairmount
Dallas, TX 75219
(214) 520-8108
Therapeutic individual, couple, group, and family counseling for gay men and lesbians. Offers education programs, professional consultation, outpatient drug/alcohol recovery program, and AIDS programs. Sliding scale fees.

Richland Hills Church of Christ Counseling Center
6250 NE Loop 820

Richland Hills, TX 76180
Metro (817) 498-1722
Provides job bank, food bank, and clothing room. Individual, couples, and drug counseling for drug abuse, depression, stress management, divorce recovery, and grief recovery. Various self-help groups. Fees vary.

The Salvation Army
5302 Harry Hines Blvd.
Dallas, TX 75235
(214) 688-4494
Administrative center for services that include counseling and work therapy for unattached, disabled, and transient men. Some services available for women and families. Free.

The Suicide and Crisis Center
2808 Swiss Ave.
Dallas, TX 75204
(214) 828-1000 (Crisis Line)
24-hour telephone crisis counseling for individuals contemplating suicide or facing a crisis. Community education and preventative services are offered. Accepts contributions.

Turtle Creek Manor
2707 Routh St.
Dallas, TX 75201
(214) 871-2454
Vocational and group counseling for people 18-60 with mental/emotional problems and/or chemical dependency. Job readiness training. Sponsored by the Texas Rehabilitation Commission, Adult Probation, and VA Hospital.

Vietnam Veterans' Readjustment Center of Fort Worth
1305 W. Magnolia St.
Fort Worth, TX 76104
(817) 921-3733
Outpatient psychological counseling, specializing in treatment of delayed combat stress. Psychological counseling available in alcohol/drug abuse, marital stress, and for psychiatric treatment. Free.

**Career
Transition Issues**

For most people, conducting a job search constitutes a crisis of sorts. Strong feelings will be aroused, and action must be taken if the crisis is to be resolved. While it's normal to have all of the following emotional responses during the course of your job search, you must manage your emotions or they'll manage you.

Anger—You must not let the fact you were fired or treated indifferently by some interviewer make you hostile on your next interview. Be aware of the object of your anger. Don't displace it onto someone else.

Depression—Of course, you're going to get disappointed and frustrated at times, but don't give in to self-pity. Your next employer wants a go-getter, not a poor-me-er.

Social withdrawal—When you're down and out it's very tempting to avoid others. Don't become a hermit. You need all the friends and contacts you can maintain. Don't apologize for being out of work. It has happened to most people.

The best antidote against getting bogged down in your own emotional turmoil is to take action:

1. *Stay physically active.* Research has shown that regular, vigorous aerobic activity combats depression and anxiety.

2. *Come up with a good plan* for finding a job and stick to it. Give your self lots to do every day. Impose deadlines on yourself. As you start making progress, you'll start feeling better.

3. *Join a support group* for other job seekers. Not only will you get encouragement, you'll also get leads and advice.

4. *Make finding a good job a full-time job.* You'll feel better and find the right position quicker.■

Selecting the Right Job
for You

Welcome to the most pleasant chapter of this book. You've figured out what you want to do, developed an acceptable resume, and used your network of contacts and other resources to research the job market and generate all sorts of interviews. If you haven't received a reasonable offer yet, you're close to it.

You have a nice kind of problem if a company makes you an offer and insists on an immediate response while you're still investigating other promising leads. The employer making this offer is essentially telling you, "We think you have everything we're looking for, and we want you to start as soon as possible." Remember, at this point you have more power with this company than at any other time in the job search, and you should not be afraid to flex it in a responsible manner. It can be difficult to stall or delay your acceptance just because other promising leads still haven't yielded firm offers. You have to use your best judgment in such a case, but you owe it to both yourself and the people who interviewed you to bring in all outstanding possibilities and *then* make your decision. Unless you're absolutely desperate, there's no reason to jump at the first offer you receive. In fact, many career specialists feel you should not take the first offer unless it is a great fit for you.

Ask the employer for a period of time, three to seven days, to review the offer and consider your options. Contact the other companies with which you were talking, and inform them that you have a pending offer. Ask them to get back to you within a set period of time (you set the time!) with a response.

If a company wants you badly enough, they'll wait a reasonable length of time for you to decide. In the meantime, use your offer to "encourage" other companies to reach a decision about your candidacy. We're not suggesting that you play hardball. That probably won't work and might even work against you. But it makes perfect sense to inform other companies who are interested in you that you have an offer. If you're sure you'd rather work for them, say so. But also say that you'll have to accept the first offer if you don't hear from them within the allotted time. Don't lie about your intentions. If you don't intend to accept the first offer, don't say that you do. Otherwise, the second (and better) company might write you off, assuming that you won't be available by the time they're ready to decide.

A job involves much more than a title and base salary. For any firm offer, be sure you understand what your responsibilities will be, what benefits you'll receive besides salary (insurance, vacation, profit sharing, training, tuition reimbursement, and the like), how much overtime is required (and whether you'll be paid for it), how much travel is involved in the job, who your superior will be, how many people you'll be supervising, and where the position might lead. (Is it a dead-end job, or are people in this slot often promoted?) In short, find out anything and everything you need to know to evaluate the offer.

For many positions, especially those requiring several years' experience, it's appropriate to ask for an offer in writing. Such a document would specify the position's title, responsibilities, reporting relationship, compensation, and include a statement of company benefits.

At the very least, before you make a firm decision, be sure to obtain a copy of the company's personnel policy. It will fill you in on such details as the number of paid sick days, overtime and vacation policy, insurance benefits, profit sharing, and the like. These so-called fringe benefits can really add up. Be certain to assign a dollar value to them to help you evaluate the financial pros and cons of each offer.

It seems obvious to us that it's unwise to choose a job exclusively on the basis of salary and benefits. You spend more of your waking hours at work than at any other activity. Don't condemn yourself to working for an impossible boss, with colleagues and subordinates you can't stand, doing work that you find boring, to accomplish goals you don't believe in.

Finding the Right Culture

Dr. Carolyn Wierson, a university coordinator of job search training, warns that you ignore a company's culture at your own peril. You can find a position that suits you to a T but still be unhappy if you don't fit the culture of the company that hires you. It takes some doing to assess an organization's culture, but it's worth your while.

Some signs are fairly obvious: What do people wear? What is the furniture like? Are office doors kept open or closed? Are there any minorities or women in positions of power? How friendly are people to you? To each other? Does anybody laugh? A very important question to ask—Do I feel comfortable here?

There are five aspects of an organization's culture to consider. Try to find out as much as you can about each. Ask yourself in which you would be most comfortable.

1. What is the relationship between a company and its environment? Does it control its own destiny, or must it depend on the mood of an adversarial home office? You probably wouldn't be wise to work for a municipal bus company if they were phasing out bus service.

2. How does a company view human nature? Good or evil? Changeable or immutable? Answers to these questions determine how employees are treated, how much supervision and control is exerted. How openly will employees communicate? Will there be opportunities for training and development?

3. What are the philosophy and mission of a company? Printed brochures are often good indicators. A good company is clear on what business it's in.

4. How do people relate to each other in a company? Is there a formal flow chart? Are there many vertical levels (defense industry)? Or is power more evenly and horizontally spread out (some new hi-tech firms)? The more horizontal, the more informal, and things generally get done through relationships.

5. How are decisions made, who makes them, and upon what basis? Facts and reason? Politics? Ideology? Good old boy network? The whims of an autocrat at the top?

The answers to these questions will determine the working atmosphere for most companies.

Compare the Offers on Paper

You've talked with each employer and taken notes about the responsibilities and compensation being offered. Where possible, you've obtained a job offer in writing. You have also read through the company's personnel policy. Now, make yourself a checklist for comparing the relative merits of each offer. We've provided a sample here, but if another format suits your purposes better, use it. The idea is to list the factors that you consider important in any job, and then assign a rating for how well each offer fills the bill in each particular area.

We've listed some of the factors that we think ought to be considered before you accept any offer. Some may not be relevant to your situation. Others that we've left out may be of great importance to you. So feel free to make any additions, deletions, or changes you want.

Once you've listed your factors, make a column for each job offer you're considering. Assign a rating (say, 1 to 5, with 1 the lowest and 5 the highest) for each factor and each offer. Then, total the score for each offer.

The offer with the most points is not necessarily the one to accept. The chart doesn't take into account the fact that "responsibilities" may be more important to you than "career path," or that you promised yourself you'd never punch a time clock again. Nevertheless, looking at the pros and cons of each offer in black and white should help you make a much more methodical and logical decision.

Factor	Offer A	Offer B	Offer C
Responsibilities	______	______	______
Company reputation	______	______	______
Salary	______	______	______
Insurance	______	______	______
Paid vacation	______	______	______
Pension	______	______	______

Profit sharing   ______   ______   ______

Tuition reimbursement   ______   ______   ______

On-the-job training   ______   ______   ______

Career path (where can
   you go from this job?)   ______   ______   ______

Company future   ______   ______   ______

Quality of product
   or service   ______   ______   ______

Location (housing
   market, schools,
   transportation)   ______   ______   ______

Boss(es)   ______   ______   ______

Other workers   ______   ______   ______

Travel   ______   ______   ______

Overtime   ______   ______   ______

Other   ______   ______   ______

______________   ______   ______   ______

______________   ______   ______   ______

TOTAL POINTS   ______   ______   ______

Salary strategy

Before you accept an offer—or dicker over salary—you need to know what other people who fill similar positions are making. The *Occupational Outlook Handbook,* put out by the U.S. Department of Labor every two years, cites salary statistics by field. Probably a better source of information is *The American Almanac of Jobs and Salaries* by John Wright, published by Avon.

What you really need to know is what other people with your qualifications and experience are making in Dallas/Fort Worth for working the job you're considering. Professional societies and associations frequently provide this sort of information. It's one more good reason to belong to one. Probably the best source of all for salary orientation is—you guessed it—your network of contacts. ∎

BOOKS ON SALARY NEGOTIATION

Cohen, Herb. *You Can Negotiate Anything.* New York: Bantam Publishing Co., 1983.
Fisher, Roger, and William Ury. *Getting to Yes.* New York: Penguin Books, 1983.
Kennedy, Marilyn Moats. *Getting the Job You Want and the Money You're Worth.* Piscataway, NJ: American College of Physician Executives, 1987.

A Final Word

Once you have accepted a job, it's important that you notify each of the people in your log of your new position, company, address, and phone number. Be sure to thank these people; let them know you appreciated their assistance. After all, you never know when you may need to ask them to help you again. You've spent weeks building up a network of professional contacts. *Keep your network alive.*

On each anniversary date of your new job, take the time to run through the self-appraisal process to evaluate your situation and the progress you are making (as measured by increased salary, responsibilities, and abilities). Consider how they compare with the objectives you set at the start of your search. Although you may be completely satisfied in your new assignment, remember that circumstances can change overnight, and you must always be prepared for the unexpected. So make an employment "New Year's Resolution" to weigh every aspect of your job annually and compare the result with what you want and expect from your life's work.

We hope that you have made good use of the job-search techniques outlined in this book. Indeed, we hope that the resulting experiences not only have won you the job you want but—equally important—also have made you a better person. Perhaps the next time you talk to an unemployed person or someone who is employed but seeking a new job, you will look at that person with new insight gained from your own search experiences. We hope you'll gladly share what you've learned about how to get a job in Dallas/Fort Worth.

Zeroing in on a great place to work

How do you know when you've found a great place to work?

We asked business writer Robert Levering, co-author of *A Great Place to Work: What Makes Some Employers So Good and Some So Bad* and *The 100 Best Companies to Work for in America,* what he considerd the key to evaluating a job proposal.

"Before you accept a job," Levering insists, "you ought to ask yourself, 'what kind of relationship am I going to have with the people I work for, with the people I'm going to work with, and with my work itself?'"

When he was tracking down "the 100 best employers in America," the rankings were based on five tangibles: pay, benefits, job security, opportunities for promotion, and ambiance. Now, however, he believes the values that rest behind the perks may be more significant than the perks themselves. Levering states, "You must trust the people you work for, have pride in what you do, and enjoy the people you work with. Simply put, the criteria for a great place to work are trust, pride, and fun.

"Let's face it, a happy marriage isn't defined by a house in the suburbs, two cars in the garage, 2.5 children, and a dog. When you find a great job, it's more than the result of just pay scales, benefits, and a chance to move up."

That doesn't mean that salary range, stock options, or a gourmet corporate cafeteria are irrelevant. Levering explains, "If you feel that you're being cheated or that the company is not paying you as much as it could, it's not just an issue of money. How your employer compensates you for your time tells you about how your employer values you, and that concerns trust.

"Similarly, pride translates into systems that let people develop their skills. Pride ensures that employees have the tools they need to do their jobs. Pride means workers get credit for their accomplishments. And if your co-workers are relaxed, pleasant to be with, and basically compatible, work is fun. Often that comes down to how much corporate politics permeates the office."

Are companies—other than the 100 best—willing to create a corporate culture based on trust, pride, and fun?

"There are positive signs," Levering says. "Businesses know that the work force has changed. Employees are now more highly educated and looking for the best job possible. Employers want to attract and retain the best people, so they want to treat their employees well. A hell of a lot of companies would like to be on the list of the 100 best places to work." ■

Where Dallas/Fort Worth Works

This chapter contains the names, addresses, and phone numbers of the area's top 1,150 employers of white-collar workers. The companies are arranged in categories according to the major products and services they manufacture or provide. Where appropriate, entries contain a brief description of the company's business and the name of the personnel director or other contact.

This listing is intended to help you survey the major potential employers in fields that interest you. It is *selective*, not exhaustive. We have not, for example, listed *all* the advertising agencies in the area, as you can find that information in the Yellow Pages. We have simply listed the top twenty-five or so, that is, the ones with the most jobs.

The purpose of this chapter is to get you started, both looking and thinking. This is the kickoff, not the final buzzer.

Browse through the whole chapter, and take some time to check out areas that are unfamiliar to you. Many white-collar skills are transferable. People with marketing, management, data processing, accounting, administrative, secretarial, and other talents are needed in a huge variety of businesses.

Ask yourself in what area your skills could be marketed. Use your imagination, especially if you're in a so-called specialized field. A dietician, for instance, might look first under Health Care, or maybe Hotels. But what about Insurance companies, Museums, Banks, or the scores of other places that run their own dining rooms for employees or the public? What about food and consumer magazines? Who makes up all those recipes and tests those products?

The hints and insider interviews that are scattered throughout this chapter are designed to nudge your creativity and suggest additional ideas for your job search. Much more detailed information on the area's top employers, and other, smaller companies, can be found in the directories and other resources suggested in Chapter 4. We can't stress strongly enough that you have to do your homework when you're looking for a job, both to unearth places that might need a person with your particular talents, and to succeed in the interview once you've lined up a meeting with the hiring authority.

A word about hiring authorities: if you've read Chapter 5, you know that the name of the game is to meet the person with the power to hire you, or get as close to that person as you can. You don't want to go to the chairman or the personnel director if the person who actually makes the decision is the marketing manager or customer service director.

Obviously, we can't list every possible hiring authority in the area's "Top 1,150." If we tried, you'd need a wagon to haul this book around.

Besides, printed directories go out of date—even those that are regularly and conscientiously revised. So always double-check a contact whose name you get from a book or magazine, including this one. If necessary, call the company's switchboard to confirm who heads a particular department or division. Here, then, are Dallas/Fort Worth's greatest opportunities. Happy hunting!

The Dallas/ Fort Worth area's top 1,150 employers are arranged in the following categories:

Accounting/Auditing Firms
Advertising/Public Relations
Aircraft and Aerospace

Architectural Firms
Auto/Truck/Transportation Equipment
Banks/Savings and Loans/Credit Unions
Book Publishers and Distributors
Broadcasting and Cable Television
Chemicals
Computers: Data Processing
Computers: Hardware/Software
Contractors/Construction
Drugs/Biological Products
Educational Institutions
Electronics
Energy, Oil, and Gas Companies
Engineering Firms
Entertainment
Film, Video, Recording, and Talent Services
Food/Beverage Producers and Distributors
Furniture and Fixtures Manufacturers
Government
Health Care
Hotels/Motels
Human Services
Insurance
Investment Bankers/Stock Brokers
Law Firms
Management Consultants
Manufacturers
Media: Print
Metal Products
Museums and Art Galleries
Paper/Packaging/Allied Products
Printers
Real Estate
Recreation/Sports/Fitness
Restaurants
Retailers/Wholesalers
Telecommunications
Travel/Transportation/Shipping
Utilities

Accounting/Auditing Firms

You may also want to check the section on **Banks** and **Investment Bankers/Stock Brokers**

For networking in **accounting** and related fields, check out the following professional organizations listed in Chapter 5:

PROFESSIONAL ORGANIZATIONS:

Certified Public Accountants
Dallas Society of Accounting Librarians
National Association of Accountants
Professional Services Marketing Association

For additional information, you can contact:

American Institute of CPAs
1211 Ave. of the Americas
New York, NY 10036
(212) 575-6200

American Society of Women Accountants
35 E. Wacker Dr.
Chicago, IL 60601
(312) 726-9030

Institute of Management Accountants
10 Paragon Dr.
Montvale, NJ 07645
(201) 573-9000

National Association of Black Accountants
200 I St., NE, #150
Washington, DC 20002
(202) 546-6222

National Society of Public Accountants
1010 N. Fairfax St.
Alexandria, VA 22314
(703) 549-6400

PROFESSIONAL PUBLICATIONS:

Accounting News
CPA Journal
CPA Letter

Journal of Accountancy
National Public Accountant

DIRECTORIES:

Accounting Firms and Practioners (American Institute of Certified Public
   Accountants, New York, NY)
Emerson's Directory of Leading U.S. Accounting Firms (Emerson's, Seattle, WA)
National Directory of Accounting Firms & Accountants (Gale Research,
   Inc., Detroit, MI)
National Directory of Certified Public Accountants (Peter Norbach
   Publishing Co., Princeton, NJ)
Texas Society of Certified Public Accountants Directory (Texas Society of
   Certified Public Accountants, Dallas, TX)
Who Audits America (Data Financial Press, Menlo Park, CA)

EMPLOYERS:

Arthur Andersen & Co.
Dallas Office
901 Main St., Suite 5600
Dallas, TX 75202
(214) 741-8300
Division Head of Management and Services: Scot Wilson

Arthur Andersen & Co.
Fort Worth Office
801 Cherry St., Suite 1200
Fort Worth, TX 76102
(817) 870-3000
Contact: Same as Dallas office

BDO Seidman
2400 Plaza of the Americas
600 N. Pearl St.
Dallas, TX 75201
(214) 220-3131
Contact: Department Head

Bailey Vaught Robertson & Co.
1999 Bryan St., Suite 2500
Dallas, TX 75201
(214) 979-0390
Contact: Prefer mail inquiries only

Belew, Averitt & Co.
700 N. Pearl St.
Plaza of the Americas
Dallas, TX 75201

(214) 969-7007
Contact: Personnel

Bland Garvey & Taylor
1202 Richardson Dr., Suite 203
Richardson, TX 75080
(214) 231-2503
Contact: Mail resume to John Garvey

Candy & Schonwald
3116 Live Oak St.
Dallas, TX 75204
(214) 826-6660
Personnel: Stacy Hoover-Bell

Cheshier & Fuller
14175 Proton Rd.
Dallas, TX 75244
(214) 387-4300
Contact: Personnel

Martin W. Cohen & Co.
1600 W. Pacific Ave., Suite 1900
Dallas, TX 75201
(214) 953-3000
Contact: Personnel

Coopers & Lybrand
Dallas Office
1999 Bryan St., Suite 3000
Dallas, TX 75201
(214) 754-5000
Personnel Director: Don Barr

Coopers & Lybrand
Fort Worth Office
301 Commerce St., Suite 1900
Fort Worth, TX 76102
Metro (817) 429-2410
Administrator: Carolyn Drews

Deloitte, Haskins & Sells
1400 Lincoln Plaza, Lock Box 4
Dallas, TX 75201
(214) 263-6894
Recruiting Manager: Monica Susman

Deloitte and Touche
2001 Bryan Tower, Suite 2400
Dallas, TX 75201
(214) 220-8000
Recruitment Director: Lindsey Green

Ernst & Young
Dallas Office
2001 Ross Ave., Suite 2800
Dallas, TX 75201
(214) 979-1700
Consulting Positions: Bill Fleming
Audit and Tax Positions: Cynthia Fox

Ernst & Young
Fort Worth Office
500 Throckmorton St., Suite 2200
Fort Worth, TX 76102
Metro (817) 335-1900
Partner: Turner Almond

Hoffman, Pederson & McBryde
7950 Elmbrook Dr., Suite 200
Dallas, TX 75247
(214) 631-4758
Contact: Miriam McBryde

Lane, Gorman Trubitt & Co.
1909 Woodall Rogers Fwy., Suite 400
Dallas, TX 75201
(214) 871-7500
Administrator: Nancy Candill

Kenneth Leventhal & Co.
2200 Ross Ave., Suite 1100
Dallas, TX 75201
(214) 969-0900
Human Resources Director: Anne Wickstrom

Peat, Marwick, Main & Co.
Dallas Office
1601 Elm St., Suite 1400
Dallas, TX 75201
(214) 754-2000
Recruiter: Michelle Robertson

Peat, Marwick, Main & Co.
Fort Worth Office
301 Commerce St.
2500 City Center Tower II
Fort Worth, TX 76102
(817) 335-2655
Partner: John Anderson

Price Waterhouse
Dallas Office
1700 Pacific Ave., Suite 1400
Dallas, TX 75201

(214) 922-8040
Human Resources Director: Terry Kepler

Price Waterhouse
Fort Worth Office
1700 City Center Tower II
301 Commerce St.
Fort Worth, TX 76102
(817) 870-5500
Sr. Manager: Rick Wessel

Tannenbaum Bindler & Co.
2323 Bryan St., Suite 700
Lock Box 107
Dallas, TX 75201
(214) 969-6990
Personnel Manager: Margaret Bentley

Grant Thorton
1445 Ross Ave., Suite 800
Dallas, TX 75202
(214) 855-7300
Office Manager: B.L. Zavatsky

Travis, Wolf, and Co.
14001 Dallas Pkwy., Suite 500
Dallas, TX 75240
(214) 661-1843
Office Manager: Walter Deuluh

Philip Vogel & Co.
12221 Merit Dr., Suite 1200
Dallas, TX 75251
(214) 386-4200
Managing Partner: Buddy Raden

Weaver & Tidwell
1500 Commerce Building
307 W. 7th St.
Fort Worth, TX 76102
(817) 332-7905
Partner: Ronnie Coulson

Advertising/Public Relations

For networking in **advertising/public relations** and related
fields, check out the following professional organizations listed in
Chapter 5:

PROFESSIONAL ORGANIZATIONS:

Advertising Club of Fort Worth
American Marketing Association
Dallas Advertising League
Dallas Professional Photographers Association
Dallas Society of Illustrators
Dallas Society of Visual Communications
Direct Marketing Association of North Texas
International Association of Business Communicators
Press Club of Dallas
Public Relations Society of America
Society for Marketing Professional Services
Southwestern Association of Advertising Agencies
Texas Association of Film & Tape Professionals
Women in Communications

For additional information, you can contact:

The Advertising Council
261 Madison Ave.
New York, NY 10016
(212) 922-1500

American Advertising Federation
1400 K St., NW
Washington, DC 20005
(202) 898-0089

American Association of Advertising Agencies
666 Third Ave.
New York, NY 10017
(212) 682-2500

Direct Marketing Association
11 W. 42nd St.
New York, NY 10036
(212) 768-7277

Public Relations Society of Ameriaca
33 Irving Place, 3rd Floor
New York, NY 10003
(212) 995-2230

PROFESSIONAL PUBLICATIONS:

Advertising Age
Adweek/Southwest
Direct Marketing Magazine
Industrial Marketing
Journal of Advertising Research

Journal of Marketing Research
Madison Avenue
Marketing and Media Decisions
PR Quarterly
Public Relations News
Public Relations Review
Marketing Week

DIRECTORIES:

Adweek Agency Directory (Adweek New England, Boston, MA)
Bradford's Directory of Marketing Research Agencies (Bradford Directory
    of Marketing Research Agencies, Centerville, VA)
International Directory of Market Companies and Services Green Book
    (American Marketing Association, New York, NY)
Marketing Consultants Directory (American Business Directories,
    Omaha, NE)
*O'Dwyer's Directory of Corporate Comunications and O'Dwyer's Directory
    of Public Relations Firms* (J.R. O'Dwyer Company, New York, NY)
Public Relations Career Directory (Career Press, Hawthorne, NJ)
Public Relations Journal—Register Issue (Public Relations Society of
    America, New York, NY)
Standard Directory of Advertising Agencies (National Register Publishing
    Co., Wilmette, IL)
Who's Who in PR (P.R. Publishing Co., Exeter, NH)

EMPLOYERS:

Anderson Fischel Thompson
Prestonwood Tower
5151 Belt Line Rd., Suite 700
Dallas, TX 75240
(214) 233-8461
Chairman of the Board: Joe Anderson
Advertising and public relations.

Berry-Brown Advertising
2602 McKinney Ave., Suite 300
Dallas, TX 75204
(214) 871-1001
Personnel Manager: Virdie Horton
Advertising and public relations.

The Bloom Agency
3500 Maple Ave.
Dallas, TX 75219
(214) 443-9900
Director of Human Resources: Dianne Bynum
Advertising and public relations.

Bozell/Dallas
201 E. Carpenter Frwy.
Irving, TX 75012
(214) 556-1100
Contact: Personnel Department
Advertising and public relations.

Champney and Associates
1440 W. Mockingbird Lane, Suite 300
Dallas, TX 75247
(214) 631-2535
Personnel: Zafar Khan
Advertising and public relations.

Dally Advertising
1320 S. University Dr., Suite 501
Fort Worth, TX 76107
(817) 332-5299
President: Scott Dally
Advertising and public relations.

Evans/Dallas
4131 N. Central Expwy., Suite 510
Dallas, TX 75204
(214) 521-6400
President: George Arnold
Advertising and public relations.

Goodman & Associates
3633 W. 7th St.
Fort Worth, TX 76107
(817) 735-9333
President: Gerry Goodman
Advertising and public relations.

Hill & Knowlton
One Dallas Centre, Suite 1500
350 N. St. Paul
Dallas, TX 75201
(214) 979-0090
Sr. Vice President: Johns Sparks
Public relations.

Keller-Crescent/Southwest
102 Decker Court, Las Colinas, Suite 100
Irving, TX 75062
(214) 541-0700
Administrative Assistant: Sue Harper
Advertising and public relations.

Knape & Knape
3131 McKinney Ave., Suite 800

Dallas, TX 75204
(214) 871-2461
Vice President and Director of PR: Steven Silvers
Advertising and public relations.

Krause & Young
501 Elm St., Suite 300
Lock Box 6
Dallas, TX 75202
(214) 741-7500
President: Jim Krause
Advertising.

Larkin, Meeder & Schweidel
7800 Stemmons Frwy., Suite 770
Dallas, TX 75247
(214) 688-7070
Office Manager: Mary Graves
Advertising.

Levinson and Hill
5215 N. O'Connor Blvd., Suite 1100
Irving, TX 75039
(214) 556-0944
Human Resources: Cyndi Morrison
Advertising and public relations.

Magnussen Advertising Agency
906 Mallick Tower
Fort Worth, TX 76102
(817) 332-1145
President: Neil Ross
Advertising.

Main Station Unlimited
901 S. Main St.
Fort Worth, TX 76104
(817) 332-1040
President: Bob Walter
Advertising and public relations.

McCann-Erickson/Dallas
10830 N. Central Expwy., Suite 246
Dallas, TX 75231
(214) 361-1135
General Manager: Santiago Hinojosa
Advertising and public relations.

McKone & Co.
1900 Westridge Dr.
Irving, TX 75038
(214) 550-7433

President: Pete McKone
Advertising and public relations.

Moroch & Associates
3625 N. Hall St., Suite 1200
Dallas, TX 75219
(214) 520-9700
Office Manager: Kathy Bell
Advertising and public relations.

Laurey Peat & Associates
2001 Ross Ave., Suite 3020
Dallas, TX 75201
(214) 871-8787
Office Manager: Debbie Meyer
Public relations.

Point Communications
14001 Dallas Pkwy., Suite 450
Dallas, TX 75240
(214) 851-1100
President: Willard Moon
Advertising and public relations.

PR/Texas
612 Grove St.
Fort Worth, TX 76102
Metro (817) 429-4682
President: Jane Schlansker
Advertising and public relations.

Puskar Gibbon Chapin
3500 Maple Ave., Suite 900
Dallas, TX 75219
(214) 528-5400
Principal: Jim Gibbon
Advertising and public relations.

Regian Associates
219 S. Main St.
Fort Worth, TX 76104
(817) 870-1128 (Toll free)
Public Relations: Julie Wilson
Advertising and public relations.

The Richards Group
10000 N. Central Expwy., Suite 1200
Dallas, TX 75231
(214) 891-5700
Office Manager: Teri Jones
Advertising.

Saunders, Lubinski & White
7610 Stemmons Frwy., Suite 100
Dallas, TX 75247
(214) 630-6160
Office Manager: Tracy Griffin
Advertising and public relations.

Team & Associates Advertising
209 S. Jennings Ave.
Fort Worth, TX 76104
(817) 332-1560
Contact: Personnel Department
Advertising and public relations.

Tracy-Locke/Dallas
200 Crescent Court
Dallas, TX 75201
(214) 969-9000
Contact: Personnel Department
Advertising and public relations.

Western International Media
2929 Carlisle St., Suite 260
Dallas, TX 75204
(214) 871-1050
Media Supervisor: Lisa Wettig
Media-buying service.

Witherspoon & Associates
1000 W. Weatherford St.
Fort Worth, TX 76102
(817) 335-1373 (Toll free)
Sr. Vice President: Mike Wilie
Advertising and public relations.

Breaking into public relations

During her senior year in college, an enterprising friend of ours began querying companies about job openings in public relations. All responded with a polite form letter, stating she must have prior experience.

Not one to be easily discouraged, she moved to Dallas after graduation, even though she didn't know anyone except her college roommate. She began writing to public relations executives and asking for five minutes of advice on how to get started in the business. She telephoned them to set up appointments and followed up the visits with thank-you notes.

One of the men she contacted was on the Cystic Fibrosis Foundation Board of Directors. When he told her the charity might consider setting up a PR department, she contacted the director and ended up running the new department.

"I'm so glad I went to work for a non-profit organization because it was the best experience I could have gotten," she says. "No one was there to spoon feed me. I built the department from scratch."

In addition to regular PR functions, she assisted with fund-raising and made arrangements for the annual dinner. She did such a superb job of setting up the event that one of the guests, a PR agency owner, offered her a job as an account executive. By that time, she had two years of experience and was ready to make a move.■

Aircraft and Aerospace

You may also want to check out the sections on **Computers** and **Electronics.**

PROFESSIONAL ORGANIZATIONS:

For information, you can write to:

Aerospace Education Foundation
1501 Lee Highway
Arlington, VA 22209

Aerospace Electrical Society
Box 24883 Village Station
Los Angeles, CA 90024

Aerospace Industries Association of America
1725 De Sales St., NW
Washington, DC 20036

American Institute of Aeronautics and Astronautics
5001 Airport Plaza Dr.
Long Beach, CA 90815

Int'l. Association of Machinists & Aerospace Workers
8411 S. Pioneer
Whittier, CA 90601

National Space Institute
600 Maryland Ave., SW
Washington, DC 20034

PROFESSIONAL PUBLICATIONS:

Aviation Week & Space Technology
Business & Commercial Aviation

DIRECTORIES:

Corporate Technology Directory (Corporate Technology Information
    Services, Woburn, MA)
World Aviation Directory & Buyers Guide (McGraw-Hill Publishing Co.,
    New York, NY)

EMPLOYERS:

Aerospace Optics
3201 Sandy Lane
Fort Worth, TX 76112
(817) 451-1141
Contact: Personnel Department
Manufactures aircraft switches.

Aerospace Technologies
7445 E. Lancaster Ave.
Fort Worth, TX 76112
(817) 429-7412
Contact: Personnel Department
Manufactures aircraft components.

Aerospatiale Helicopter Corp.
2701 Forum Dr.
Grand Prairie, TX 75051
Metro (214) 641-0000
Contact: Personnel Office
Reassembles and modifies helicopters for commercial and
government use.

Associated Air Center
8321 Lemmon Ave.

Dallas, TX 75209
(214) 350-4111
Human Resources Coordinator: Barbra Henderson
Maintains and customizes aircraft.

Aviall of Texas
P.O. Box 7199
Dallas, TX 75209
(214) 956-5400
Contact: Personnel Department
Services and repairs turbine engines, installs avionic systems, refurbishes general aviation airframes, and operates terminal hangar and refueling complex at Dallas Love Field. Also distributes engine and aircraft-related parts and supplies.

BEI Defense Systems Co.
11312 S. Pipeline Rd.
Euless, TX 76060
(817) 267-8191
Personnel Manager: Pat McDaniel
Manufactures rocket systems, rocket fuses, warheads, and rocket motors.

Bell Helicopter/Textron
600 E. Hurst Blvd.
Hurst, TX 76053
(817) 280-2011
Contact: Personnel Department
Government contractor involved in research and manufacturing of helicopters.

Dyncorp
6801 Calmont Ave.
Fort Worth, TX 76116
(Contact company by mail only)
Employment Manager: Daphne Geary
Government service contractor for aircraft maintenance and modification.

EDM of Texas
14042 Distribution Way
Farmers Branch, TX 75234
(214) 241-2501
Controller: Bill Wade
Repairs aircraft parts.

GEC Avionics
6410 Southwest Blvd., Suite 128
Fort Worth, TX 76109
(817) 763-0281
Contact: Atlanta office at (404) 448-1947
Develops and produces electronic devices used in aircraft.

General Aviation Industries
7150 Midway Rd.
Fort Worth, TX 76118
(817) 284-4848
Personnel Director: Bonnie Nix
Government defense contractor for airplane parts.

General Dynamics Corp.
Grants Lane
Fort Worth, TX 76106
(817) 777-2000
Contact: Employment Office
Major employer and government contractor that manufactures aircraft, radar systems, and related equipment in the Fort Worth division.

Glover Machine Co.
210 S. Morocco St.
Dallas, TX 75211
(214) 331-8373
Personnel Director: Ygnacio Lopez
Manufactures aircraft parts.

HAC Corp.
537 Camden Dr.
Grand Prairie, TX 75051
(214) 263-4387
Personnel: Teena Wright
Manufactures aircraft parts and does composite bondings.

K-C Aviation
7350 Cedar Springs Rd.
Dallas, TX 75235
(214) 902-7535
Human Resources Recruiter: Jacque Leopard
Aircraft maintenance and modification.

LTV Aerospace and Defense Co.
P.O. Box 650003
Dallas, TX 75265-0003
(214) 266-7789
Attn: Employment Division
Government contractor, producing aircraft, missiles, launch vehicles, and space vehicle components.

Menasco Aerosystems Division
4000 Hwy. 157
Euless, TX 76039
(817) 283-4471

Personnel Supervisor: Kathy Johnson
Multi-industry firm, producing marine weapons, handling systems, aircraft landing gear, helicopter rotor assemblies, and heat-treated metals.

Murdock Engineering Co. of Texas
5100 W. Airport Frwy.
Irving, TX 75062
(214) 790-1122
Contact: Personnel Administration Manager
Manufactures aircraft parts and equipment, flexible pipe fittings for marine and oil industries, and bonded metal parts.

Progressive
1030 N. Commercial Blvd.
Arlington, TX 76017
Metro (817) 467-0031
Aircraft machine shop.

Putoma Corp.
5101 E. California Pkwy.
Fort Worth, TX 76119
Metro (817) 429-5416
Office Manager: Wanda Nicholson
Manufactures aircraft parts.

Stratoflex
220 Roberts Cutoff Rd.
Fort Worth, TX 76114
(817) 738-6543
Employee Relations: Terry Benton
Manufactures hose fittings for aircraft and automobiles.

Texstar
802 Ave. J East
Grand Prairie, TX 75050
(214) 647-1366
Contact: Personnel Department
Manufactures canopies for different aircraft.

Apparel and Textiles

You may also want to check the **Retailers/Wholesalers** section.

For networking in the **apparel and textile industries** and related fields, check out the following professional organizations listed in Chapter 5:

PROFESSIONAL ORGANIZATIONS:

American Fashion Association
American Society of Interior Designers
Fashion Group Inc. of Dallas

For additional information, you can write to:

Educational Foundation for the Fashion Industries
227 W. 27th St.
New York, NY 10001

Federation of Apparel Manufacturers
450 7th Ave.
New York, NY 10001

National Association of Textile and Apparel Distributors
401 7th Ave.
New York, NY 10001

Textile Research Institute
Box 625
Princeton, NJ 08540

PROFESSIONAL PUBLICATIONS:

Apparel Industry Magazine
Textile Products
Textile Research Journal
Textile World
Women's Wear Daily

DIRECTORIES:

American Apparel Contractors' Association Directory (American Apparel
     Contractors' Association, Atlanta, GA)
Davison's Textile Blue Book (Davison Publishing Co., Ridgewood, NJ)
Modeling Agencies Directory (American Business Directories, Omaha, NE)

EMPLOYERS:

Byn-Mar
2952 Ladybird Lane
Dallas, TX 75220
(214) 350-7011
Head Designer: Vicki Inabett
Operations Manager: Sandra Robinson
Manufactures women's clothing.

Cheerleader Supply Co.
9150 Markville Dr.
Dallas, TX 75241
(214) 231-6364
Payroll/Personnel Director: Katrina Russell
Manufactures cheerleader's apparel.

Victor Costa
7600 Ambassador Row
Dallas, TX 75247
(214) 634-1133
Contact: Personnel
Manufactures women's clothing.

Designers Collection
901 Regal Row
Dallas, TX 75247
(214) 634-8040
Contact: Personnel
Manufactures table linens.

The Haggar Co.
6113 Lemmon Ave.
Dallas, TX 75209
(214) 352-8481
Contact: Human Resources
Manufactures men's and women's clothing.

Jerell
1431 Regal Row
Dallas, TX 75247
(214) 637-5300
Contact: Personnel Office
Manufactures women's and juniors' clothing.

Jones of Dallas Manufacturing
8505 Chancellor Row
Dallas, TX 75247
(214) 638-0321
Contact: Personnel
Manufactures women's clothing.

Justin Boot Co.
300 S. Jennings Ave.
Fort Worth, TX 76104
(817) 332-4385
Personnel Manager: Bill Ledbetter
Manufactures cowboy boots.

Niver Western Wear
1221 Hemphill St.
Fort Worth, TX 76104

(817) 336-2389
Office Manager: Dorris Scanlan
Manufactures Western clothing.

Prophecy Corp.
1302 Champion Circle
Carrollton, TX 75006
(214) 247-1900
Contact: Human Resources
Manufactures women's sportswear.

RLM Fashion Industries
2220 Canton St.
Dallas, TX 75201
(214) 747-4812
Contact: Personnel
Manufactures women's apparel.

Resistol Hats
601 Marion Dr.
Garland, TX 75042
(214) 494-0511
Contact: Personnel Department
Manufactures cowboy hats and other headwear.

Sidran Sportswear
2875 Merrell Rd.
Dallas, TX 75229
(214) 352-7979
Contact: Personnel Manager
Manufactures men's Western clothing.

Sunny South Fashions
7777 Hines Place
Dallas, TX 75235
(214) 637-4333
Personnel Director: Paula Hultsman
Manufactures women's sportswear.

Williamson-Dickie Manufacturing Co.
509 W. Vickery St.
Fort Worth, TX 76104
(817) 336-7201
Employee Relations Supervisor: Estelle Lewis
Manufactures women's and men's work clothing.

Howard B. Wolf
3809 Parry Ave.
Dallas, TX 75226
(214) 823-9941
Sr. Vice President: Eugene Friesen
Manufactures women's clothing.

Architectural Firms

You may also want to check the sections on **Contractors/ Construction, Engineering,** and **Real Estate.**

For networking in **architecture** and related fields, check out the following professional organizations listed in Chapter 5:

PROFESSIONAL ORGANIZATIONS:

American Institute of Architects
American Society of Landscape Architects
Institute of Business Designers

For additional information, you can contact:

American Institute of Architects
1735 New York Ave., NW
Washington, DC 20006
(202) 626-7300

National Council of Architectural Registration Boards (NCARB)
1735 New York Ave., NW
Washington, DC 20006
(202) 783-6500

Society of American Registered Architects
1245 S. Highland Ave.
Lombard, IL 60148
(708) 932-4622

PROFESSIONAL PUBLICATIONS:

AIA Journal
Architectural Forum
Architectural Record
Practicing Architect
Progressive Architecture

DIRECTORIES:

AIA Membership Directory (American Institute of Architects, New York, NY)
Directory of Contract Service Firms (C.E. Publications, Kirkland, WA)
Profile: Firm & Membership Directory (American Institute of Architects, Washington, DC)

EMPLOYERS:

Benson, Hlavaty & Associates
1717 Main St., Suite 3550
Dallas, TX 75201
(214) 698-2700
President: Martti Benson

Beran & Shelmire
Two Turtle Creek Village, Suite 1313
Dallas, TX 75219
(214) 522-7980
President: Overton Shelmire

Dahl Braden PTM
3500 Maple Ave., Suite 1100
Dallas, TX 75219
(214) 520-0077
Associate: Jerry Sutton

Corgan Associates Architects
501 Elm St., Suite 500
Dallas, TX 75202
(214) 748-2000
Contact: Department Head

F&S Partners
3535 Travis St., Suite 201
Dallas, TX 75204
(214) 559-4851
Vice President: Bill Grady

Good Fulton Farrell
3102 Oak Lawn Ave.
Dallas, TX 75219
(214) 528-5599
Principal: Duncan Fulton

Haldeman, Powell, Johns
15303 Dallas Pkwy., Suite 300
Dallas, TX 75248
(214) 701-9000
Contact: Department Head

Hardy McCullah/MLM Architects
12221 Merit Dr., Suite 280
Dallas, TX 75251
(214) 385-1900
Office Manager: Earlene Romano

Harper Kemp Clutts and Parker
4131 N. Central Expwy., Suite 400

Dallas, TX 75204
(214) 528-8644
Treasurer: Howard Parker

Hatfield Halcomb Architects
18333 Preston Rd., Suite 300
Dallas, TX 75252
(214) 931-9151
Director of Operations: Jim Stuart

Hellmuth/Obata & Kassabaum
6688 N. Central Expwy., Suite 700
Dallas, TX 75206
(214) 739-6688
Sr. Vice President: Dan Jeakins

Henningson, Durham & Richardson
12700 Hillcrest Rd., Suite 125
Dallas, TX 75230
(214) 960-4000
Contact: Executive Vice President

Hodges & Associates
13642 Omega Rd.
Dallas, TX 75244
(214) 387-1000
Contact: Department Head

JPJ Architects
5910 N. Central Expwy., Suite 120
Dallas, TX 75206
(214) 987-8000
Office Manager: George Hicks

Albert S. Komatsu & Associates
550 Baily Ave., Suite 102
Fort Worth, TX 76107
(817) 429-7463
President: Karl Komatsu

Frank Meier Architects
3500 Oak Lawn Ave.
Dallas, TX 75219
(214) 528-0020
President: Jim Phillips

Page Southerland Page
3500 Maple St., Suite 700
Dallas, TX 75219
(214) 522-3900
Partner: Cliff Lloyd

Parker/Croston Partnership
3311 Hamilton Ave.
Fort Worth, TX 76107
(817) 332-8464
Contact: Charles Kelley

RTKL Associates
2828 Routh St., Suite 200
Dallas, TX 75201
(214) 871-8877
AIA Principal: Joe Scalabrin

Rees Associates
511 E. John Carpenter Frwy., Suite 222
Irving, TX 75062
(214) 630-7337
Vice President: Ralph Blackman

SHWC, Inc.
P.O. Box 619087
Dallas, TX 75261
(214) 550-0700
Partner: Jeryl Jordan
Inquire by mail.

Harwood K. Smith & Partners
1111 Plaza of the Americas North
Dallas, TX 75201
(214) 969-5599
Executive Vice President: Wade Driver

Taylor, Gahl, Spensland Architects
5001 Spring Valley Rd., Suite 800E
Dallas, TX 75224
(214) 620-9262
Partner: Dallas Taylor

Phillip W. Wheeler Architects
8235 Douglas Ave., Suite 900
Dallas, TX 75205
(214) 691-2900
Contact: Chase Corher

Womack Architects
3000 McKinney Ave.
Dallas, TX 75204
(214) 754-8700
Personnel Director: Rick Garza

WRA Architects
7557 Rambler Rd., Suite 400
Dallas, TX 75231

(214) 750-0077
President: Raymond Arhelger

Yandell and Heller
512 Main St., Suite 1500
Fort Worth, TX 76102
(817) 335-3000
President: Roger Yandell
Architecture and engineering design services.

Auto/Truck/Transportation Equipment

You may also want to look at the section on **Travel and Transportation.**

PROFESSIONAL ORGANIZATIONS:

For more information, you can write to:

Automotive Service Industry Association
444 N. Michigan Ave.
Chicago, IL 60611

Society of Automotive Engineers
400 Commonwealth Dr.
Warrendale, PA 15096

PROFESSIONAL PUBLICATIONS:

Auto Age
Autocar & Motor
Automotive Industries
Automotive News
Chilton's Motor Age
Drag Racing News
Four-Wheeler Magazine
Jobber Topics
Motor Trend
Truck & Off-Highway Industries
Trux

DIRECTORIES:

ASIA Membership Directory (Automotive Service Industries Association, Chicago, IL)
Automotive Age, Buyers Guide Issue (M.H. West Publishing Co., Van Nuys, CA)

Automotive News, Market Data Book Issue (Crain Communications, Detroit, MI)
Jobber Topics, Annual Marketing Directory Issue (Irving-Cloud Publishing Co., Chicago,IL)

EMPLOYERS:

Big 4 Automotive
400 South Freeway
Fort Worth, TX 76104
(817) 332-3171
General Manager: Wayne Mitchell
Warehouse distributor for automotive parts.

Cummins Southern Plains
600 N. Watson Rd.
Arlington, TX 76011
Metro (817) 640-6801
Personnel Director: Don Watson
Distributes and services diesel engines.

Darr Equipment Co.
549 Jim Wright Frwy.
Fort Worth, TX 76108
Metro (817) 429-9226
Contact: Dallas Personnel Office at (214) 445-0060
Caterpillar dealership and parts distributor.

FM Industries
8600 Will Rogers Blvd.
Fort Worth, TX 76140
(817) 293-4220
Personnel Manager: Jack Adams
Manufactures hydraulic cushioning devices for railroad freight cars.

Fruehauf Corp.
4600 Blue Mound Rd.
Fort Worth, TX 76106
(817) 625-2181
Contact: Personnel Department
Manufactures semi-trailers.

General Motors Corp.
2525 E. Abram St.
Arlington, TX 76010
(817) 625-2085
Contact: Personnel Department
Major manufacturer of Oldsmobiles and Chevrolets.

Interstate Battery System of America
12770 Mevit Dr.
Dallas, TX 75251

(214) 991-1444
Recruiter: Janie Brilain
Battery distributor.

Long Mile Rubber Co.
6820 Forrest Park Rd.
Dallas, TX 75235
(214) 350-7851
Contact: Personnel Department
Manufactures tire retreads.

Mass Merchandisers
909 W. North Carrier Pkwy.
Grand Prairie, TX 75050
(214) 647-7891
Contact: Department Head
Wholesaler of automotive supplies, housewares, and other non-food items.

SCS Frigette Corp.
1200 W. Risinger Rd.
Fort Worth, TX 76134
(817) 293-5313
Personnel Manager: Jane Turner
Manufactures automotive air conditioners and parts.

TIC United Corp.
4645 N. Central Expwy.
Dallas, TX 75205
(214) 559-0580
Vice President of Personnel: Harrold Hatley
Manufactures farm machinery; steel forgings.

Texas Kenworth Co.
4040 Irving Blvd.
Dallas, TX 75247
(214) 920-7300
Contact: Executive Offices
Heavy-duty truck sales and service.

Banks/Savings and Loans/Credit Unions

You may also want to check out the sections on **Accounting** and **Investment Bankers/Stock Brokers.**

For networking in the **banking industry** and related fields, check out the following professional organizations listed in Chapter 5:

PROFESSIONAL ORGANIZATIONS:

Dallas Bankers Association
Dallas Business League
National Association of Bank Women

For additional information, you can contact:

American Bankers Association
1120 Connecticut Ave., NW
Washington, DC 20036
(202) 663-5000

Bank Marketing Association
309 W. Washington Blvd.
Chicago, IL 60646
(312) 782-1442

Mortgage Bankers Association of America
1125 15th St., NW
Washington, DC 20005
(202) 861-6500

National Association of Bank Women
500 N. Michigan Ave.
Chicago, IL 60611
(312) 661-1700

National Bankers Association (minority bankers)
122 C St., NW
Washington, DC 20001
(202) 783-3200

United States League of Savings Institutions
1709 New York Ave., NW
Washington, DC 20006
(202) 637-8900

PROFESSIONAL PUBLICATIONS:

ABA Banking Journal
American Banker
Bank Administration
Bank Marketing Magazine
Banker & Tradesman
Bankers Magazine
Bankers Monthly
Mortgage Banking
Savings Institutions

DIRECTORIES:

American Bank Directory (McFadden Business Publications, Norcross, GA)
American Banker's Guide to the First 5,000 U.S. Banks (American Banker, New York, NY)
Money Market Directory (Money Market Directories, Charlottsville, VA)
Moody's Bank & Finance Manual (Moody's Investor Service, New York, NY)
Polk's Bank Directory (R.L. Polk, Nashville, TN)
Rand McNally Bankers Directory (Thompson Financial Information, Skokie, IL)
Texas Savings & Loan Directory (Texas State Directory Press, Austin, TX)
The U.S. Savings Institutions (Thompson Financial Information, Skokie, IL)

EMPLOYERS:

American Airlines Employees Federal Credit Union
4255 Amon Carter Blvd.
Fort Worth, TX 76155
Metro (817) 963-6000
Contact: Personnel Department

Bank One Texas
1717 Main St.
Dallas, TX 75265
(214) 290-2000
Contact: Human Resources Department

Colonial Savings
2626 W. Frwy.
Fort Worth, TX 76102
(817) 390-2000
Personnel Director: Martho Erngy

Community Credit Union
5400 Independence Pkwy.
Plano, TX 75023
(214) 596-3300
Human Resources Director: Liz German

Cullen/Frost Bank of Dallas
2001 Bryan St.
Dallas, TX 75201
(214) 979-2000
Senior Vice President and Cashier: William R. Mathis, Jr.

Dallas Teachers Credit Union
4600 Ross Ave.
Dallas, TX 75204
(214) 824-6371
Personnel Director: Les McKee

Educational Employees Credit Union
1617 W. 7th St.
Fort Worth, TX 76102
(817) 336-5508
Contact: Human Resources

Federal Reserve Bank of Dallas
400 S. Akard St.
Dallas, TX 75202
(214) 651-6111
Contact: Human Resources Department

First City, Texas/Dallas
1700 Pacific Ave.
Dallas, TX 75201
(214) 939-8384
Contact: Human Resources Department

First City National Bank/Arlington
201 E. Abram St.
Arlington, TX 76010
Metro (817) 588-0100
Contact: Dallas Human Resources Department at (214) 939-8000

Guaranty Federal Savings and Loan Assoc.
8333 Douglas Ave., Human Resources, 3rd Floor
Dallas, TX 75225
(214) 360-3360
Employment Coordinator: Janie Chrisenberry

LTV Federal Credit Union
425 W. Jefferson Blvd.
Grand Prairie, TX 75051
(214) 263-5171
Vice President of Personnel: Mike Hedlund

NCNB Texas
Main Bank
P.O. Box 831000
Dallas, TX 75283
(214) 922-5000
Personnel Director: John Lamb

NorthPark National Bank
1300 NorthPark Center
Dallas, TX 75225
(214) 890-5100
Sr. Vice President of Human Resources: Culver Wilson

TEAM Bank/Dallas
6300 Harry Hines Blvd.
Dallas, TX 75235

(214) 559-8254
Human Resources Department

TEAM Bank/Fort Worth
403 W. 4th St.
Fort Worth, TX 76113
(817) 884-4000
Contact: Laura Fisher for professional positions and Carol LeBlanc for support positions

Texas Commerce Bank, NA
500 E. Border St.
Arlington, TX 76004
Metro (817) 469-3100
Personnel: Suzzanne Kittrell

Texas Commerce Bank, NA
2200 Ross Ave., 7th Floor
Dallas, TX 75201
(214) 922-2300
Human Resources: Dee Cochran

Texas Independent Bank
5221 N. O'Connor Rd., Suite 1300
Irving, TX 75356
(214) 869-4600
Personnel: Tiffani Burke

Book Publishers and Distributors

You might also want to check out the section on **Media.**

For networking in **book publishing** and related fields, check out the following professional organizations listed in Chapter 5:

PROFESSIONAL ORGANIZATIONS:

Society of Children's Book Writers
Southwestern Booksellers Association
Women in Communications

For additional information, you can contact:

American Booksellers Association
122 E. 42nd St.
New York, NY 10017
(212) 463-8450

Association of American Publishers
1718 Connecticut Ave., NW
Washington, DC 20009
(202) 232-3335

Southwestern Booksellers Association
3404 S. Ravinia Dr.
Dallas, TX 75233

PROFESSIONAL PUBLICATIONS:

American Bookseller
Editor & Publisher
Library Journal
Publishers Weekly
Small Press

DIRECTORIES:

American Book Trade Directory (R.R. Bowker, New York, NY)
Editor & Publisher International Yearbook (Editor & Publisher, New York, NY)
Literary Market Place (R.R. Bowker, New York, NY)
Publishers Directory (Gale Research, Detroit, MI)

EMPLOYERS:

Harcourt Brace Jovanovich
8551 Esters Blvd.
Irving, TX 75063
(214) 929-4666
Contact: M.G. Halsey
Regional sales office of educational publishing company.

Houghton Mifflin Co.
13400 Midway Rd.
Dallas, TX 75244
(214) 980-1100
Contact: Personnel
Regional sales and warehouse division of educational publishing company.

MAPSCO
5308 Maple Ave.
Dallas, TX 75235
(214) 521-2131
Contact: Department Head
Publishes street maps and reference guides.

Prentice Hall School Division
641 W. Mockingbird Lane
Dallas, TX 75247
(214) 631-0955
Regional Sales Manager: Reece Washington
Textbook sales and marketing division.

Sweet Publishing
3950 Fossil Creek Blvd., Suite 201
Fort Worth, TX 76137
(817) 232-5661
Personnel Director: Kippi Bridger
Publishes Bible school curriculum

Taylor Publishing Co.
1550 W. Mockingbird Lane
Dallas, TX 75235
(214) 637-2800
Contact: Personnel Department
Publishes yearbooks and general interest books.

Broadcasting and Cable Television

You may also want to look at the section on **Film and Video.**

For networking in **TV, radio, cable TV,** and related fields, check out the following professional organizations listed in Chapter 5:

PROFESSIONAL ORGANIZATIONS:

Dallas Communications Council
Dallas/Fort Worth Association of Black Communicators
Network of Hispanic Communicators
Press Club of Dallas
Society of Professional Journalists
Texas Association of Film and Tape Professionals
Women in Communications

For additional information, you can contact:

American Federation of Television & Radio Artists
260 Madison Ave.
New York, NY 10016
(212) 532-0800

Association of Independent TV Stations
1200 18th St., NW
Washington, DC 20036
(202) 887-1970

International Radio & Television Society
420 Lexington Ave.
New York, NY 10170
(212) 867-6650

National Academy of Television Arts and Sciences
111 W. 57th St.
New York, NY 10019
(212) 586-8424

National Association of Broadcasters
1771 N St., NW
Washington, DC 20036
(202) 429-5300

National Cable Television Association
1724 Massachusetts Ave., NW
Washington, DC 20036
(202) 775-3550

Radio-Television News Directors Association
1717 K St., NW
Washington, DC 20006
(202) 659-6510

PROFESSIONAL PUBLICATIONS:

Billboard
Broadcasting Press Digest
Cable Marketing
Cable World
Cablevision Magazine
Communications News
Radio Only
Radio World
Television Broadcast
Variety

DIRECTORIES:

Broadcasting Cable Sourcebook (Broadcasting Publishing Co.,
    Washington, DC)
Broadcasting Yearbook (Broadcasting Publishing Company, Washington, DC)
Television and Cable Fact Book (Warren Publications, Washington, DC)
TV/Radio Age Ten-City Directory (TV Editorial Corporation, New York, NY)

EMPLOYERS:

KAAM-AM
15851 Dallas Pkwy., Suite 1200

Dallas, TX 75248
(214) 263-0008
Personnel Director: Mary Young
Big Band and great singer music.

KCBI-FM
411 Ryan Plaza Dr.
Arlington, TX 76011
Metro (817) 792-3800
Director of Operations: Johanna Fisher
24-hour religious radio music.

KDAF-TV
8001 John Carpenter Frwy.
Dallas, TX 75247
(214) 634-8833
Contact: Personnel Department
Channel 33 independent TV station.

KDFI-TV
433 Regal Row
Dallas, TX 75247
(214) 637-2727
Contact: Department Head
Channel 27 independent TV station.

KDFW-TV
400 N. Griffin St.
Dallas, TX 76102
(214) 720-4444
Contact: Personnel Department
Channel 4 CBS-TV affiliate.

KEGL-FM
222 W. Las Colinas Blvd., Suite 1400
Irving, TX 75039
(214) 869-9700
Contact: Department Head
Contemporary hits.

KERA-FM
3000 Harry Hines Blvd.
Dallas, TX 75201
Metro (214) 871-1390
PBS-affiliated public affairs programs and jazz/classical radio music.

KERA-TV
3000 Harry Hines Blvd.
Dallas, TX 75201
Metro (214) 871-1390
Channel 13 PBS-TV station.

**Public
broadcasting
job hotline**

You can phone KERA for a recorded listing of job openings. Just dial (214) 871-1390, ext. 598. Or send your resume to the attention of the Personnel Dept. at the KERA stations' address. You can also come by to fill out an application from 8:00am to 5:00pm, Monday to Friday.

Karen Denard, host of KERA's "Karen Denard's Evening Talk Show" advises broadcasting hopefuls: "I recommend that you volunteer and join professional groups. When you do a little bit for others and include yourself in organizational work, serendipitous things do happen. You hear of opportunities and receive information you might not have gotten otherwise."■

KESS-FM
7700 John Carpenter Frwy.
Dallas, TX 75247
Metro (214) 263-0700
Office Manager: Carmen Aguilera
24-hour Spanish radio music.

KFJZ-AM
2214 E. 4th St.
Fort Worth, TX 76111
Metro (817) 429-1630
General Manager: Joe Vasquez
Spanish music from sunrise to sunset.

KHSX-TV
1957 E. Irving Blvd.
Irving, TX 75060
(214) 721-0104
General Manager: Bradley Foltyn
Channel 49 Christian independent TV station.

KHYI-FM
545 E. John Carpenter Frwy., Suite 1560
Irving, TX 75062
Metro (214) 263-3695
Business Manager: Kelli Fox
Contemporary-hit radio music.

KJMZ-AM/FM
9900 McCree Rd.
Dallas, TX 75238

Metro (214) 263-0400
Contact: Department Head
Urban contemporary radio music.

KKDA-FM
621 N.W. 6th St.
Grand Prairie, TX 75053
Metro (214) 263-9911
Office Manager: Evelyn Broughton
24-hour urban contemporary radio music.

KLIF-AM
3500 Maple Ave., Suite 1600
Dallas, TX 75219
(214) 526-2400
Program Director: Floyd Andrews
24-hour all-talk radio.

KLUV-FM
4131 N. Central Expwy.
Dallas, TX 75204
Metro (214) 263-3187
Contact: Personnel Department
24-hour solid gold radio music.

KMEZ-FM
1229 Corporate Dr. West
Arlington, TX 76006
Metro (817) 691-1075
Contact: Department Head
Easy-listening music.

KMGC-FM
1353 Regal Row
Dallas, TX 75247
Metro (214) 263-2960
Office Manager: Glen Wagner
Light rock/light jazz radio music.

KOAI-FM
8235 Douglas Ave., Suite 300
Dallas, TX 75225
(214) 891-3400
New age, light jazz radio music.

KPBC-AM
3201 Royalty Row
Irving, TX 75062
Metro (214) 445-1700
Station Manager: Doug Burnes
Program Director: Bill Dennis
24-hour adult Christian contemporary radio music.

KPLX-FM
3500 Maple Ave., Suite 1600
Dallas, TX 75219
Metro (214) 526-2400
Program Director: Bobby Craig
Contemporary country radio music.

KRLD-AM
1080 Metromedia Place
Dallas, TX 75247
Metro (214) 647-5753
News Director: Rick Erickson
Sales Manager: Dan Gorski
All-news radio station, CBS affiliate.

KSCS-FM
1 Broadcast Hill
Fort Worth, TX 76103
Metro (817) 429-2330
General Manager: Victor Sansone
Contemporary country radio music.

KSKY-AM
4144 N. Central Expwy.
Dallas, TX 75204
(214) 827-5759
General Manager: Bill Simmons
24-hour religious radio music.

KSSA-AM
3500 Maple Ave.
Dallas, TX 75219
Metro (214) 528-1600
General Manager: Mike Bradly
Spanish contemporary radio music.

KTVT-TV
5233 Bridge St.
Fort Worth, TX 76103
Metro (817) 654-1100
Contact: Department Head
Channel 11 independent TV station.

KTXA-TV
1712 E. Randol Mill Rd.
Arlington, TX 76011
Metro (817) 265-2100
Contact: Personnel Department
Channel 21 independent TV station.

KTXQ-FM
4131 N. Central Expwy., Suite 700

Dallas, TX 75204
Metro (214) 263-0804
Contact: Department Head
Album rock radio music.

KVIL-FM
5307 E. Mockingbird Lane, Suite 500
Dallas, TX 75206
Metro (214) 263-6539
Contact: Department Head
Adult contemporary radio music.

KVTT-FM
11061 Shady Trail
Dallas, TX 75229
Metro (214) 263-8713
Station Manager: Brandon Donnell (office help);
Operations Manager: Devin Wickham
Religious non-commercial radio music.

KXAS-TV
3900 Barnett St.
Fort Worth, TX 76103
Metro (817) 429-1550
Contact: Personnel Department
Channel 5 NBC-TV affiliate.

KXTX-TV
3900 Harry Hines Blvd.
Dallas, TX 75219
(214) 521-3900
Contact: Department Head
Channel 39 independent TV station.

KZPS-FM
15851 Dallas Pkwy., Suite 1200
Dallas, TX 75248
(214) 263-0008
Personnel Director: Mary Young
Classic hit radio music.

Sammons Communication
Dallas Office
3010 LBJ Freeway
Dallas, TX 75234
(214) 484-8888
Contact: Department Head
North Texas cable company.

Southern Baptist Radio-Television Commission
6350 West Frwy.
Fort Worth, TX 76150

(817) 737-4011
Contact: Department Head
Baptist broadcast network producing radio and TV shows.

TCI Cablevision of Texas
121 N. Greenville Ave.
Allen, TX 75002
(214) 328-2882
Contact: Administrative Office
Cable company with franchise to serve Dallas, Farmers Branch, and Mesquite.

Texas State Network
7901 John W. Carpenter
Dallas, TX 75247
(214) 688-1133
Contact: Department Head
Statewide radio news network.

WBAP-AM
1 Broadcast Hill
Fort Worth, TX 76103
Metro (817) 429-2330
General Manager: John Hare
Country radio music.

WFAA-TV
Communications Center
606 Young St.
Dallas, TX 75202
(214) 748-9631
Personnel Department: Jennifer Barnum
Channel 8 ABC-TV affiliate.

WRR-FM
P.O. Box 159001
Dallas, TX 75315
(214) 670-8888
Assistant Manager: Mary Lou Rodriguez
24-hour classical radio music. Inquire by mail.

Broadcasting—tough and competitive

If you're fresh out of school and want to break into the Dallas-Fort Worth broadcast market, radio commentator Alex Burton has one word of advice, "Wait."

"There's no reason any broadcaster in this market should accept someone without experience. Those with degrees should go to a smaller market so they can unlearn everything they learned in school," Burton says.

While working in smaller towns, get a broad-based education on what makes a radio station run. Volunteer to do EVERYTHING, Burton recommends. That means sales, sports, news, copywriting, deejaying, and even engineering.

"Engineering experience helps you know what is possible, so you're not at the mercy of an engineer, and what to do in case your equipment breaks down," he says.

When you have at least six months of experience, begin building your tape of your best pieces and critique them as if it's someone else's. Then you can take your best work to apply in D/FW's tough broadcast market, which is the ninth largest in the nation.

After working at 18 stations, Burton says, "I would never suggest that anyone go into the broadcasting business. It's such a tenuous life. So few people have contracts. You work long hours, strange hours. It's hard on the wife and kids," he says.

The image of the hard-living, hard-drinking broadcaster is deceptive. "The only people who stay in the business are the ones who do their work straight—all the time," Burton confides.■

Chemicals

You may also want to look at the section on **Drugs.**

For networking in the **chemical industry** and related fields, check out the following professional organization listed in Chapter 5:

PROFESSIONAL ORGANIZATIONS:

American Institute of Chemical Engineers

For additional information, you can write to the following:

American Chemical Society
1155 16th St., NW
Washington, DC 20036

Chemical Specialties Manufacturers Association
1001 Connecticut Ave.
Washington, DC 20036

PROFESSIONAL PUBLICATIONS:

Chemical Engineering News
Chemical Week

DIRECTORIES:

Analytical Chemistry Lab Guide (American Chemical Society, Washington, DC)
Chemical and Engineering News Facts and Figures Issue (American Chemical
    Society, Washington, DC)
Chemical Week: Buyer's Guide Issue (Chemical Week, New York, NY)
Chemical Week: Financial Survey of the 300 Largest Companies (Chemical Week,
    New York, NY)
OPD Buyers Directory: The Green Book (Schnell Publishing, New York, NY)

EMPLOYERS:

American Cyanamid Co.
7611 John Carpenter Frwy.
Dallas, TX 75247
(214) 631-2130
Manager: Jerry Elizondo
A diversified corporation with several area divisions: Agriculture, Formica Corp., Household Products, Lederle Laboratories, and Cyro Acrylics.

Ashland Chemical
8201 N. Central Expwy.
Dallas, TX 75216
(214) 371-0794
Personnel Manager: Susan Bartholomew
Supplies solvents and chemicals and handles hazardous waste
disposal.

Atlas Powder Co.
15301 Dallas Pkwy., Suite 1200
Dallas, TX 75248
(214) 387-2400
Contact: Human Resources Manager
Manufactures commercial explosives.

Buckley Oil & Chemical Co.
1809 Rock Island St.
Dallas, TX 75207
(214) 421-4147
President: Bess Buckley
Buys and sells alcohol, ketones, hexane, lacquer, enamel, motor oil,
paint stripper, and screen cleaners.

Chemical Lime Co.
3700 Hulen St.
Fort Worth, TX 76107
(817) 429-3077
Human Resources: Tom Stokes
Manufactures and distributes powdered lime.

Delta Distributors
11344 Plano Rd.
Dallas, TX 75243
(214) 341-0510
Sales Manager for sales positions: Tom Mrazek
Plant Supervisor for plant positions: Clay Wade
Distributes acetates, acids, ethers, ektones, and pine oil.

Dow Chemical USA
1 Galleria Tower
13355 Noel Rd., Suite 1025
Dallas, TX 75240
(214) 702-2300
Contact: Linda Neal for clerical positions
Contact: Company headquarters in Midland, MI, (517) 636-1000, for
sales and lab positions
Produces agricultural and industrial chemicals, including herbicides,
insecticides, plastics, and latex.

DuBois Chemicals Division
8770 S. Central Expwy.
Dallas, TX 75239

(214) 376-6491
Branch Manager: Ron Robbins
Produces industrial and institutional chemicals.

Harcros Chemicals
2627 Weir St.
Dallas, TX 75212
(214) 638-8034
Branch Manager: Gary Hutchings
Distributes industrial and oil field chemicals, laundry, dry cleaning
supplies, and pest control chemicals.

Jones-Blair Co.
2728 Empire Central Dr.
Dallas, TX 75235
(214) 353-1600
Human Resources: Jean Lair
Produces and distributes paints and coatings.

NCH Corp.
2727 Chemsearch Blvd.
Irving, TX 75062
(214) 438-0211
Contact: Personnel
Maintenance of industrial and chemical products.

Plastics Manufacturing Co.
2700 S. Westmoreland Rd.
Dallas, TX 75233
(214) 330-8671
Contact: Billy Crow for office positions and C. R. Whited for plant
positions
Produces resin adhesives and plastic dinnerware.

Poly-America
2000 W. Marshall Dr.
Grand Prairie, TX 75051
(214) 647-4374
Contact: Personnel Department
Manufactures polyethylene film for agriculture and commercial uses.

Southwestern Petroleum Corp.
534 N. Main St.
Fort Worth, TX 76107
(817) 332-2336
Personnel Director: Margaret Castillo
Manufactures protective coatings and specialty lubricants.

Texas Refinery Corp.
840 N. Main St.
Fort Worth, TX 76106
(817) 332-1161

Personnel Manager: Linda Burger
Produces industrial coatings, lubricants, and industrial cleaners.

Valley Solvents
2573 NE 33rd St.
Fort Worth, TX 76111
(817) 831-0001
Branch Manager: Lavon Thompson
Distributes industrial solvents and chemicals.

Virginia KMP Corp.
4100 Platinum Way
Dallas, TX 75237
(214) 330-7731
Personnel: Pat Chaney
Produces water-treating chemicals and manufactures air-conditioning
and refrigeration components.

Zoecon Corp.
12005 Ford Rd., Suite 800
Dallas, TX 75234
(214) 243-2321
Contact: Heidi Hodge
Two area locations produce a variety of insecticide products, including
baited traps and dog and cat flea collars.

Computers: Data Processing

You may also want to look at the sections on **Electronics** and
Computers: Hardware/Software.

For networking in the **data processing industry** and related
fields, you can contact these professional organizations listed in
Chapter 5:

PROFESSIONAL ORGANIZATIONS:

Association of Information Systems Professionals
Association of Records Managers and Administrators
Women in Computing

For more information about the data processing industry, you can
write to:

Data Processing Management Association
505 Busse Highway
Park Ridge, IL 60068
(312) 825-8124

Women in Information Processing
Lock Box 39173
Washington, DC 20016

PROFESSIONAL PUBLICATIONS:

Data Communications
Datamation

DIRECTORIES:

Data Processing Equipment Directory (American Business Directories,
    Omaha, NE)
Data Processing Services Directory (American Business Directories,
    Omaha, NE)
Data Sources (Ziff-Davis, New York, NY)
Datamation: The Top 100 Companies in the DP Industry (Cahners
    Publishing, Newton, MA)
*Peterson's Job Opportunies for Engineering, Science, and Computer
    Graduates* (Peterson's Guides, Princeton, NJ)
Thomas Register Office Automation Buyers' Guide (Thomas Publishing,
    New York, NY)

EMPLOYERS:

AIC Analysts Corp.
9901 E. Valley Ranch Pkwy., Suite 3010, L.B. 27
Irving, TX 75063
(214) 869-1881
Staff Recruiter: Shirley Hollywood
Consulting firm for systems analysts.

Commercial Computer Service
1503 S. University Dr.
Fort Worth, TX 76107
(817) 335-6411
Operations Manager: George Radford
Provides packaged programs, systems programming, and data
preparation.

Computer Assistance
2711 LBJ Frwy., Suite 160
Farmer's Branch, TX 75234
(214) 243-1256
Contact: Recruiter
Provides consulting, designing, and programming services.

CompuTrac
222 Municipal Dr.
Richardson, TX 75080

(214) 234-4241
Contact: Department Head
Computerized law firm management systems.

Control Data Business Management Services
6700 LBJ Freeway, Suite 3100
Dallas, TX 75240
(214) 385-5750
Contact: Anthony N. Mitcham for customer service positions and Jack Hatfield for sales and installation positions
Service bureau company that provides batch services for payroll and other financial needs.

Cutler-Williams
4000 McEwen Rd.
Dallas, TX 75244
(214) 960-7053
Contact: Recruiting
Information management services company.

Electronic Data Systems Corp.
Recruitment Department
12200 Park Central Dr., Suite 200
Dallas, TX 75251
(214) 604-6000
Contact: Recruiting
Designs, programs, consults, and operates computer services for major commercial and governmental customers worldwide.

Input
2307 Oak Lane, Suite 100
Grand Prairie, TX 75051
(214) 263-4761
President: True Horton
Data processing service bureau.

Leardata Info-Services
5910 N. Central Expwy.
Dallas, TX 75206
(214) 360-9008
President: Chris Smith
Provides contract data processing.

Lomas Information Systems
2001 Bryan Tower
Dallas, TX 75235
(214) 879-5711
Contact: Human Resources Department
Provides data processing for Lomas & Nettleton and contract services for mortgage and savings and loan companies.

Texas American Services Co.
1900 Don Dodson Dr.
Bedford, TX 76021
(817) 884-4000
Contact: Personnel Department
Data processing.

Computers: Hardware/Software

You may also want to look at the sections on **Computers: Data Processing** and **Electronics.**

For networking in the **computer and electronics industries,** check out these organizations listed in Chapter 5:

PROFESSIONAL ORGANIZATIONS:

**Association of Information Systems Professionals
Women in Computing**

For additional information, you can contact:

ADAPSO-The Computer Software and Services Industry Association
1616 N. Ft. Myers Dr.
Arlington, VA 22209
(703) 522-5055

Association for Computer Operations Management
742 E. Chapman Ave.
Orange, CA 92666
(714) 997-7966

Association of Computer Professionals
230 Park Ave., #460
New York, NY 10169
(212) 599-3019

Association for Computing Machinery
11 W. 42nd St.
New York, NY 10036
(212) 869-7440

IEEE Computer Society
1730 Massachusetts Ave., NW
Washington, DC 20036
(202) 371-0101

National Association of Desktop Publishers
Museum Wharf
300 Congress St.
Boston, MA 02110
(617) 426-2800

PROFESSIONAL PUBLICATIONS:

Byte
Computer Report
Electronic Business
Electronic News
MIS News
PC Magazine
PC Week
PC World
Personal Computing

DIRECTORIES:

Directory of Computer Installations (Computer Management Research, New York, NY)
EIA Trade Directory (Electronics Industry Association, Washington, DC)
Guide to High Technology Companies (Corporate Technology Information Services, Inc., Woburn, MA)
Peterson's Job Opportunies for Enginnering, Science, and Computer Graduates (Peterson's Guides, Princeton, NJ)
Who's Who in Electronics (Harris Publications, Twinsburg, OH)

EMPLOYERS:

Amdahl Corp.
9441 LBJ Frwy., Suite 400
Dallas, TX 75243
(214) 234-8553
Contact: Department Head
Manufactures and sells computers.

Amstrad
1915 Westridge Dr.
Irving, TX 75038
(214) 518-0668
Contact: Department Head
Computer manufacturer.

Apple Computers
12770 Merit Dr., Suite 1000
Dallas, TX 75251
(214) 770-5800

Human Resources Department
Sales office for Apple personal computers.

CE Services
2895 113th St.
Grand Prairie, TX 75050
(214) 641-0070
Contact: Personnel Department
Computer hardware service company.

Computer Language Research
2395 Midway Rd.
Carrollton, TX 75006
(214) 250-7000
Contact: Human Resources Department
Provides time-sharing services for tax applications.

CompuTrac Corporation
17950 Preston Rd., Suite 750
Dallas, TX 75252
(214) 733-3911
President: Robert Markovich
Sells computer systems for financial institutions and retailers.

CSC Logic
9330 LBJ Frwy., Suite 500
Dallas, TX 75243
(214) 238-1898
V.P. of Human Resources: Lori Tucker
Provides software for insurance firms.

Digital Equipment
4851 LBJ Frwy., Suite 1100
Dallas, TX 75244
(214) 702-4000
Contact: Personnel Department
Manufacturer of computers and computer devices.

GenRad
1601 N. Collins Blvd.
Richardson, TX 75080
(214) 234-3357
Contact: Human Resources in Concord, MA, (508) 369-4400
Designs and manufactures computer-controlled test, measurement, and development systems in three high-technology markets.

Harris Corp.
16001 N. Dallas Pkwy.
Dallas, TX 75248
(214) 386-2000

Contact: Human Resource Department
Manufactures, designs, sells, and services high-technology
communications and information processing equipment, including
computer terminals, line printers, card punchers, and readers.

Hogan Systems
5080 Spectrum Dr., Suite 400 E
Dallas, TX 75248
(214) 386-0020
Facilities Administrator: Shirley Wilkerson
Develops, markets, maintains, and supports integrated line of
standard banking applications software packages.

International Business Machines Corp.
2727 LBJ Frwy.
Dallas, TX 75381
(214) 620-6683
Contact: Central Employment Office
Manufactures, sells, and services computers and office equipment.

International Business Machines Corp.
Fort Worth Office
201 Main St.
Fort Worth, TX 76102
(817) 870-4000
Contact: Central Employment Office
Computer and electronic components manufacturer and service.

Micronyx
1901 N. Central Expwy., Suite 400
Richardson, TX 75080
(214) 690-0595
Human Resources Director: Joanna Symmonds

NCR Corp.
450 E. John Carpenter Frwy.
Irving, TX 75062
(214) 650-2100
Contact: Personnel Department
Sells and services computer systems and financial and retail terminals.

National Data Corp.
12005 Ford Rd., Suite 520
Dallas, TX 75234
(214) 620-1851
Contact: Home office in Atlanta, GA, (404) 982-8372
Sells computer systems and software to banking and health care
organizations.

Reynolds & Reynolds Co.
1010 Ave. J. East
Grand Prairie, TX 75050

(214) 647-1722
Regional Human Resources Manager: Scott Brown
Sells and services computers.

Rubicon Corp.
1217 Digital Dr.
Richardson, TX 75081
(214) 231-6591
Contact: Personnel Manager
Provides computer software for the medical industry.

Tandem Computers
12770 Merit Dr., Building 8, Suite 200
Dallas, TX 75251
Metro (214) 960-5000
Human Resources Representative
Manufactures, sells, and services computers.

Total Assets Protection
2301 E. Lamar Blvd., Suite 500
Arlington, TX 76006
(817) 640-8800
Contact: Personnel Office
Computer consulting.

Xerox Corp.
222 W. Las Colinas Blvd.
Irving, TX 75039
(214) 830-4000
Contact: Employment Office
One of world's largest manufacturers of computer systems, copy
machines, and other electronic products.

Contractors/Construction

You may also want to look at the sections on **Architecture,
Engineering,** and **Real Estate.**

For networking in the **construction** industry and related fields,
check out the following trade and professional organizations listed in
Chapter 5:

PROFESSIONAL ORGANIZATIONS:

**American Society of Heating, Refrigeration & Air-
Conditioning Engineers
American Society of Landscape Architects
American Subcontractors Association
Associated General Contractors**

Builders Association of Fort Worth/Tarrant County
**Home & Apartment Builders Association of Metropolitan
   Dallas**
Mechanical Contractors Association of Dallas
National Association of Women in Construction
Sheet Metal and Air Conditioning Contractors

For additional information, you can contact:

Associated Builders & Contractors
729 15th St., NW
Washington, DC 20005
(202) 637-8800

Associated General Contractors of America
1957 E St., NW
Washington, DC 20006
(202) 393-2040

Construction Management Association of America
12355 Sunrise Valley Dr., #640
Reston, VA 22091
(703) 391-1200

Construction Specifications Institute
601 Madison St.
Alexandria, VA 22314
(703) 391-1200

National Association of Home Builders of the U.S.
15th and M Sts., NW
Washington, DC 20005
(202) 822-0200

National Association of Minority Contractors
1333 F St., NW, #500
Washington, DC 20004
(202) 347-8259

National Association of Women in Construction
327 S. Adams St.
Fort Worth, TX 76104
(817) 877-5551

PROFESSIONAL PUBLICATIONS:

Associated Construction Publications
Builder
Building & Contractor
Building Design & Construction
Construction Review
Constructor

Dixie Contractor
ENR: Engineering News Record

DIRECTORIES:

Associated Builders & Contractors Membership Directory (Associated
    Builders & Contractors, Washington, DC)
Blue Book of Major Homebuilders (CMR Systems, Crofton, MD)
Construction Equipment, Construction Giants (Cahners Publishing, Des
    Plaines, IL)
Constructor Directory Issue (Associated General Contractors of America,
    Washington, DC)
ENR Directory of Contractors (McGraw-Hill, New York, NY)
Who's Who in Engineering (Engineers Joint Council, New York, NY)

EMPLOYERS:

APAC-Texas
1901 Cold Springs Rd.
Fort Worth, TX 76102
(817) 336-0521
Personnel Director: Bobby Gay
Contractor for highway, street, and parking facilities.

Austin Industries
3535 Travis St.
Dallas, TX 75204
(214) 443-5500
Personnel Manager: Evelyn Hulshouser or Robert Ford
General contractor, including commercial, residential, and road
construction.

J.W. Bateson
10150 Monroe Dr.
Dallas, TX 75229
(214) 357-1891
Contact: Don Sumrell
General contractor.

Brandt Engineering Co.
11245 Indian Trail
Dallas, TX 75229
(214) 241-9411
Contact: Personnel Department
Commercial and residential contractor.

Thomas S. Byrne
900 Summit Ave.
Fort Worth, TX 76102
(817) 335-3394

V.P. of Construction: Richard M. Patterson
Commercial construction.

Centex Corp.
3333 Lee Pkwy.
Dallas, TX 75219
(214) 559-6500
Employee Communications Coordinator: Dianne Clifton
Residential and commercial construction.

The Freeman Companies
8801 Ambassador Row
Dallas, TX 75247
(214) 638-6450
Contact: Department Head
Full-service contractor.

Frymire Engineering Co.
2818 Satsuma Dr.
Dallas, TX 75229
Metro (214) 263-0201
Commercial and residential contractor, heating, air conditioning,
plumbing, and electrical.

HCB Contractors
1401 Elm St.
4600 InterFirst One
Dallas, TX 75202
(214) 747-8541
V.P. of Human Resources: Jerry Cooper
Commercial construction.

Haws & Tingle General Contractors
909 W. Magnolia Ave., Suite 2
Fort Worth, TX 76104
Metro (817) 429-8310
Superintendent of Field Office: Waldo Strein
President: Paul R. Tingle
General contracting.

JRL Birtram
325 Trinity Court
Arlington, TX 76010
Metro (817) 261-2991
Contact: Personnel Department
Concrete, asphalt, and utility construction.

LH Lacy Co.
10888 Shady Trail
Dallas, TX 75220
(214) 357-0146

Personnel Director: Michelle Bannon
Structural architectural restoration.

Medco
2625 Elm St., Suite 216
Dallas, TX 75226
(214) 820-2492
Contact: Personnel Department
General contractor.

Redman Industries
2550 Walnut Hill Lane, Suite 200
Dallas, TX 75229
(214) 353-3600
Contact: Personnel Department
Mobile home construction.

Speed Fab-Crete Corp.
1150 E. Mansfield Hwy.
Kennedale, TX 76060
(817) 572-0351
Contact: Department Head
General contractor and pre-cast concrete manufacturer.

Walker Construction Co.
4028 Daley Dr.
Fort Worth, TX 76180
(817) 284-9208
Controller: Glenn Jones
Commercial building construction.

Drugs/Biological Products

You may also want to look at the section on **Chemicals.**

For more information, you can write to:

PROFESSIONAL ORGANIZATIONS:

American Pharmaceutical Association
2215 Constitution Ave., NW
Washington, DC 20037

Association of Biotechnology Companies
1666 Connecticut Ave, Suite 330
Washington, DC 20009

National Association of Pharmaceutical Manufacturers
747 Third Ave.
New York, NY 10017

National Association of Retail Druggists
205 Daingerfield Rd.
Alexandria, VA 22314

Pharmaceutical Manufacturers Association
1100 15th St., NW
Washington, DC 20005

PROFESSIONAL PUBLICATIONS:

American Druggist
Biotechnology
Cosmetics and Toiletries
Cosmetic World
Drug Topics
Soap/Cosmetics/Chemical Specialties

DIRECTORIES:

Biotechnology Directory (Stockton Press, New York, NY)
Drug Topics Red Book (Medical Economics Data Co., Montvale, NJ)
Genetic Engineering & Biotechnology Related Firms Worldwide Directory
     (Mega-Type Publishing, Princeton Junction, NJ)
NACDS Membership Directory (National Association of Chain
     Drugstores, Alexandria, VA)
NWDA Membership Directory (National Wholesale Druggists
     Association, Alexandria, VA)
Pharmaceutical Manufacturers of the U.S. (Noyes Data Corp., Park Ridge, NJ)

EMPLOYERS:

AKM Distributing Co.
10681 N. Stemmons Frwy.
Dallas, TX 75220
(214) 869-0595
Vice President: Carolyn McLellan
Manufactures vitamins, health, and beauty aids.

Abbott Laboratories
1921 Hurd Dr.
Irving, TX 75038
(214) 257-6000
Contact: Personnel Department
Mail applications/resumes to:
Alcon Laboratories
Placement and Development T1-3

P.O. Box 6600
Ft. Worth, TX 76115
Designs, develops, and manufactures automated diagnostic medical instruments.

Alcon Laboratories
6201 South Frwy.
Fort Worth, TX 76134
(817) 293-0450
Jobline: (817) 551-4575
Contact: Placement Office
Produces ophthalmic products, including contact lens solutions and eye care products.

Carrington Lab
1300 E. Rochelle Blvd.
Irving, TX 75062
(214) 541-2278
Contact: Personnel Department
Produces phamaceutical products.

Colgate-Hoyt: GEL-KAM
14335 Gillis Rd.
Dallas, TX 75244
(214) 233-2800
Manufactures dental products.

Dexide
7509 Flagstone Dr.
Fort Worth, TX 76118
(817) 589-1454
Personnel: Larry Larsen
Manufactures surgical scrub devices.

FoxMeyer Drug Co.
1220 Senlac Dr.
Carrollton, TX 75006
(214) 446-9090
Contact: Department Head
Manufactures pharmaceuticals.

Nortex Drug Distributors
1021 N. Central Expwy., Suite 20
Plano, TX 75075
(214) 424-2127
Contact: Individual store manager
Parent company for Drug Emporium chain.

Quest Medical
4103 Billy Mitchell St.
Dallas, TX 75244

(214) 387-2740
Human Resources Manager: Corinne OlszowkaAssembles medical and surgical products for I.V. therapy.

Surgikos
2500 Arbrook Blvd.
Arlington, TX 76014
Metro (817) 467-0211
Jobline: (817) 784-4800
Contact: Personnel Department
Johnson & Johnson subsidiary that produces disposable latex gloves.

Educational Institutions

For networking in **education** and related fields, check out the following professional organizations listed in Chapter 5:

PROFESSIONAL ORGANIZATIONS:

Dallas Association for the Education of Young Children
Dallas Association of Educational & Office Personnel
Dallas Association of Texas Professional Educators
Dallas Music Teachers Association
Dallas School Administrators Association
Educational Secretaries Association of Grand Prairie
Irving Association of Educational Office Personnel
Mesquite Educational Secretaries Association
Richardson Music Teachers Association
Texas Music Teachers Association

For additional information, you can write to:

American Association of School Administrators
1801 N. Moore St.
Arlington, VA 22209

American Association of University Women
2401 Virginia Ave., NW
Washington, DC 20037

Association of Independent Colleges and Universities
1 Dupont Circle
Washington, DC 20036

Association of School and Business Officials
1760 Reston Ave.
Reston, VA 22090

Council for Educational Development and Research
1201 16th St., NW
Washington, DC 20036

National Education Association
1201 16th St., NW
Washington, DC 20036

PROFESSIONAL PUBLICATIONS:

Chronicle of Higher Education
Education Week
Instructor
Teaching K-8
Today's Catholic Teacher

DIRECTORIES:

College Board Guide to High Schools (College Board, New York, NY)
Peterson's Guide to Four Year Colleges (Peterson's Guides, Princeton, NJ)
QED's School Guide (Quality Education Data, Denver, CO)

EMPLOYERS:

Public School Districts

Arlington Independent School District
1203 W. Pioneer Pkwy.
Arlington, TX 76013
Metro (817) 261-2581
Executive Director of Personnel: Dr. Doug Shouse
Enrollment: 42,000

Birdville Independent School District
6125 E. Belknap St.
Haltom City, TX 76117
(817) 831-5700
Personnel: Robert L. Cox, Sue Martin, or Carl Reuther
Enrollment: 17,150

Carrollton-Farmers Branch Independent School District
1445 N. Perry Rd.
Carrollton, TX 75006
(214) 323-5700
Personnel Director: Jo Ann Patton
Enrollment: 15,100

Castleberry Independent School District
315 Churchill Rd.

Fort Worth, TX 76114
(817) 737-7235
Superintendent: Dr. Clarence L. Winn
Enrollment: 2,750

Cedar Hill Independent School District
270 S. Hwy. 67
Cedar Hill, TX 75104
(214) 291-1581
Personnel Director: Kathline Bailey
Enrollment: 4,000

Dallas Independent School District
3807 Ross Ave.
Dallas, TX 75204
(214) 827-0202
Contact: Personnel Department
Enrollment: 130,000

DeSoto Independent School District
200 E. Belt Line Rd.
DeSoto, TX 75115
(214) 223-6666
Personnel Director: Gloria Berry
Enrollment: 6,000

Duncanville Independent School District
802 S. Main St.
Duncanville, TX 75137
(214) 296-4761
Personnel Director: Carl Smith
Enrollment: 10,000

Eagle Mountain-Saginaw Independent School District
1200 Old Decatur Rd.
Saginaw, TX 76179
(817) 232-0880
Deputy Superintendent: Truett Absher
Enrollment: 4,700

Everman Independent School District
608 Townley Dr.
Everman, TX 76140
(817) 568-3500
Personnel Officer: Nelda Winnett
Enrollment: 3,300

Fort Worth Independent School District
3210 W. Lancaster Ave.
Fort Worth, TX 76107
(817) 336-8311

Assistant Superintendant: J.D. Skipp
Enrollment: 75,500

Garland Independent School District
720 Stadium Dr.
Garland, TX 75040
(214) 494-8201
Personnel Director: Roger Harrington (elementary); Gary Reeves (secondary)
Enrollment: 35,100

Grand Prairie Independent School District
202 W. College St.
Grand Prairie, TX 75053
(214) 264-6141
Personnel Director: Aurora Jacinto
Enrollment: 16,500

Grapevine-Colleyville Independent School District
3051 Ira E. Woods Ave.
Grapevine, TX 76051
(817) 488-9588
Personnel: Margaret Montgomery
Enrollment: 7,100

Highland Park Independent School District
7015 Westchester Dr.
Dallas, TX 75205
(214) 521-4103
Contact: Personnel Department
Enrollment: 4,000

Hurst-Euless-Bedford Independent School District
1849 Central Dr.
Bedford, TX 76022
(817) 283-4461
Personnel Department
Enrollment: 17,200

Irving Independent School District
901 N. O'Connor Rd.
Irving, TX 75061
(214) 259-4575
Assistant Superintendant: Jerry Christian
Enrollment: 21,850

Kennedale Independent School District
120 W. Mansfield Hwy.
Kennedale, TX 76060
(817) 478-1166
Contact: Personnel
Enrollment: 1,600

Lake Worth Independent School District
6800 Telephone Rd.
Lake Worth, TX 76135
(817) 237-1491
Administrative Assistant: Mattie Millican
Enrollment: 1,500

Lancaster Independent School District
1105 Westridge Ave.
Lancaster, TX 75146
(214) 227-2747
Contact: Personnel Department
Enrollment: 4,000

Mansfield Independent School District
605 E. Broad St.
Mansfield, TX 76063
(817) 473-5600
Personnel: Martha Reed
Enrollment: 8,000

Mesquite Independent School District
405 E. Davis St.
Mesquite, TX 75149
(214) 288-6411
Personnel: Dr. Robert Murdock
Enrollment: 24,000

Plano Independent School District
1517 Ave. H
Plano, TX 75074
(214) 881-8100
Contact: Jeff Bailey for secondary positions and Jo Anne Priest for elementary and support positions
Enrollment: 28,700

Richardson Independent School District
400 S. Greenville Ave.
Richardson, TX 75081
(214) 301-3333
Contact: Peg Griffith
Enrollment: 31,700

White Settlement Independent School District
401 S. Cherry Lane
White Settlement, TX 76108
(817) 367-1350
Superintendent: Clabe Welch
Enrollment: 3,800

Wilmer-Hutchins Independent School District
3820 E. Illinois Ave.

Dallas, TX 75216
(214) 376-7311
Personnel: Joyce Aldrige
Enrollment: 4,000

Universities and Colleges

Amber University
1700 Eastgate Dr.
Garland, TX 75041
(214) 279-6511
Personnel: Dr. Algia Allen
Business and technology undergraduate and graduate university.
Enrollment: 1,000

Baylor College of Dentistry
3302 Gaston Ave.
Dallas, TX 75246
(214) 828-8100
Personnel: John Gilbert
Private college for dentists, dental hygienists, and graduate students.
Enrollment: 400

Baylor University School of Nursing
3700 Worth St.
Dallas, TX 75246
(214) 820-3361
Office Manager: Barbra Worth
Personnel Dean: Phyllis Karns
Four-year R.N. program.
Enrollment: 150

Collin County Community College District
2200 W. University
McKinney, TX 75070
Contact: Personnel Department
Community college.
Enrollment: 10,000

Criswell Center For Biblical Studies
4010 Gaston Ave.
Dallas, TX 75246
(214) 821-5433
Personnel: Dr. Leo Bradley
Graduate and undergraduate Bible studies program.
Enrollment: 375

Dallas Baptist University
7777 W. Kiest Blvd.
Dallas, TX 75211
(214) 331-8311

Personnel Department
Private liberal arts school offering undergraduate and graduate
programs.
Enrollment: 2,700

Dallas County Community College District
701 Elm St.
Dallas, TX 75202
(214) 746-2149
Jobline: (214) 746-2438
Contact: Individual campus
Offers associate degrees at seven campuses, including Brookhaven
College, Cedar Valley College, Eastfield College, El Centro College,
Mountain View College, North Lake College, and Richland College.
Approximate enrollment: 50,000

Dallas Theological Seminary
3909 Swiss Ave.
Dallas, TX 75204
(214) 824-3094
Personnel Director: Jim Anderson
Non-denominational graduate seminary.
Enrollment: 1,000

Devry Institute of Technology
4250 N. Belt Line Rd.
Irving, TX 75038
(214) 258-6330
Human Resources Manager: Glyn Williams
Private institution offering training and placement in electronics,
technology, and computer science with associate and bachelor's
degrees.
Approximate enrollment: 2,400

Harris College of Nursing
P.O. Box 32899
Fort Worth, TX 76129
(817) 921-7652
Personnel Dean: Patricia Scearse
Four-year undergraduate nursing program associated with Texas
Christian University.
Enrollment: 200

Southern Methodist University
P.O. Box 232
Dallas, TX 75275
(214) 692-2000
Contact: Personnel Department
Private university offering undergraduate and graduate programs.
Enrollment: 9,150

Southwestern Baptist Theological Seminary
P.O. Box 22000
Fort Worth, TX 76122
(817) 923-1921
Contact: Personnel Department
World's largest Baptist graduate theological seminary.
Approximate enrollment: 5,000

Tarrant County Junior College District
1500 Houston St.
Fort Worth, TX 76102
(817) 336-7851
Administrative Office Assistant: Martha Martinez
Community college offering associate degrees at TCJC Northeast
Campus, TCJC Northwest Campus, TCJC South Campus, and
Community Campus in downtown Fort Worth.
Approximate enrollment: 25,000

Texas Christian University
2800 S. University Dr.
Fort Worth, TX 76129
Jobline: (817) 921-7791
Contact: Personnel Department
Private university affiliated with the Christian Church, offering
undergraduate and graduate programs.
Enrollment: 7,000

Texas College of Osteopathic Medicine
3500 Camp Bowie Blvd.
Fort Worth, TX 76107
Metro (817) 429-9120
(817) 735-2000
Personnel Director: Rand Horseman
State medical school for osteopathic doctors.
Enrollment: 450

Texas Wesleyan University
1201 Wesleyan St.
Fort Worth, TX 76105
(817) 531-4403
Personnel Department
Private Methodist college, offering undergraduate and graduate
programs.
Enrollment: 1,500

University of Dallas
1845 E. Northgate Dr.
Irving, TX 75062
(214) 445-0110
Personnel Director: Mary Laughlin

Private Catholic university offering undergraduate and graduate programs.
Enrollment: 2,600

The University of Texas at Arlington
800 S. Cooper St.
Arlington, TX 76019
Metro (817) 273-2011
Contact: Personnel Department
Largest area state university, offering undergraduate and graduate programs.
Enrollment: 21,000.

University of Texas at Dallas
2601 N. Floyd Rd.
Richardson, TX 75080
(214) 690-2111
Personnel Director: Jerry Robinson
State university, offering undergraduate and graduate programs.
Enrollment: 7,500

The University of Texas Health Science Center at Dallas
5323 Harry Hines Blvd.
Dallas, TX 75235
(214) 688-3111
Contact: Employment Office
State health science center, which includes the Southwestern Medical School, Southwestern Graduate School of Biomedical Sciences, and the School of Allied Health Sciences.
Enrollment: 2,200

Electronics

Be sure also to look at the sections on **Aircraft and Aerospace, Computers: Hardware/Software,** and **Telecommunications.**

For networking in the **electronics** industry and related fields, check out these organizations listed in Chapter 5:

PROFESSIONAL ORGANIZATIONS:

Electrical Women's Round Table
Texas Electronics Association

For additional information, you can write to:

Electronics Industry Association
2001 I St., NW
Washington, DC 20006

Institute of Electrical & Electronics Engineers
345 W. 47th St.
New York, NY 10017

North American Telecommunications Association
2000 M St., NW
Washington, DC 20036

PROFESSIONAL PUBLICATIONS:

Communications Week International
Electronic Business
Electronic News
Telecommunications Reports
Telephone Engineer and Management
Telephony

DIRECTORIES:

American Electronics Association Directory (American Electronics
    Association, Santa Clara, CA)
Corporate Technology Directory (Corporate Technology Information
    Services, Woburn, MA)
Directory of High Technology Firms (Greater Dallas Chamber of
    Commerce, Dallas, TX)
EIA Trade Directory (Electronics Industry Association, Washington, DC)
Who's Who in Electronics (Harris Publications, Twinsburg, OH)

EMPLOYERS:

AT&T Information Systems
2777 Stemmons Frwy., Suite 1425
Dallas, TX 75207
(214) 308-5542
Job hotline: (903) 876-1996
Employment Supervisor: Bill Henderson
Sales, service, and maintenance for AT&T products.

Airborn Connectors
4321 Airborn Dr.
Addison, TX 75001
(214) 931-3200
Personnel Manager: Nancy Carroll
Manufactures electronic connectors.

American Medical Electronics
250 E. Arapaho Rd.
Dallas, TX 75081
(214) 918-8300

Human Resources Director: Lovonne Chimbel
Manufactures proprietary medical equipment.

Business Records Co.
1111 W. Mockingbird Lane
Dallas, TX 75247
(214) 688-1800
Human Resources: Abe Ruben
Micrographically records and electronically indexes special records.
Also has elections services and county data entry service.

Continental Electronics
4212 S. Buckner Blvd.
Dallas, TX 75227
(214) 381-7161
Employment Manager: Jacki Dale
Manufactures high-power radio transmitters for radio stations.

E-Systems
1200 S. Jupiter Rd.
Garland, TX 75042
(214) 272-0515
Contact: Staffing Office
Corporate headquarters for major worldwide developer and producer
of high-technology electronic systems and products for government
uses.

Hall-Mark Electronics Corp.
11333 Pagemill Dr.
Dallas, TX 75243
(214) 343-5000
Employment Recruiter: Maria Gonzales
Distributes electronic components.

Honeywell
14643 Dallas Pkwy., Suite 800
Dallas, TX 75240
(214) 701-2800
Contact: Department Head
Researches, develops, manufactures, and sells advanced technology
products for information processing, electronics, automation, and
controls industries.

Howell Instruments
3479 W. Vickery Blvd.
Fort Worth, TX 76107
(817) 336-7411
Personnel Manager: Corene Cloud
Manufactures ground test equipment for jet engines.

International Power Machine Corp.
2975 Miller Park North

Garland, TX 75242
(214) 272-8000
Personnel Manager: Judy Hemphill
Manufactures UPS systems.

Motorola Mobile Products Division
5555 N. Beach St.
Fort Worth, TX 76117
(817) 232-6000
Staffing Manager: Gary Gillespie
Research and development of cellular phones.

Recognition Equipment
2701 E. Grauwyler Rd.
Irving, TX 75061
(214) 579-6000
Human Resources Manager: Willemia Shaw
Designs and manufactures image processing, OCR, and networking
technologies.

Siecor Corp.
9275 Hwy. 377 North
Keller, TX 76248
(817) 431-1521
Personnel Manager: Penny Church
Manufactures telephone apparatus, electronic components, and fiber
optics.

Spectradyne
1501 N. Plano Rd.
Richardson, TX 75081
(214) 234-2721
Contact: Human Resources Department
Manufactures, sells, and services television entertainment systems.

Tandy Corp.
1800 One Tandy Center
Fort Worth, TX 76102
(817) 390-3700
Contact: Personnel Department
Manufactures and sells consumer electronic parts and equipment,
including microcomputers, cellular mobile telephones, and satellite
dishes.

Teccor Electronics
1801 Hurd Dr.
Irving, TX 75038
(214) 580-1515
Personnel Manager: Myran Dill
Manufactures electronic power controls, semiconductor power
devices, solid state relays, silicon chips, and rectifiers.

Texas Instruments
13500 N. Central Expwy.
Richardson, TX 75265
(214) 995-3125
Contact: Employment Center
Largest Texas-based high-tech firm. Designs, develops, and manufactures semiconductor memories, microprocessors, large-scale integrated circuits, electronic calculators, home and professional computers, electronic data terminals, and electro-optics equipment.

Thermalloy
2021 W. Valley View Lane
Dallas, TX 75234
(214) 243-4321
Contact: Personnel Department
Manufactures electronic components and systems, including semiconductor equipment and semiconductor insulating covers.

UTL Corp.
1508 W. Mockingbird Lane
Dallas, TX 75235
(214) 638-6688
Personnel Administrator: Janet Foran
Manufactures electronic warfare systems.

Varo
2800 W. Kingsley Rd.
Garland, TX 75046
(214) 840-5446
Contact: Staffing Office
Manufactures defense systems.

Westronics
5001 Blue Mound Rd.
Fort Worth, TX 76106
(817) 625-2311
Contact: Personnel Department
A division of Baker-Hughes that manufactures potentiometric indicators and recorder and digital data systems.

Wiltel Communications Systems
1544 Valwood Pkwy., Suite 106
Carrollton, TX 75006
(214) 620-8300
Sells and services phone systems.

Energy, Oil, and Gas Companies

For networking in the **energy** industry and related fields, check out the following organizations listed in Chapter 5:

PROFESSIONAL ORGANIZATIONS:

Dallas Geological Society
Desk & Derrick Club
Fort Worth Association of Petroleum Landmen
Society of Petroleum Engineers

For more information, you can write to:

American Gas Association
1515 Wilson Blvd.
Arlington, VA 22209

American Petroleum Institute
211 N. Ervay St.
Dallas, TX 75201

PROFESSIONAL PUBLICATIONS:

Drilling
Engineering & Mining Journal
Mining Newsletter
National Petroleum News
Oil and Gas Journal
Public Power
Solar Beat

DIRECTORIES:

Mining Companies Directory (American Business Directories, Omaha, NE)
National Petroleum News Factbook (Hunter Publishing, Des Plaines, IL)
Oil and Gas Directory (Geophysical Directory, Houston, TX)
Oil and Gas Exploration and Development Directory (American Business
    Directories, Omaha, NE)
Solar Industry Journal (Solar Energy Industries Association, Washington, DC)
US Oil Industry Directory (Penwell Publishing, Tulsa, OK)
Whole World Oil Directory (National Register Publishing Company,
    Wilmette, IL)

EMPLOYERS:

American International Manufacturing Corp.
3300 N. Sylvania Ave.
Fort Worth, TX 76111
Metro (817) 429-6715
Human Resources Director: Richard Sheehan
Manufactures oil field equipment.

American Petrofina
8350 N. Central Expwy., Suite 1300
Dallas, TX 75206
(214) 750-2400
Corporate Recruiter: Paula Green
Exploration and production of petroleum and petrochemical products.

Arch Petroleum Co.
777 Taylor St., Suite II-A
Fort Worth, TX 76102
Metro (817) 429-0691
Contact: Personnel Department
Oil and gas exploration and production.

Atlantic Richfield Company
1601 Bryan St.
Dallas, TX 75201
(214) 880-2500
Director of Human Resources: Vetta Stiles
Oil and gas exploration and production.

Aztec Manufacturing Co.
400 N. Tarrant Rd.
Arlington, TX 76036
(817) 297-4361
Director of Industrial Relations: Bill Arnold
Manufactures oil tubing and processing drilling pipe.

CALTEX Petroleum Corp.
125 E. John W. Carpenter Frwy.
Irving, TX 75039
(214) 830-1000
Contact: Personnel Department
Oil refining and marketing.

Delphi Gas Pipeline Corp.
1700 Pacific Ave., L.B. 10
Dallas, TX 75201
(214) 954-2000
Employment Supervisor: Keith Huffman
Headquarters for drilling company that produces natural gas from properties.

Dresser Industries
1600 Pacific Ave.
Dallas, TX 75201
(214) 740-6000
Personnel Manager: Danny Sanchez
Supplies technology, products, and services used by energy-related
industries in the development of petroleum, natural gas, and coal.

Endevco
8080 N. Central Expwy., 12th Floor
Dallas, TX 75206
(214) 691-5536
Payroll Administrator: Valery Davis
Energy development company.

ENSERCH Corp.
1817 Wood St.
Dallas, TX 75201
(214) 651-8700
Contact: Employment Office
Petroleum exploration and production, natural gas transmission and
distribution, engineering and construction, oil field services, and
major utilities.

EXXON Capital Corporation
4545 Fuller Dr., Suite 250
Dallas, TX 75015
(214) 650-7000
Contact: Personnel Department
Oil and gas exploration and marketing.

GNC Energy Corp.
2811 McKinney Ave., Suite 340 West Lobby
Dallas, TX 75204
(214) 979-0353
Owner: W.H. Hudson
Exploration surveys.

Halliburton Co.
3600 Lincoln Plaza
500 N. Akard St.
Dallas, TX 75201
(214) 978-2600
Vice President Administration: Karen Stewart
Headquarters for one of the world's largest and most diversified oil
field services, and engineering and construction organizations. Also
has casualty and life insurance companies.

Harbison-Fischer Manufacturing Co.
901 N. Crowley Rd.
Crowley, TX 76036
(817) 297-2211

Personnel Director: Leon Gregory
Manufactures oil field equipment, subsurface oil well pumps, and pumping equipment.

Holly Corp.
100 Crescent Ct., Suite 1600
Dallas, TX 75201-1880
(214) 979-0210
Contact: Personnel Director Don Prout in Artesia, NM, (505) 748-3311
Refining and marketing of petroleum products.

Hunt Oil Co.
1445 Ross at Field
Dallas, TX 75202
(214) 978-8020
Recruiter: Paula Smith
Oil and gas production, real estate, and agribusiness.

ICO
6500 West Frwy., Suite 220
Fort Worth, TX 76116
Metro (817) 429-9005
Benefits Coordinator: Tina Pruitt
Services oil field equipment.

Kendavis Holding Co.
106 W. 6th St.
Fort Worth, TX 76102
(817) 335-6748
Vice President of Industrial Relations: Bob Ruffin
Provides support services to oil companies.

Knox Oil of Texas
4835 LBJ Frwy., Suite 800
Dallas, TX 75244
(214) 960-9663
Contact: Department Head
Wholesale and retail petroleum production.

LTV Energy Products Co.
2441 Forest Lane
Garland, TX 75042
(214) 487-3000
Personnel Administrator: Joyce Powell
Manufacturer and distributor of oil field supplies.

Maxus Energy Corp.
717 N. Harwood St.
Dallas, TX 75201
(214) 953-2000

Personnel Director: Mark Gentry
Oil and gas exploration and production.

Maynard Oil Co.
8080 N. Central Expwy., Suite 660
Dallas, TX 75206
(214) 891-8880
Contact: Katherine Shaffer
Exploration, development, and production of oil and natural gas.

Meridian Oil Co.
801 Cherry St.
Fort Worth, TX 76102
(817) 429-3080
Human Resources Representative: Linda Harris
Oil and gas exploration and production.

Mobil Oil Corp.
1201 Main St.
Dallas, TX 75202
(214) 658-2111
Contact: Employee Relations
Petroleum refining and distribution.

NRM and Edisto Resources
2121 San Jacinto Tower, Suite 2600
Dallas, TX 75201
(214) 742-9751
Contact: Personnel Department
Oil and gas exploration and production.

ORYX Energy Co.
5656 Blackwell
Dallas, TX 75231
(214) 715-4000
Personnel: Steve Church
Oil and gas exploration and production.

Pacific Enterprises
LTV Center, Suite 1000
2001 Ross Ave.
Dallas, TX 75201
(214) 979-6900
Contact: Personnel Department
Exploration, development, production, and acquisition of crude oil, natural gas, and other natural resources.

Peerless Manufacturing Co.
2819 Walnut Hill Lane
Dallas, TX 75229
(214) 357-6181

Contact: Personnel Director
Manufactures products for oil and gas industry.

Penrod Drilling Co.
2200 Thanksgiving Tower
Dallas, TX 75201
(214) 880-1700
Human Resources Director: Louis Mullenix
Oil and gas driller.

Petro Hunt Corp.
3900 Thanksgiving Tower
Dallas, TX 75201
(214) 922-0135
Personnel: Bill Heidelberg
Oil and gas production.

Placid Oil Co.
3900 Thanksgiving Tower
1601 Elm St.
Dallas, TX 75201
(214) 880-1389
Personnel: Darlene Williams
Oil and gas production and exploration.

Schulmberger Well Services
4100 Spring Valley Rd., Suite 600
Dallas, TX 75244
(214) 385-4040
Relocation Coordinator: Valerie Horne
Oil field services.

SEDCO Forex
3232 McKinney Ave.
Dallas, TX 75204
(214) 720-8700
Contact: Personnel Department
Offshore oil drilling company.

Statex Petroleum
300 E. Carpenter Frwy., Suite 1100
Irving, TX 75062
(214) 541-1155
Vice President: Dhar Carman
Oil and gas exploration and production.

Sunshine Mining Co.
300 Crescent Court, 15th Floor
Dallas, TX 75201
(214) 855-8700
Silver mining and exploration for natural gas.

Teledyne Geotech
3401 Shiloh Rd.
Garland, TX 75041
(214) 271-2561
Human Resources Manager: Ernest Stephens
Manufactures scientific equipment for oil and gas, seismology, and meteorology industries.

Teledyne Merla
300 Kirby St.
Garland, TX 75042
(214) 276-8561
Personnel Manager: Diane Iannucci
Designs, manufactures, and services oil and gas production equipment for the petroleum industry.

Triton Energy Corp.
8008 Cedar Springs
Dallas, TX 75235
(214) 691-5200
Contact: Vice President of Human Resources
Oil, gas, and coal exploration and production.

Union Pacific Resources Co.
801 Cherry St.
Fort Worth, TX 76102
(817) 877-6000
Vice President of Human Development: Marshall Utterson
Petroleum exploration and production.

Whitehall Corp.
2659 Nova Dr.
Dallas, TX 75229
(214) 247-8747
Contact: Department Head
Oil and gas exploration and production.

Woodbine Petroleum
1445 Ross Ave., Suite 3660
Dallas, TX 75202
(214) 855-6263
Vice President: Cricket Livengood
Oil and gas exploration and production.

Engineering Firms

You may also want to look at the sections on **Architecture** and **Contractors/Construction.**

For networking in **engineering** and related fields, check out the following professional organizations listed in Chapter 5:

PROFESSIONAL ORGANIZATIONS:

American Institute of Chemical Engineers
American Society of Civil Engineers
American Society of Heating, Refrigeration and Air-Conditioning Engineers
American Society of Mechanical Engineers
American Society of Safety Engineers
Society of Hispanic Professional Engineers
Society of Women Engineers
Texas Environmental Health Association
Texas Society of Professional Engineers

For additional information you can contact:

American Society of Civil Engineers
1 Walnut St.
Boston, MA 02108
(617) 227-5551

American Society of Civil Engineers
345 E. 47th St.
New York, NY 10017
(212) 705-7496

American Society of Mechnanical Engineers
345 E. 47th St.
New York, NY 10017
(212) 705-7722

Institute of Electrical & Electronics Engineers
345 E. 47th St.
New York, NY 10017
(212) 705-7900

National Society of Professional Engineers
1420 King St.
Alexandria, VA 22314
(703) 684-2800

Society of Women Engineers
345 E. 47th St.
New York, NY   10017
(212) 705-7855

PROFESSIONAL PUBLICATIONS:

Building Design & Construction
Chemical Engineering News
Construction Weekly
ENR: Engineering News Record
Proceedings

DIRECTORIES:

Directory of Contract Service Firms (C.E. Publications, Kirkland, WA)
IEEE Directory (Institute of Electrical and Electronics Engineers, New York, NY)
Official Register (American Society of Civil Engineers, New York, NY)
Professional Engineering Directory (National Society of Professional Engineers, Alexandria, VA)
Who's Who in Engineering (American Assoc. of Engineering Societies, Washington, DC)
Who's Who in Technology (Gale Research, Detroit, MI)

EMPLOYERS:

Arjo Engineers
4311 Oak Lawn Ave.
Dallas, TX 75219
(214) 233-4478
Chairman of the Board: Argen Pearce
Specialties: Office buildings, shopping centers, educational facilities, and hospitals.

Black & Veatch Engineering and Architects
5728 LBJ Frwy., Suite 300
Dallas, TX 75240
(214) 770-1500
Recruitment Director: Bill Davis
Specialties: Municipal water and wastewater.

Bridgefarmer & Associates
1300 S. Sherman St., Suite 290
Richardson, TX 75081
(214) 231-8800
Sr. Vice President: John Blackledge
Specialties: Highways, railroads, and bridges.

Brockette Davis Drake
3535 Travis St., Suite 100
Dallas, TX 75204
(214) 522-9540
Contact: Prefer mail inquiries only
Specialties: Civil and structural engineering.

Carter & Burgess
1100 Macon St.
Fort Worth, TX 76102
(817) 335-2611
Personnel Supervisor: Ken Pusey
Specialties: Engineering, planning, landscape architecture, and surveying.

CH2M Hill
5339 Alpha Rd., Suite 300
Dallas, TX 75240
(214) 980-2170
Personnel Director: Theresa Martinez
Specialties: Wastewater and hazardous wastes.

Datum Engineering
6516 Forest Park Rd.
Dallas, TX 75235
(214) 358-0174
Engineering Department: Tom Herrin
Specialties: Corporate facilities, universities, and airports.

DeShazo, Starek & Tang
330 Union Station
Dallas, TX 75202
(214) 748-6740
President: John DeShazo
Specialties: Transportation planning and traffic engineering.

Steve Dunn & Partners
2520 Fairmount St.
Dallas, TX 75201
(214) 871-1107
Vice President of Finance: Bill Alexander
Specialties: Office buildings and health care facilities.

Greiner Engineering Sciences
909 E. Las Colinas Blvd., Suite 1900
Lock Box 44
Irving, TX 75039
(214) 869-1001
Director of Human Resources: Thomas R. Smith
Specialties: Highways and airports.

Gunnin-Campbell Consulting Engineers
3625 N. Hall St., Suite 500
Dallas, TX 75219
(214) 559-2600
President: Stephen J. Campbell
Specialties: Mid- and high-rise office buildings and hotels.

Albert H. Halff Associates
8616 Northwest Plaza Dr.
Dallas, TX 75225
(214) 739-0094
Contact: Personnel Department
Specialties: Flood plain management, office/industrial parks, and environmental engineering.

Howard Needles Tammen & Bergendoff
14114 Dallas Pkwy., Suite 630
Dallas, TX 75240
(214) 661-5626
Office Coordinator: Claire Caldwell
Specialties: Highway design and municipal engineering.

Huitt-Zollars
3131 McKinney Ave., Suite 600
Dallas, TX 75204
(214) 871-3311
Contact: Larry Huitt or Bob Zollars
Specialties: Hydrology/hydraulics and land development.

Bernard Johnson
7800 Stemmons Frwy., Suite 730
Dallas, TX 75247
(214) 631-7200
Sr. Vice President: Bill Glasgow
Specialties: Engineering for city governments and other public groups.

Kimley-Horn and Associates
12660 Coit Rd., Suite 300
Dallas, TX 75251
(214) 386-7007
Personnel Director: Jack Janco, 3001 Weston, Cary, NC 27513
Specialties: Transportation engineering.

Lockwood Andrews & Newnam
2710 N. Stemmons Frwy., Suite 1200
Dallas, TX 75207
(214) 630-1414
Operations Manager: Jack Moseley
Specialties: Public works engineering.

Lockwood Greene Engineers
4201 Spring Valley Rd., Suite 1500
Dallas, TX 75244
(214) 991-5505
Human Resources Manager: Judy Schosield
Specialties: Advanced technology and manufacturing facilities.

Romine, Romine & Burgess
300 Greenleaf St.
Fort Worth, TX 76107
(817) 336-4633
Office Manager: Patti McKittrick
Specialties: Mechanical and electrical engineers.

Rone Engineers
11234 Goodnight Lane
Dallas, TX 75229
(214) 241-4517; Metro (214) 263-1555
President: Bob Patton
Specialities: Geotechnical, environmental, and materials testing consultants.

Southwestern Laboratories
2575 Lone Star Dr.
Dallas, TX 75212
(214) 263-1133
President: Chester Drash
Specialties: Industrial, institutional, commercial buildings, and construction materials testing.

Teague, Nall & Perkins
915 Florence St.
Fort Worth, TX 76102
(817) 336-5773
Principal: John H. Nall, Jr.
Specialties: Consulting engineering.

Turner, Collie & Braden
5710 LBJ Frwy., Suite 370
Dallas, TX 75240
(214) 960-9651
Vice President: Thomas Burke
Specialties: Highways and airports.

Entertainment

For networking in the **entertainment** industry, check out the following professional organizations listed in Chapter 5:

PROFESSIONAL ORGANIZATIONS:

American Guild of Organists
Dallas Arts Council
Pro-Musica
Society for Theatrical Artists Guidance and Enhancement

For more information, you can write to:

American Federation of Arts
41 E. 65th St.
New York, NY 10021

American Guild of Authors and Composers
6430 Sunset Blvd.
Hollywood, CA 90028

Amusement and Music Operators Association
1101 Connecticut Ave., NW
Washington, DC 20036

Arts and Business Council
130 E. 40th St.
New York, NY 10016

PROFESSIONAL PUBLICATIONS:

ArtCom
Backstage
BAM
Billboard
Mix
Music Journal
Performance
Show Buisness
Variety

DIRECTORIES:

Back Stage Shoot/Commerical Production (Knowledge Industry
     Publications, White Plains, NY)
Contemporary Musicians (Gale Research, Detroit, MI)
Music Business (Music Industry Resources, San Anselmo, CA)

EMPLOYERS:

Billy Bob's Texas
2520 Rodeo Plaza
Fort Worth, TX 76106
(817) 624-7117
Personnel: Ruth Churkey
World's largest honky-tonk with indoor bull-riding arena, concerts by
national entertainers, gift shops, and restaurants.

Caravan of Dreams
312 Houston St.
Fort Worth, TX 76102
Metro (817) 429-4000
General Manager: Maria Golia
Jazz/blues nightclub, featuring local and national entertainers,
theater, and restaurant.

Casa Manana Theatre
3101 W. Lancaster Ave.
Fort Worth, TX 76107
(817) 332-9319
Company Manager: Debbie Brown
Theater with summer musicals, children's plays, and theatrical
productions.

Dallas Alley
2019 N. Lamar St.
Dallas, TX 75202
(214) 988-0581
Contact: Fill out applications from 9 a.m.-6 p.m. Monday-Friday
Nightclub complex.

The Dallas Opera
3102 Oak Lawn Ave., Suite 450, LB130
Dallas, TX 75219
(214) 443-1043
Opera association.

Dallas Repertory Theatre
150 NorthPark Center
Dallas, TX 75225
(214) 692-5611

Executive Producer: Douglas Parker
Legitimate theater.

Dallas Symphony Orchestra
2301 Flora St., Suite 300
Dallas, TX 75201-2413
(214) 871-4000
Contact: Personnel

Dallas Theater Center
3636 Turtle Creek Blvd.
Dallas, TX 75219
(214) 526-8210
General Manager: Carl Wittenburg
Legitimate theater.

Dallas Zoo
621 E. Clarendon Dr.
Dallas, TX 75203
(214) 946-5154
Contact: Personnel Office
City zoo.

Fort Worth Ballet
6845 Green Oaks Rd.
Fort Worth, TX 76116
(817) 763-0207
Executive Director: David Mallette
Ballet company.

Fort Worth Opera Association
3505 W. Lancaster Ave.
Fort Worth, TX 76107
(817) 731-0833
General Manager: Pat Crowley
Opera company.

Fort Worth Symphony Orchestra
4401 Trail Lake Dr.
Fort Worth, TX 76109
(817) 921-2676
General Manager: John Toohey

Fort Worth Zoological Park
2727 Zoological Park Dr.
Fort Worth, TX 76110
(817) 870-7050
Assistant Director: Elaine McGowan
More than 4,000 animals and exhibits.

Funny Bone Comedy Club
2525 E. Arkansas Lane, Suite 253

Arlington, TX 76010
Metro (817) 265-2277
Manager: Gary Johnston
Comedy club with local and national entertainers.

Hip Pocket Theatre
1627 Fairmount Ave.
Fort Worth, TX 76104
(817) 927-2833
General Manager: Holly Leach
Outdoor theater.

Shakespeare Festival of Dallas
3630 Harry Hines Blvd., Suite 306
Dallas, TX 75219
(214) 559-2778
Contact: Executive Director
Produces annual Shakespeare play series.

Showco
201 Regal Row
Dallas, TX 75247
(214) 263-5944
Contact: Mail resume
Sound and lighting company.

Six Flags Over Texas
2201 Road To Six Flags
Arlington, TX 76010
Metro (817) 640-8900
Contact: Personnel Office
Family theme park.

Stage West
312 Houston St.
Fort Worth, TX 76102
(817) 332-6238
Artistic Director: Jerry Russell
Legitimate theater.

State Fair of Texas
P.O. Box 26010
Dallas, TX 75226
(214) 565-9931
Contact: Personnel for staff positions and Texas Employment
Commission for seasonal jobs during annual fair in October.

Texas Stadium
2401 E. Airport Frwy.
Irving, TX 75062
(214) 438-7676

Director of Operations: Ron Underwood
Major stadium for Dallas Cowboys football games and other events.

Theatre Three
2800 Routh St.
Dallas, TX 75201
(214) 871-2933
Director of Administration: Chris Hansdorff
Non-profit legitimate theater.

Wet 'N Wild
1800 E. Lamar St.
Arlington, TX 76006
Metro (817) 265-3566
Contact: Personnel department at Arlington and Garland water parks
Water park.

Theatrical career often noble but low paying

Theater Three Executive Producer and Director Jac Alder appreciates the struggle involved when people pursue a career in the theater. He was an architect for seven years before his avocation became his vocation.

His interests motivated him to get more involved in the theater, although he says, "I have not given up architecture. In the service of the theater, I design sets. I use every bit of training I got as an architect on virtually a daily basis. Right now I'm standing over a computer doing a spread sheet on construction costs."

Alder describes how terrified parents have approached him and said, "My God, my son or daughter is in theater. What's going to happen?"

"They can't see it as a paying profession and they are right," he says.

He tells parents that the theater teaches young people to work in a team situation, meet deadlines, and deal with great ideas of the Western World.

"My feeling is that any task can be followed with a sense of ethics and a sense of industry," Alder says. "If any job offers you an opportunity to do that, you've got a wonderful life. Theater involves creativity, responsibility, and all the things that we think are important." ■

Film, Video, Recording, and Talent Services

You may also want to look at the section on **Broadcasting and Cable Television.**

For networking in **film, video,** and related fields, check out these professional organizations listed in Chapter 5:

PROFESSIONAL ORGANIZATIONS:

Dallas Communications Council
Dallas Producers Association
Dallas Screenwriters Association
Texas Association of Film & Tape Professionals
Women of the Motion Picture Industry

For additional information, you can write to:

Academy of Motion Picture Arts & Sciences
8949 Wilshire Blvd.
Beverly Hills, CA 90211

American Film Institute
6430 Sunset Blvd.
Hollywood, CA 90028

PROFESSIONAL PUBLICATIONS:

American Film
Back Stage
Billboard
Box Office
Film Comment
Film Journal
Variety

DIRECTORIES:

Audio-Visual Communications: Who's Who (Media Horizons, New York, NY)
Audio-Visual Buyer's Guide (PTN Publishing Company, Melville, NY)
Back Stage Shoot/Commercial Production (Knowledge Industry
     Publications, White Plains, NY)
Billboard International Buyers Guide (Billboard Publishers, New York, NY)

EMPLOYERS:

AVW Audio Visual
2241 Irving Blvd.
Dallas, TX 75241
(214) 634-9060
Contact: Department Head
Sells and leases equipment; produces tapes for customers.

Dallas Communications Complex
The Studios at Las Colinas
6301 N. O'Connor Rd.
Irving, TX 75039
(214) 869-0700
Vice President: Jennifer Loeb
Film and sound studios, manages offices for support services for the
commercial and entertainment film business.

Dallas Sound Lab
Four Dallas Communications Complex, Suite 119
6305 N. O'Connor Rd.
Irving, TX 75039
(214) 869-1122
Accepts resumes by mail only.
Contact: Johnny Marshall
Specializes in post-production audio services for film and video,
including film/video interlock and scoring; mixing, demos, and
albums.

Kim Dawson Agency
1643 Apparel Mart
Dallas, TX 75258
(214) 638-2414
Contact: Department Head
Talent and modeling agency for film, television, radio, theater, and
fashion promotions.

Fort Worth Productions
1227 Magnolia Ave.
Fort Worth, TX 76104
(817) 336-0777
Accepts resumes by mail only.
Contact: Lyn Downing
Independent television production company, providing
programming for network syndicators, public broadcasting, and cable.

Goodnight Audio
11260 Goodnight Lane
Dallas, TX 75229
(214) 241-5182
Studio Manager: Jennifer Spencer
Complete 24-track recording studio.

January Sound Studios
3341 Towerwood Dr., Suite 205
Dallas, TX 75234
(214) 243-3735
Studio Manager: Denis Lowe
Sound studio, featuring two full-service 24-track studios.

Richard Kidd Productions
5610 Maple Ave.
Dallas, TX 75235
(214) 638-5433
Contact: Barbara Ratliff
Full-service production company for film, video, and A/V
presentations.

Magnum Audio-Visual
1333 Maryland Dr.
Irving, TX 75061
(214) 554-0533
Contact: Claire Tuallier
Industrial shows, audio, and video production work.

Omega Audio & Productions
7027 Twin Hills, Suite #5
Dallas, TX 75231
(214) 891-9585
Senior Engineer: Steve Lowney
Complete remote audio multi-track recording service for records, film,
and video.

Southwest Teleproductions
2649 Tarna Dr.
Dallas, TX 75229
(214) 243-5719
Contact: J.P. Shives or Lee Harrison for operations positions and
Suzanne Morris for administrative
Production and post-production services for 35mm and 16mm film
and videotape.

Bill Stokes Associates
5642 Dyer St.
Dallas, TX 75206
(214) 363-0161
C.E.O.: Bill Stokes
Full production facility for 35mm and 16mm commercials, industrials,
and feature films.

Video Post and Transfer
2727 Inwood Rd.
Dallas, TX 75235
(214) 350-2676
Send resumes by mail only.

Personnel: Ray Howell
Complete video post-production services, including film-to-tape transfer, graphics, animation, and special effects.

Zimmersmith
6311 N. O'Connor Rd., Suite 113
Dallas Communications Complex, Bldg. #3
Irving, TX 75039
(214) 869-4611
Production Coordinator: Vickie Leeper
Full-service music production company.

"Models are born, not made"

On an average day, 30 phone calls and 15 letters are directed to George Dawson, talent coordinator for the Kim Dawson Agency, Inc. Here's what he tells eager applicants who want to break into the area's growing fashion, film, and talent industries:

Send several color photographs along with your measurements, height, phone number, and address where you can be reached. "Most people think you have to pay for expensive portfolio photographs, and that's not the case," Dawson says.

Out of 50 or 60 inquiries, he may find one person who has the potential to make it in the highly competitive Dallas market. Many people don't meet one necessary requirement—height. A women must be 5 feet, 8 inches, to 5 feet, 11 inches and a man should be between 5 feet, 11 inches and 6 feet, 2 inches.

Dawson interviews promising candidates. If he thinks they have potential, he advises them to get a series of quality pictures taken. If those turn out well, the person is signed with the agency and assisted in putting together a "composite" (photo sheet) and portfolio.

"The first year can be rough financially for new models," Dawson says. "They should be prepared to moonlight during the first six months to a year because few novices make a livable income."

People who sign with the agency can take modeling and grooming classes, but it's not a requirement. "We never tell a person they will be a model after taking a certain number of courses," he says. "Models are usually born, not made." ■

Food/Beverage Producers and Distributors

You may also want to look at the section on **Restaurants.**

For networking in the **food industry** and related fields, check out the following professional organizations listed in Chapter 5:

PROFESSIONAL ORGANIZATIONS:

Southwestern Meat Packers Association
Women's Association of Allied Beverage Industries

For additional information, you can write to:

Food Marketing Institute
1750 K St., NW
Washington, DC 20006

National Association of Beverage Importers
1025 Vermont Ave.
Washington, DC 20005

National Food Distributors Association
111 E. Wacker Drive
Chicago, IL 60601

National Food Processors Association
1401 New York Ave.
Washington, DC 20005

National Frozen Food Association
PO Box 398
Hershey, PA 17033

National Soft Drink Association
1101 16th St., NW
Washington, DC 20036

Wine & Spirits Wholesalers of America
1025 15th St., NW
Washington, DC 20005

PROFESSIONAL PUBLICATIONS:

Beverage World
Food and Beverage Newsletter
Food Management
Foodservice Product News
Impact
Institutional Distribution
Market Watch
Progressive Grocer
Wine Investor
Wine Spectator
Wines and Vines

DIRECTORIES:

Directory of the Canning, Freezing, Preserving Industry (Edward C. Judge
    & Sons, Westminster, MD)
Impact Yearbook: A Directory of the Wine and Spirits Industry (M.
    Shanken Communications, New York, NY)
Modern Brewery Age Blue Book (Business Journals, Norwalk, CT)
National Frozen Food Association Directory (National Frozen Food
    Association, Harrisburg, PA)
Texas Retail Grocers Association Directory (Texas Retail Grocers
    Association, Austin, TX)

EMPLOYERS:

Affiliated Food Stores
100 Nat Gibbs Dr.
Keller, TX 76248
Metro (817) 498-4042
Personnel Manager: Mike Malone
Food store chain.

American Produce & Vegetable Co.
4721 Simonton Rd.
Dallas, TX 75244
(214) 233-5750
Personnel: Cynthia Esquivel
Distributes canned and fresh food to hotels, caterers, restaurants, and
airlines.

Arrow Industries
2625 Belt Line Rd.
Carrollton, TX 75006
(214) 416-6500
Contact: Personnel Department
Packages dry food products.

Mrs Baird's Bakeries
Dallas Office
5230 E. Mockingbird Lane
Dallas, TX 75205
(214) 526-7201
Contact: Personnel Department
Produces bread and baked goods.

Mrs Baird's Bakeries
Fort Worth Office
7301 South Frwy.
Fort Worth, TX 76134
(817) 293-6230
Contact: Personnel Department
Same as Dallas.

Borden
5327 S. Lamar St.
Dallas, TX 75215
(214) 565-0332
Personnel Manager: Lou Ray
Produces milk, ice cream, and dairy products.

Cabell's Dairy
4017 Commerce St.
Dallas, TX 75226
(214) 234-6761
Personnel Manager: Gary McNeil
Produces and distributes dairy products.

Campbell Taggert
6211 Lemmon Ave.
Dallas, TX 75209
(214) 358-9211
Manager of Personnel Administration: Ellen Einsohn
Produces white breads, earth grains, and sweet goods.

Coca-Cola Bottling Co. of North Texas
3400 Fossil Creek Blvd.
Fort Worth, TX 76137
(817) 232-8600
Contact: Personnel Department
Bottlers of soft drink beverage.

Continental Grain Co.
2301 Terminal Rd.
Fort Worth, TX 76106
(817) 624-4171
Operations Manager: Roger Sellers
Buys and sells grains.

Coors Distributing Co.
2550 McMillan Pkwy. S.
Fort Worth, TX 76137
(817) 831-4211
Contact: Personnel Director
Beer distributor.

Cullum Companies
14303 Inwood Rd.
Dallas, TX 75244
(214) 661-9700
Employment Training Manager: Marylin Smith
Operates chain of supermarkets, drug stores, wholesale grocery
distribution, and meat packing, including Tom Thumb Page Food &
Drug Centers.

Jimmy Dean Meat Co.
10430 Shady Trail
Dallas, TX 75220
(214) 350-6755
Contact: Personnel
Produces sausage and prepared meats.

Jacob E. Decker & Sons Food Co.
3200 W. Kingsley Rd.
Garland, TX 75041
(214) 278-6192
Human Resources Director: Vicki Minden
Processes bacon, sausage, boiled ham, and smoked and cured pork.

Design Foods
3709 E. First St.
Fort Worth, TX 76111
(817) 831-0981
Personnel Manager: Janet Kelley
Produces meats for institutional and commercial customers.

Dr Pepper/7UP Cos.
8144 Walnut Hill Lane
Dallas, TX 75231
(214) 360-7000
Contact: Personnel Department
Soft drink beverage bottlers.

Frito-Lay
National Headquarters
7701 Legacy Dr.
Plano, TX 75024
(214) 351-7000
Contact: Professional Placement
Produces and markets snack products.

Glazer's Wholesale Distributors
10750 Denton Dr.
Dallas, TX 75220
(214) 357-1245
Contact: Department Head
Wholesale wine and liquor distributor.

Deli Express
2005 108th St., Suite 504
Grand Prairie, TX 75050
(214) 647-0371
Personnel Manager: Wes Eatman
Produces and distributes wholesale sandwiches, snacks, and Mexican
food.

George A. Hormel & Co.
4114 Mint Way
Dallas, TX 75224
(214) 784-9055
Contact: Personnel Office at (507) 437-5611
Processes and distributes fresh and canned meat products, frozen and
prepared foods, and institutional food.

ITT Continental Baking Co.
9000 Denton Dr.
Dallas, TX 75235
(214) 358-0232
Contact: Personnel Department
Produces and distributes bread and bakery items.

Jewel-Osco
1100 Executive Dr. West, Suite 100
Richardson, TX 75083
(214) 238-7231
Contact: Human Resources Department
Grocery and drug store chain.

Keebler Co.
3900 Meecham Blvd.
Halton City, TX 76117
Metro (817) 577-2933
Personnel: Al Goday
Distributes cookie, cracker, and snack products.

Ben E. Keith Co.
601 E. 7th St.
Fort Worth, TX 76102
Metro (817) 429-8488
Contact: Department Head
Beer distributor and wholesaler of frozen foods and produce.

Kreck Foods
4115 S. Lamar St.
Dallas, TX 75215
(214) 421-8226
Contact: Personnel Department
Produces processed meats and meat products.

Kroger Food Co.
1901 Gateway Dr.
Irving, TX 75038
(214) 580-3000
Contact: Human Resources Department
Major food retailer and operator of food processing, dairies, bakeries, and egg-producing facilities.

Manor Baking Co.
3500 Manor Way
Dallas, TX 75235
(214) 357-1754
Personnel: Vera Carver
Produces bread and bakery products.

Miller Brewing Co.
7001 South Frwy.
Fort Worth, TX 76134
(817) 551-3350
Personnel Manager: Steve Hanke
Produces, bottles, and distributes beer and malt beverages.

Owens Country Sausage
1403 Lookout Dr.
Richardson, TX 75082
(214) 235-7181
Vice President: Lindsey Borden
Produces sausage and pork products.

Pepsi-Cola Bottling Group
4532 Hwy. 67
Mesquite, TX 75150
(214) 324-8500
Bottles soft drink beverage.

Pilgrim's Pride Corp.
2411 Ferris St.
Dallas, TX 75226
(214) 421-7625
Personnel: Claudia Stamp
Poultry wholesaler.

Quaker Oats Co.
13745 Jupiter Rd.
Dallas, TX 75238

(214) 340-0370
Personnel Manager: Jolyne Thorne
Distributor for foods, pet foods, and specialty chemicals.

Rodriguez Festive Foods
899 N. Houston St.
Fort Worth, TX 76106
(817) 429-1980
Personnel Manager
Produces Mexican food products.

Southland Corp.
4711 N. Haskell Rd.
Dallas, TX 75204
(214) 828-7107
Contact: Personnel Department
Corporate headquarters for 7-Eleven convenience stores and dairy
products producer.

Supreme Beef Co.
5219 2nd Ave.
Dallas, TX 75210
(214) 428-1761
Personnel Safety Director: Gayla Hensley
Beef processing plant.

Sysco Food Systems
14330 Gillis Rd.
Farmers Branch, TX 75244
(214) 233-9700
Personnel Director: Kyle Killingsworth
Institutional food distributor.

Vandervoort Dairy Foods
900 S. Main St.
Fort Worth, TX 76104
(817) 332-7551
Contact: Texas Employment Commission for production positions and
send resumes for management positions
Dairy foods processor.

White Swan
1515 Big Town Blvd.
Mesquite, TX 75149
(214) 388-7700
Contact: Personnel Department
Institutional food distributor.

Willow Distribution
2601 Cockrell Ave.
Dallas, TX 75215
(214) 426-5636

Contact: Department Head
Beer distributor.

Winn-Dixie Texas
5500 South Frwy.
Fort Worth, TX 76115
(817) 921-1100
Contact: Department Head
Grocery store chain and dairy products producer.

Furniture and Fixtures Manufacturers

For networking in the **furniture and fixtures** industry and related fields, check out this professional organization listed in Chapter 5.

PROFESSIONAL ORGANIZATIONS:

International Furnishings and Design Association

To help you learn more about the furniture industry, you can write to:

International Home Furnishings Association
405 Merchandise Mart Plaza
Chicago, IL 60654

PROFESSIONAL PUBLICATIONS:

Home Furnishings Review
Textile Products and Processes
Textile World

DIRECTORIES:

Furniture Manufacturers Directory (American Business Directories, Omaha, NE)
Who's Who in Furniture Distribution (National Wholesale Furniture Association, High Point, NC)

EMPLOYERS:

Duro Metal Manufacturing Co.
410 Hilburn St.
Dallas, TX 75217
(214) 391-3181
Plant Manager: Frank Ramirez
Office Manager: Pricilla Siegel

Executive V.P. for Sales Positions: Chuck Siegel
Manufactures bed frames, mirror supports, bed rails, and trundle beds.

Inca Metal Products Corp.
501 E. Purnell St.
Lewisville, TX 75067
(214) 436-5581
Contact: Department Head
Manufactures workbenches, shop desks, and industrial shelving.

Levolor Corp.
1750 Monetary Lane
Carrollton, TX 75006
(214) 245-4776
Personnel Director: Melinda Swartwot
Manufactures window coverings.

Massould Furniture Manufacturing Co.
8208 Moberly Lane
Dallas, TX 75227
(214) 388-8655
Plant Manager: Dwain Seabolt
Manufactures household furniture, including sofas, loveseats, and
chairs.

Pillowtex Corp.
4111 Mint Way
Dallas, TX 75237
(214) 333-3225
Contact: Personnel Department
Manufactures bedding, pillows, mattress pads, and comforters.

Simmons Co.
8600 Harry Hines Blvd.
Dallas, TX 75235
(214) 637-0460
Contact: Personnel Department
Manufactures mattresses and box springs.

Smith System Manufacturing Co.
1714 E. 14th St.
Plano, TX 75074
(214) 424-6591
Personnel Manager: Ron Smith
Manufactures furniture for schools and offices.

Southland Bedding Co.
1207 W. Crosby Rd.
Carrollton, TX 75006
(214) 242-7666
Owner: Larry Bannister

General Manager: Grady McAlum
Manufactures bedding.

Stamco-Stationers Manufacturing Co.
420 S. Ballinger St.
Fort Worth, TX 76104
Metro (817) 332-8311
President: Jim Pipes
Manufactures executive office tables.

Universal Carrier Co.
613 Easy St.
Garland, TX 75043
(214) 276-8335
Personnel Manager: Lucy Maines
Manufactures wire and tubular products.

Vecta Contract
1800 S. Great Southwest Pkwy.
Grand Prairie, TX 75051
(214) 641-2860
Human Resources Manager: Betty McCrey
Manufactures contemporary office furniture.

Government

For networking in **government** and related fields, check out these professional organizations listed in Chapter 5:

PROFESSIONAL ORGANIZATIONS:

American Planning Association
Dallas County Library Association
Federal Employed Women
Fort Worth Librarians Association
Public Library Administrators of North Texas
Texas Recreation & Park Society
Texas Society of Professional Surveyors
Urban Management Assistants of North Texas

For additional information, you can contact:

American Federation of Government Employees
80 F St., NW
Washington, DC 20001
(202) 737-8700

Civil Service Employees Association
P.O. Box 125, Capital Station

143 Washington Ave.
Albany, NY 12210
(518) 434-0191

National Association of Government Employees
2011 Crystal Dr., #206
Arlington, VA 22202
(703) 979-0290

PROFESSIONAL PUBLICATIONS:

AFSCME 93 News
AFSCME Leader
The Beacon
Federal Times
FedNews
The Municipal Forum
Public Employee Newsletter
Public Management

DIRECTORIES:

Braddock's Federal-State-Local Government Directory (Braddock
    Communications, Alexandria, VA)
Directory of Texas City Officials (Texas Municipal League, Austin, TX)
Legislative Directory (North Central Texas Council of Government,
    Arlington, TX)
Texas Legislative Handbook (Legislative Associates, Dallas, TX)

EMPLOYERS:

City Government

Town of Addison
16801 Westgrove Dr.
Addison, TX 75248
(214) 450-2817
Jobline: (214) 450-2815
Benefits Coordinator: Marilyn LeBlanc

City of Arlington
501 Main St.
Arlington, TX 76004
Metro (817) 265-3311
Employment Specialist: Leonard Jefferson

City of Balch Springs
3117 Hickory Tree Rd.
Balch Springs, TX 75180

(214) 550-6070
Contact: City Manager

City of Bedford
2000 Forest Ridge Dr.
Bedford, TX 76021
Metro (817) 952-2100
Contact: Personnel Department

City of Burleson
141 W. Renfro St.
Burleson, TX 76028
(817) 295-1113
Personnel: Ginger Allen

City of Carrollton
1945 Jackson Rd.
Carrollton, TX 75006
(214) 466-3000
Jobline (214) 466-3376
Contact: Personnel Department

City of Cedar Hill
502 Cedar St.
Cedar Hill, TX 75104
(214) 291-5100
Director of Community Services: Greg Porter

City of Cockrell Hill
4125 W. Clarendon Dr.
Cockrell Hill, TX 75211
(214) 330-6333
City Secretary: Mary Lynn Cole

City of Colleyville
5400 Bransford Rd.
Colleyville, TX 76034
Metro (817) 498-7180
Contact: Department Head

City of The Colony
5151 N. Colony Blvd.
The Colony, TX 75056
(214) 370-5667
Personnel Director: Katherine Benavides-Martinez

City of Dallas
1500 Marilla St., 6A North
Dallas, TX 75201
(214) 670-3552
Jobline: (214) 670-5908
Contact: Personnel Department

City of DeSoto
200 S. Hampton Rd.
DeSoto, TX 75115
(214) 223-6316
Contact: Personnel Department

City of Duncanville
203 E. Wheatland Rd.
Duncanville, TX 75116
(214) 780-5006
Personnel Director: Greg Weaver

City of Euless
201 N. Ector Dr.
Euless, TX 76039
(817) 685-1400
Contact: Personnel Department

City of Everman
212 N. Race St.
Everman, TX 76140
(817) 293-0525
Personnel Assistant: David Honeycutt

City of Farmers Branch
13000 William Dodson Pkwy.
Farmers Branch, TX 75234
(214) 247-3131
Personnel Specialist: Sondra Coldwell

City of Forest Hill
6800 Forest Hill Dr.
Forest Hill, TX 76140
(817) 293-3695
Contact: Department Head

City of Fort Worth
1000 Throckmorton St.
Fort Worth, TX 76102
(817) 870-7750
Temporary Services Coordinator: Barbara Reyna

City of Garland
203 N. 5th St.
Garland, TX 75046
(214) 205-2000
Jobline (214) 205-2349
Contact: Personnel Department

City of Grand Prairie
326 W. Main St.
Grand Prairie, TX 75050

(214) 660-8190
Contact: Personnel Department

City of Grapevine
413 Main St.
Grapevine, TX 76051
Metro (817) 481-0300
Contact: Personnel Department

City of Haltom City
5024 Broadway Ave.
Haltom City, TX 76117
J(817) 834-7341
Personnel Assistant: Ruby Leath

Town of Highland Park
4700 Drexel Dr.
Dallas, TX 75205
(214) 521-4161
Contact: Personnel Department

City of Hurst
1505 Precinct Line Rd.
Hurst, TX 76054
(817) 281-6160
Personnel Manager: Doris Elston

City of Irving
825 W. Irving Blvd.
Irving, TX 75061
(214) 721-2532
Contact: Personnel Department

City of Lake Worth
6720 Telephone Rd.
Lake Worth, TX 76135
(817) 237-1211
Personnel: Dorothy Praily

City of Lancaster
211 N. Henry St.
Lancaster, TX 75146
(214) 227-2111
Assistant City Manager: Evelyn Kelly

City of Mansfield
1305 E. Broad St.
Mansfield, TX 76063
(817) 473-9371
Personnel Officer: Barbara Parker

City of Mesquite
1515 N. Galloway Ave.
Mesquite, TX 75149
(214) 216-6218
Personnel: Sherry Miller

City of North Richland Hills
7301 NE Loop 820
North Richland Hills, TX 76180
(817) 281-0041
Personnel Director: Ron McKinney

City of Plano
1520 Ave. K
Plano, TX 75074
(214) 424-6531
Joblines: Professional (214) 578-7116; and Maintenance
(214) 578-7117
Contact: Personnel Department

City of Richardson
411 Arapaho Rd.
Richardson, TX 75080
(214) 238-4150
Jobline: (214) 238-4150
Contact: Personnel Department

City of Richland Hills
3200 Diana Dr.
Richland Hills, TX 76118
(817) 595-6600
City Secretary: Pauline Kemp

City of Saginaw
333 W. McLeroy Blvd.
Saginaw, TX 76179
(817) 232-4640
Payroll Supervisor: Janice England

City of Seagoville
702 N. Hwy. 175
Seagoville, TX 75159
(214) 287-2050
Personnel Director: Cindy Brown

City of University Park
3800 University Blvd.
Dallas, TX 75205
(214) 363-1644
Personnel Director: Louanne Best

City of Watauga
7101 Whitley Rd.
Watauga, TX 76148
(817) 281-8047
City Receptionist: Cindy Brandon

County Government

Dallas County
600 Commerce St.
Dallas, TX 75202
(214) 749-8637
Contact: Personnel Department

Tarrant County
100 E. Weatherford St.
Fort Worth, TX 76196
(817) 884-1188
Personnel Director: Gerald Wright

State of Texas

Fort Worth State School
5000 Campus Dr.
Fort Worth, TX 76119
(817) 534-4831
Assistant Personnel Director: Francis Sherbert

Human Services
Regional Office
631 106th St.
Arlington, TX 76011
Metro (817) 640-5090
Contact: Personnel Office

Parks & Wildlife
Fort Worth Office
5200-A Airport Frwy.
Fort Worth, TX 76117
(817) 831-3128
Contact: Office Manager

Public Health
Region 5 Office
2561 Matlock Rd.
Arlington, TX 76015
Metro (817) 261-2911
Contact: Personnel Department

Public Safety
Region 1

350 W. Interstate 30
Garland, TX 75043
(214) 226-7611
Contact: Personnel Department

Public Safety
Fort Worth District Office
624 NE Loop 820
Hurst, TX 76053
(817) 284-1490

Rehabilitation Commission
Regional Office
3005 Alta Mere Dr.
Fort Worth, TX 76116
(817) 731-7343
Human Resource Officer: Jesus Quiroga

Texas Department of Transportation
Dallas District Office
9700 E. R. L. Thornton Frwy.
Dallas, TX 75228
(214) 320-6100
District Human Resources Officer: Stephen D. Thomas

Texas Department of Transportation, Highway Division
Fort Worth District Office
2501 SW Loop 820
Fort Worth, TX 76133
(817) 292-6510
Contact: Personnel Department

Texas Employment Commission
Administrative Office
8300 John W. Carpenter Frwy.
Irving, TX 75247
(214) 631-6050
Contact: Personnel Office

United States Government

Agriculture Department
Food & Nutrition Division
1100 Commerce St., Room E21
Dallas, TX 75242
(214) 767-0224
Personnel Specialists: Lupe Gomez, Cindy Guy, or Alex Annan

Agriculture Department
Fruit and Vegetable Division
819 Taylor St., Room 8B08
Fort Worth, TX 76102

(817) 334-2624
Director: Bryon White

Army Corps of Engineers
Fort Worth District Office
819 Taylor St., Room 4A18
Fort Worth, TX 76102
(817) 334-2208
Contact: Gerald Slusher for engineers positions and Texas
Employment Commission for other positions

Carswell Air Force Base
7 MSSQ/MSCS
Carswell Air Force Base, TX 76127
(817) 782-7829
Contact: Chief of Civilian Personnel or Texas Employment
Commission

Dallas Naval Air Station
CCPO Building 12
Dallas, TX 75211
(214) 266-6129
Contact: Civilian Personnel

Department of Defense
106 Decher Ct., Suite 300
Irving, TX 75062-2795
(214) 650-4878
Contact: Personnel RCP-3

Department of Education
Regional Office
1200 Main Tower Bldg., Room 2125
Dallas, TX 75202
(214) 767-3651
Personnel Director: Pauline Torres

Environmental Protection Agency
Regional Office
1445 Ross Ave.
Dallas, TX 75202
(214) 655-6444
Contact: Personnel Director

Federal Bureau of Investigation
Dallas Office
1801 N. Lamar St., Suite 300
Dallas, TX 75202
(214) 720-2200
Applicant Coordinator: Tom Cotton

General Services Administration
Personnel Division
819 Taylor St., 7CPT
Fort Worth, TX 76102
(817) 334-2361
Contact: Personnel Department

Department of Health and Human Services
Dallas Office
1200 Main Tower, Suite 930
Dallas, TX 75201
(214) 767-3126
Jobline: (214) 767-4930
Contact: Staffing Specialist

Department of Housing & Urban Development
Fort Worth Office
1600 Throckmorton St.
Fort Worth, TX 76102
(817) 885-5541
Personnel Officer: James G. Garcia, Jr.

Internal Revenue Service
Dallas Office
IRS Personnel
1100 Commerce St., Room 11A20
Dallas, TX 75242
(214) 767-9387
Staffing Specialist: Rose Riley

Interstate Commerce Commission
Fort Worth Office
411 W. 7th St., Suite 510
Fort Worth, TX 76102
(817) 334-3101
Contact: Mail resume to office

Department of Justice
Dallas Office, Anti-trust Division
1100 Commerce St., Room 8C6
Dallas, TX 75242
(214) 767-8051
Office Service Specialist: Lucy Lumberass

Department of Justice
Fort Worth Office
10th St. and Lamar St., Room 310
Fort Worth, TX 76102
(817) 334-3291
Personnel Officer: Janie Esclavon

Department of Labor
Office of Information
525 Griffin St.
Dallas, TX 75202
(214) 767-6812
Contact: Personnel Department

Department of Labor
Fort Worth Office, Room 7A08
819 Taylor St.
Fort Worth, TX 76102
(817) 334-3341
Contact: Dallas Labor Department office

Office of Personnel Management
1100 Commerce St., Room 6B12
Dallas, TX 75242
(214) 767-8235
Jobline: (214) 767-8035
Contact: Write for job listings

Postal Service
Main Post Office-Dallas
401 Interstate 30
Dallas, TX
(214) 741-5508
Contact: Personnel Department

Postal Service
Main Post Office-Fort Worth
4600 Mark IV Pkwy.
Fort Worth, TX 76161
(817) 625-3366
Contact: Personnel Department

Small Business Administration
Regional Office
8625 King George Dr., Building C
Dallas, TX 75235
(214) 767-7649
Contact: Mary Jo Smith

Department of Transportation
Southwest Regional Office
DOT, Federal Aviation Administration
4400 Blue Mound Rd.
Fort Worth, TX 76193
(817) 624-5838
Contact: Employment Section

Department of Treasury
Dallas Office

1200 Main St., Room 2550
Dallas, TX 75202
(214) 767-2250
Management Analyst: Sharon Rhine

Veterans Administration
Dallas Office
1100 Commerce St., Room 1B29
Dallas, TX 75242
(800) 827-2012
Contact: Office of Personnel Management

Health Care

For networking in the **health care** industry, check out the following professional organizations listed in Chapter 5:

PROFESSIONAL ORGANIZATIONS:

American Association for Respiratory Therapy
American Association of Medical Transcription
Christian Medical Society
Dallas Association of Speech Pathology and Audiology
Dallas County Chiropractic Society
Dallas Dietetic Association
Dallas Group Psychotherapy Society
Dallas Metropolitan Black Nurses Association
Dallas Psychological Association
Fort Worth District Dental Society
Licensed Vocational Nurses Association
North Texas Optometric Society
Nurses Association
Official Professional Nursing Bureau
Society of Diagnostic Medical Sonographers
Texas Association of Certified Registered Nurse Anesthetists
Tarrant County Psychological Association
Texas Nurses Association
Texas Society of Medical Assistants

For additional information, you can contact:

American Health Care Association
1201 L St., NW
Washington, DC 20005
(202) 842-4444

American Hospital Association
840 N. Lake Shore Dr.

Chicago, IL 60611
(312) 280-6000

American Medical Association
515 N. State St.
Chicago, IL 60610
(312) 464-5000

American Public Health Association
1015 15th St., NW
Washington, DC 20005
(202) 789-5600

Federation of American Health Systems
1111 19th St., NW
Washington, DC 20036
(202) 833-3090

PROFESSIONAL PUBLICATIONS:

AHA News
American Journal of Medicine
American Journal of Nursing
American Journal of Public Health
HMO Practice
Hospital & Health Services Administration
Hospitals
Modern Healthcare
Nations Health
Nursing Outlook

DIRECTORIES:

AHA Guide to the Health Care Field (American Hospital Association,
  Chicago, IL)
Directory of Hospital Personnel (Medical Device Register, Stamford, CT)
Saunders Health Care Directory (W.B. Saunders, Philadelphia, PA)

EMPLOYERS:

All Saints Episcopal Hospital
1400 8th Ave.
Fort Worth, TX 76104
(817) 926-2544
Employment Manager: Jack Lewis

Arlington Memorial Hospital
800 W. Randol Mill Rd.
Arlington, TX 76012

Metro (817) 265-5581
Personnel Director: Aleyne Brochet

Baylor University Medical Center
3500 Gaston Ave.
Dallas, TX 75246
(214) 820-1111
Assistant Personnel Director: Beverly Bradshaw

Cook's Fort Worth Children's Medical Center
801 W. 7th St.
Fort Worth, TX 76104
(817) 885-4000
Personnel Director: David Blackwell

Dallas/Fort Worth Medical Center
2709 Hospital Blvd.
Grand Prairie, TX 75051
Metro (214) 647-1141
Employee Coordinator: Linda Cox

Dallas VA Medical Center
4500 S. Lancaster Rd.
Dallas, TX 75216
(214) 376-5451
Staffing Specialist: Kim Fenton

Fort Worth Osteopathic Medical Center
1000 Montgomery St.
Fort Worth, TX 76107
(817) 735-3535
Contact: Personnel Office

Garland Community Hospital
2696 W. Walnut
Garland, TX 75042
(214) 276-7116
Personnel Director: Ed Winkelmeyer

Grapevine Medical Center
1650 W. College St.
Grapevine, TX 76051
Metro (817) 481-1588
Jobline: (817) 329-2677

HCA Medical Center of Plano
3901 W. 15th St.
Plano, TX 75075
(214) 519-1174
Contact: Personnel Department

HCA Medical Plaza Hospital
900 8th Ave.
Fort Worth, TX 76104
(817) 336-2100
Jobline: (817) 347-5793
Human Resources Director: Katherine Mackey

HCA South Arlington Medical Center
3301 Matlock Rd.
Arlington, TX 76013
Metro (817) 467-7486
Contact: Personnel Department

Harris Hospital-H.E.B.
1600 Hospital Pkwy.
Bedford, TX 76022
Metro (817) 355-7950
Contact: Personnel Department

Harris Methodist Fort Worth
1301 Pennsylvania Ave.
Fort Worth, TX 76104
(817) 882-2000
Employment Supervisor: Gay Kelley

Humana Hospital-Medical City Dallas
7777 Forest Lane
Dallas, TX 75230
(214) 661-7000
Contact: Personnel Department

Irving Community Hospital
1901 N. MacArthur Blvd.
Irving, TX 75061
(214) 579-8100
Recruitment Manager: Linda Bryan

Mansfield Community Hospital
1802 Hwy. 157 North
Mansfield, TX 76063
(817) 473-6101
Executive Secretary: Michele Shero

Medical Care International
5080 Spectrum Ave., Suite 300 W.
Dallas, TX 75248
(214) 490-3190
Director of Employee Benefits: Connie Pritchett

Memorial Hospital of Garland
2300 Marie Curie Dr.
Garland, TX 75042

(214) 487-5000
Contact: Personnel Office

Mesquite Community Hospital
3500 Hwy. I 30
Mesquite, TX 75150
(214) 270-3300
Personnel: Cindy Poole

Methodist Medical Center
301 W. Colorado Blvd.
Dallas, TX 75208
(214) 944-8181
Contact: Personnel Department

Northeast Community Hospital
1301 Airport Frwy.
Bedford, TX 76021
(817) 283-6700
Contact: Personnel Office

Parkland Memorial Hospital
5201 Harry Hines Blvd.
Dallas, TX 75235
(214) 590-8000
Contact: Personnel Department

Presbyterian Hospital of Dallas
8200 Walnut Hill Lane
Dallas, TX 75231
(214) 696-7863
Contact: Personnel Department

R.H.D. Memorial Medical Center
7 Medical Pkwy.
Farmers Branch, TX 75381
(214) 247-1000
Contact: Personnel Department

Republic Health Corp.
15303 Dallas Pkwy., Suite 1400
Dallas, TX 75248
(214) 851-3100
Recruitment Manager: Herb Cox

Richardson Medical Center
401 W. Campbell Rd.
Richardson, TX 75080
Metro (214) 231-1441
Contact: Personnel Department

St. Joseph Hospital
1401 S. Main St.
Fort Worth, TX 76104
(817) 336-9371
Contact: Personnel Department

St. Paul Medical Center
5909 Harry Hines Blvd.
Dallas, TX 75235
(214) 879-1000
Nurse Recruiter: Carey Morris; Allied Recruiter: Mary Hunt

Sanus Texas Health Plan
8600 Freeport Pkwy., Suite 3040
Irving, TX 75063
(214) 621-8143
Contact: Department Heads

John Peter Smith Hospital
1500 S. Main St.
Fort Worth, TX 76104
(817) 921-3431
Contact: Personnel Department

Texas Scottish Rite Hospital
2222 Welborn St.
Dallas, TX 75219
(214) 521-3168
Director of Human Resources: James D. Sturgis

Timberlawn Psychiatric Hospital
4600 Samuell Blvd.
Dallas, TX 75228
(214) 381-7181
Recruitment Director: James Clark

Hotels/Motels

You might also want to look at the section on **Restaurants.**

For networking in the **hospitality** industry and related fields, you can contact these professional organizations listed in Chapter 5:

PROFESSIONAL ORGANIZATIONS:

Dallas Restaurant Association
Hotel and Motel Association of Greater Dallas

For additional information, you can contact:

American Hotel & Motel Association
1201 New York Ave., NW
Washington, DC 20005
(202) 289-3100

Hotel Sales & Marketing Association International
1300 L St., NW
Washington, DC 20005
(202) 789-0089

International Special Events Society
46 Turner St.
Boston, MA 02135
(617) 254-2557

Meeting Planners International Infomart
1950 Stemmins Freeway
Dallas, TX 75207
(214) 746-5222

PROFESSIONAL PUBLICATIONS:

Hotel & Motel Management
Lodging Magazine
Meeting Manager
Meeting News
Meetings & Conventions

DIRECTORIES:

Directory of Hotel and Motel Systems (American Hotel Association,
Directory Corporation, Washington, DC)
Hotels and Motels Directory (American Business Directories, Omaha,
NE)
Meetings and Conventions–Gavel International Directory Issue (Reed
Travel Group, Seacaucus, NJ)
Successful Meetings Sourcebook (Bill Communications, New York, NY)

EMPLOYERS:

Adolphus Hotel
1321 Commerce St.
Dallas, TX 75202
(214) 742-8200
Personnel Director: Karen Ranker

Clarion Hotel
1241 W. Mockingbird Lane

Dallas, TX 75247
(214) 630-7000
Contact: Human Resources

Crescent Court Hotel
400 Crescent Court
Dallas, TX 75201
(214) 871-3200
Contact: Personnel Department

Dallas/Fort Worth Airport Marriott
8440 Freeport Pkwy.
Irving, TX 75063
(214) 929-8800
Human Resources Director: Ken Brown

Dallas Marriott Park Central
7750 LBJ Frwy.
Dallas, TX 75251
(817) 233-4421
Contact: Human Resources

Dallas Marriott Quorum
14901 Dallas Pkwy.
Dallas, TX 75240
(214) 661-2800
Director of Human Resources: Bob O'Brien

Doubletree at Lincoln Center
5410 LBJ Frwy.
Dallas, TX 75240
(214) 934-8400
Contact: Human Resources

Embassy Suites Hotel
3880 W. Northwest Hwy.
Dallas, TX 75220
(214) 357-4500
Director of Human Resources: Kassy Tanner

Fairmont Hotel
1717 N. Akard St.
Dallas, TX 75201
(214) 720-2020
Personnel Director: Ray Hassan

Four Seasons Hotel and Resort
4150 N. MacArthur Blvd.
Irving, TX 75038
(214) 717-0700
Human Resources Manager: Brenda Ruben

The Grand Kempinski Dallas
15201 Dallas Pkwy.
Dallas, TX 75248
(214) 386-6000
Contact: Personnel Department

Green Oaks Inn/Conference Center
6901 West Frwy.
Fort Worth, TX 76116
(817) 738-7311
Personnel Director: Karin Naron

Harvey Hotel-DFW Airport
4545 W. John Carpenter Frwy.
Irving, TX 75063
(214) 929-4500
Personnel Manager: Olivia Monograss

Hyatt Regency Dallas
300 Reunion Blvd.
Dallas, TX 75207
(214) 651-1234
Employment Manager: Paul Pederson

Hyatt Regency DFW
P.O. Box 619014
International Pkwy.
DFW Airport, TX 75261
(214) 453-8400
Employment Manager: Marie Tijerina

Hyatt Regency Fort Worth
815 Main St.
Fort Worth, TX 76102
Metro (817) 429-1234
Contact: Personnel Director

Loews Anatole Hotel
2201 N. Stemmons Frwy.
Dallas, TX 75207
(214) 748-1200
Employment Manager: April Vogelsang

The Mansion on Turtle Creek Hotel
2821 Turtle Creek Blvd.
Dallas, TX 75219
(214) 559-2100
Contact: Human Resources

Park Inn Plaza
1914 Commerce St.
Dallas, TX 75201

(214) 747-7000
Contact: Personnel Department

Plaza of the Americas Hotel
650 N. Pearl St.
Dallas, TX 75201
(214) 979-9000
Human Resources Director: Linda Wissen

Radisson Suite Hotel
700 E. Ave. H
Arlington, TX 76011
Metro (817) 640-0440
Contact: Department Head

Sheraton Dallas Hotel
400 N. Olive St.
Dallas, TX 75201
(214) 922-8000
Contact: Personnel Department

Sheraton Inn Mockingbird West
1893 W. Mockingbird Lane
Dallas, TX 75235
(214) 634-8850
Assistant General Manager: Paul Allen

Sheraton Park Central Hotel
12720 Merit Dr.
Dallas, TX 75251
(214) 385-3000
Director of Human Resources: Tracy Page

Stouffer Dallas Hotel
2222 Stemmons Frwy.
Dallas, TX 75207
(214) 631-2222
Personnel Assistant: Chris Martz

The Westin Hotel Galleria
13340 Dallas Pkwy.
Dallas, TX 75240
(214) 934-9494
Personnel Director: Patty Evans

Worthington Hotel
200 Main St.
Fort Worth, TX 76102
(817) 870-1000
Recruiter: Jacqueline Graham

Big rewards in hospitality business

The hotel business offers people unparalleled opportunities, says a managing director of a large Dallas hotel. Often, executives work their way up from the bottom as he did.

While still in high school, this manager began busing tables and working as a waiter and bartender. He didn't intend to stay in the business after college graduation until he realized that he could get a job at a higher management level at a hotel than if he transferred into another field.

He moved swiftly through the ranks from catering director to food and beverage manager and finally to general manager of one of the largest hotels in the Southwest.

He advises aspiring hotel managers to get a degree in business and be willing to start in a less glamorous position to establish a solid understanding of the operation.

"The hotel business is more of a lifestyle than a career because of the odd hours of working on holidays and weekends," he says. "But the rewards are great for people who prove their abilities." ■

Human Services

For more information, you can write to:

PROFESSIONAL ORGANIZATIONS:

Center for Human Services
5530 Wisconsin Ave.
Chevy Chase, MD 20815

National Association of Social Workers
7981 Eastern Ave.
Silver Spring, MD 20910

Volunteers of America
3813 N. Causeway Blvd.
Metairie, LA 70002

PROFESSIONAL PUBLICATIONS:

Children and Youth Services
The Nonprofit Times
Society

DIRECTORIES:

Directory of Community Resources for Fort Worth and Tarrant County
    (United Way, Fort Worth, TX)
Directory of Hotlines and Crisis Intervention Centers (Covenant House,
    New York, NY)
Directory of Services (Community Council of Greater Dallas)
National Directory of Children and Youth Services (Marion Peterson,
    Longmont, CO)
National Directory of Private Social Agencies (Croner Publications,
    Jericho, NY)

EMPLOYERS:

American Cancer Society
Area V Office
8900 John Carpenter Frwy.
Dallas, TX 75247
(214) 631-3850
Contact: Personnel Department
Charitable organization that provides counseling, cancer screening,
public and professional education, and conducts research.

American Cancer Society
Texas Division
2222 Montgomery St.
Fort Worth, TX 76107
(817) 737-3185
Contact: Department Head
Parallels Dallas office.

American Heart Association
National Center Office
7320 Greenville Ave.
Dallas, TX 75231
(214) 373-6300
Contact: Personnel Department
Volunteer health association for science, research, and education.

American Red Cross
Dallas County Chapter
2300 McKinney Ave.
Dallas, TX 75201
(214) 871-2175
Contact: Human Resources Department
Services provided for military families, 24-hour disaster assistance, and
community volunteer programs.

American Red Cross
Tarrant County Chapter
1515 Sylvania Ave.
Fort Worth, TX 76111
(817) 335-9137
Contact: Personnel Department
Provides first-aid classes, disaster training programs, community
volunteer service, military family assistance, and transportation for
the elderly.

Arthritis Foundation
3145 McCart Ave.
Fort Worth, TX 76110
(817) 926-7733
Executive Director: Marty Cook
Public education and special help for arthritis victims.

Association for Retarded Citizens
National Headquarters
P.O. Box 1047
Arlington, TX 76004
Metro (817) 261-6003
Contact: Personnel Department
Information and referral services for mentally retarded and their
families. Also includes respite care, citizen advocacy, and continuing
education for mentally retarded adults.

Boy Scouts of America
National Office
1325 Walnut Hill Lane
Irving, TX 75038
(214) 580-2122
Contact: Employment Office
Headquarters for national organization that sponsors education and
character-building programs for boys seven years old through high
school.

Boys' and Girls' Club of Greater Dallas
4816 Worth St.
Dallas, TX 75246
(214) 821-2950

Controller: Craig Price
Physical, educational, and vocational guidance program for boys and girls between the ages of 6 and 18.

Buckner Baptist Benevolences
5200 S. Buckner Blvd.
Dallas, TX 75227
(214) 328-3141
Contact: Department Head
Baptist General Convention of Texas supports adoption services, Buckner's Children's Home, Ryburn Home For Aging, and Mary E. Trew Home for Aging.

Catholic Charities Diocese of Dallas
3845 Oak Lawn Ave.
Dallas, TX 75219
(214) 526-2772
Administrator: Sharon Hoskin
Manages the Catholic Counseling Service, Marillac Social Center, St. Joseph Youth Center, St. Joseph Residence, and migration and refugee services.

Catholic Charities Diocese of Fort Worth
1404 Hemphill St.
Fort Worth, TX 76104
(817) 921-5381
Contact: Department Head,
Programs for underprivileged families, counseling, foster care, and adoption service. Also manages St. Theresa's Home.

Community Council of Greater Dallas
2121 Main St., Suite 500
Dallas, TX 75201
(214) 741-5851
Financial Officer: Vicki White
Organization for public and non-profit voluntary service agencies. Council provides information and referral to social services, publishes a directory, conducts surveys, and provides management assistance and planning.

Dallas County Mental Health and Mental Retardation Center
1341 W. Mockingbird Lane, Suite 1000E
Dallas, TX 75247
(214) 637-4600
Contact: Personnel Department
Comprehensive community mental health and mental retardation program with hospital, day treatment, and outpatient services.

Fort Worth State School
5000 Campus Dr.
Fort Worth, TX 76119

How To Get a Job

Metro (817) 429-0810
Personnel: Francis Sherbert
Residential campus and non-residential programs for mentally retarded.

Girl Scout Council
4411 Skillman Ave.
Dallas, TX 75206
(214) 823-1342
Assistant Executive Director: Sue Duron
Worldwide organization for girls between the ages of 5 and 17.

Edna Gladney Center
2300 Hemphill St.
Fort Worth, TX 76110
Metro (817) 429-1461
Director of Maternity Services: Elaine Brown
Unwed mother services and adoption agency.

Goodwill Industries of Dallas
2800 N. Hampton Rd.
Dallas, TX 75212
(214) 638-2800
Personnel Manager: Joy Jones
Rehabilitation services for handicapped adults. Operates stores with donated and repaired merchandise. Has job placement and vocational testing departments.

Jewish Federation of Greater Dallas
7900 Northaven Rd.
Dallas, TX 75230
(214) 739-2737
Contact: Personnel Director
Plans and coordinates health, recreation, and social services for the Dallas Jewish community, including the Dallas Home For Jewish Aged, Jewish Community Center of Dallas, and Jewish Family Services.

Jewish Social Service Agency
6801 Dan Danciger Rd.
Fort Worth, TX 76133
(817) 294-2660
Contact: Sylvia Persky
Plans and coordinates health, recreation, and social services for the Tarrant County Jewish community, including the Dan Danciger Jewish Community Center and Jewish Social Agency.

March of Dimes, Birth Defects Foundation
North Texas Chapter
5720 LBJ Frwy., Suite 180
Dallas, TX 75240
Metro (214) 988-7126

Director of Operations: Richard Stout
Provides public health education, conducts fund-raising campaigns,
and provides services for polio patients.

Mothers Against Drunk Driving
National Headquarters
511 E. John Carpenter Frwy.
Dallas, TX 75062
Personnel Manager: Debbie Charles
Provides education for responsible drinking.

Multiple Sclerosis Association
Tarrant County
617 7th Ave., Suite 405
Fort Worth, TX 76104
(817) 877-1222
Executive Director: Nancy Walters
Counseling, support groups, physical therapy, and education.

Multiple Sclerosis Society
North Texas Chapter
8214 Westchester Dr.
Dallas, TX 75225
(214) 373-1400
Administrative Assistant: Diane Jochum
Sponsors education programs, supports research, and provides patient
services and counseling.

National Kidney Foundation of Texas
13500 Midway Rd., Suite 101
Dallas, TX 75244
(214) 934-8057
Executive Director: Marla Roberts
Provides education about kidney disease, supports research, and
sponsors organ donor program.

Sickle Cell Anemia Association of Texas
617 7th Ave., Suite 402
Fort Worth, TX 76104
(817) 332-5300
Office Manager: Janice Oliver
Screening, counseling, and educational programs.

Tarrant County Mental Health & Mental Retardation Services
1319 Summit Ave.
Fort Worth, TX 76102
(817) 335-5371
Contact: Personnel Department

Provides treatment, training, and social services for mental health patients in Tarrant County, including programs for the elderly, alcohol center, family services, diagnosis service, sheltered workshops, and industrial training for the retarded.

United Way of Metropolitan Dallas
901 Ross Ave.
Dallas, TX 75202
(214) 978-0000
V.P. of Human Resources: Calvin Smith
Voluntary non-profit organization providing support to local, state, and national health agencies, family agencies, and character-building organizations. Conducts annual fund-raising campaign. Coordinates allocations of contributed funds.

United Way of Metropolitan Tarrant County
210 E. 9th St.
Fort Worth, TX 76102
(817) 878-0000
Contact: Department Head
Parallels Dallas division.

YMCA-Dallas Metropolitan Offices
601 N. Akard St.
Dallas, TX 75201
(214) 880-9622
V.P. of Human Resources and Training: Vera Mackie
Recreational and social activities for all ages and sexes at 17 area branches.

YMCA-Tarrant County Offices
540 Lamar St.
Fort Worth, TX 76102
(817) 335-6147
Contact: Personnel or individual branches
Offers similar programs as Dallas YMCA at 10 Tarrant County centers.

YWCA-Metropolitan Dallas
4621 Ross Ave.
Dallas, TX 75204
(214) 821-9595
Contact: Department Head
Provides social and recreational activities, licensed day care, and year-round special programs at seven branches.

YWCA-Tarrant County
512 W. 4th St.
Fort Worth, TX 76102
(817) 332-6191
Contact: Personnel Department
Provides residential and support services for women, child care, Y-Teens, and handicapped programs.

Employment programs for seniors

Job-hunting techniques that work for younger people aren't always as effective for individuals over the age of 55. The good-ol'-boy network begins breaking down for senior citizens as their friends retire.

It's especially hard on people who didn't plan on working past a certain age and thought they could live off savings, Social Security benefits, or pensions. Everyone thinks, this won't happen to me, but inflation and health costs can wipe out savings.

As a result, older workers sometimes need special help, and the Senior Community Service Employment Program is one of several in the Dallas/Fort Worth area that can provide it. Applicants must take a free physical and meet Department of Labor income guidelines for the economically disadvantaged.

They receive training and counseling to prepare for a part-time job and are placed in non-profit agencies. After working there for six months to a year, workers are encouraged to find work in the public or private sector.

Call (214) 520-6380 for information about the program, which is funded by the U.S. Department of Labor and sponsored by the American Association of Retired Persons and the National Retired Teachers Association. The agency's address is 2727 Inwood Rd., Suite 100, Dallas, TX 75235.

Other senior employment programs include:

Forty Plus of Dallas
301 E. Carillon Tower
13601 Preston Rd.
Dallas, TX 75240
(214) 991-9932
Self-help peer support group for unemployed professionals over age 40. Program offers a mentor system, weekly guest speakers, mock

interviews, and office computers available for resume preparation. Fee is $700 total, to be paid out: $50 application fee, $150 acceptance fee, and $50 a month plus $10 dues, which are ongoing.

Senior Community Service Project

The MASTERS Program
712 W. Magnolia Ave.
Fort Worth, TX 76104
(817) 870-8798
Mature Associates Skills Training and Referral Services (MASTERS) is a job-training and placement program for people 55 years old and older. The program provides job-search assistance, on-the-job training, job placement, and limited counseling. All applicants must be residents of Fort Worth, Euless, Haltom City, White Settlement, or Arlington.

Seniors in Community Service

Dallas Urban League
2121 Main St., Suite 410
Dallas, TX 75201
(214) 747-4734
Assists minority groups and low-income individuals who are 55 and older. Individuals undergo assessment of skills and two-week job-hunting/training course. Assists in finding full-time and part-time jobs in private companies with benefits.■

Insurance

For networking in **insurance** and related fields, check out the following professional organizations listed in Chapter 5:

PROFESSIONAL ORGANIZATIONS:

Dallas Association of Life Underwriters
Independent Insurance Agents of Dallas
Insurance Women of Dallas

For additional information, you can contact:

Amercian Council of Life Insurance
1001 Pennsylvania Ave., NW
Washington, DC 20006
(202) 624-2000

American Insurance Association
1130 Connecticut Ave., NW
Washington, DC 20036
(202) 828-7100

National Association of Life Underwriters
1922 F St., NW
Washington, DC 20006
(202) 331-6000

Society of Certified Insurance Counselors
P.O. Box 27027
Austin, TX 78755
(512) 345-7932

PROFESSIONAL PUBLICATIONS:

Best's Review
Business Insurance
Independent Agent
Insurance Advocate
The Insurance Agent
Insurance Times
National Underwriter
Underwriter's Report

DIRECTORIES:

Best's Directory of Insurance Agencies (A.M. Best Co., Oldwick, NY)
Best's Insurance Reports (A.M. Best Co., Oldwick, NY)
Insurance Almanac (Underwriter Publishing Co., Englewood, NJ)
Texas Insurance Directory (Insurance Field Co., Louisville, KY)
Underwriters Handbook (National Underwriter Company, Cincinnati, OH)

EMPLOYERS:

Aetna Life & Casualty
2350 Lakeside Blvd.
Richardson, TX 75082
(214) 470-7000
Commercial Division: Krista Herfort

Alexander & Alexander of Texas
Dallas Office
717 N. Harwood St., 19th Floor
Lock Box 8
Dallas, TX 75201
Metro (214) 263-1366
Personnel Manager: Meryl Frank

Alexander & Alexander of Texas
Fort Worth Office
6100 Western Place, Suite 100
Fort Worth, TX 76113
Metro (817) 429-3653
Personnel Administrator: Maria Jones

Allstate Insurance Co.
8711 Freeport Pkwy.
Irving, TX 75063
Metro (214) 650-8100
Human Resources Manager: Bill Ayo

American Life & Accident Insurance Co.
2909 N. Buckner Blvd.
Dallas, TX 75228
(214) 321-9700
Personnel Director: Chris Gaddis

Associates Insurance Group
250 E. John Carpenter Frwy.
Irving, TX 75062
(214) 541-3800
Contact: Human Resources Department

Auto Club Insurance Agency
4425 N. Central Expwy.
Dallas, TX 75205
(214) 526-7911
Personnel: Melanie Osborn

Blue Cross-Blue Shield of Texas
901 S. Central Expwy.
Richardson, TX 75080
Metro (214) 669-5364
Contact: Employment Department

Chubb Group of Insurance Companies
717 N. Harwood St., Suite 300
Dallas, TX 75201
(214) 754-0777
Human Resources Manager: Janice Wilsford

Combined Insurance Co. of America
3141 Hood St., Suite 700
Dallas, TX 75219
(214) 521-6340
Contact: Personnel Department

Commercial Union Insurance Co.
9330 Amberton Pkwy.
Dallas, TX 75243
(214) 783-6100
Recruiting Director: Ruby Jones

Corrigan Jordan Insurance Agency
4301 Westside, Suite 200
Dallas, TX 75209
(214) 754-0022
Office Manager: Terry Cook

Employers Insurance of Texas
1301 Young St.
Dallas, TX 75202
(214) 760-6100
Contact: Human Resources

Fidelity Union Life Insurance Co.
P.O. Box 500
Dallas, TX 75221
(214) 978-7004
Contact: Human Resources

Fireman's Fund Insurance Co.
1999 Bryan St., 9th Floor
Dallas, TX 75201

(214) 220-4000
Recruiter: Jeanine Cremers

Great Southern Life Insurance Co.
500 N. Akard St.
Dallas, TX 75201
(214) 954-7651
Contact: Personnel Department

Group Life & Health Insurance Co.
901 S. Central Expwy.
Richardson, TX 75080
(214) 669-6900
Contact: Personnel Department

Hartford Insurance Group
5001 LBJ Frwy.
Dallas, TX 75244
(214) 980-1900
Personnel Manager: Carol Neff

Jackson National Life Insurance Co. of Texas
P.O. Box 515769
Dallas, TX 75251
(214) 991-9193
Regional Vice President: Amanda Stevens

Kirby Head-Teas Insurance
One Summit Ave., Suite 400
Fort Worth, TX 76102
(817) 336-2721
Partner: Clovis Putnam

Life Insurance Co. of the Southwest
1300 W. Mockingbird Lane
Dallas, TX 75247
(214) 638-7100
Personnel: Kelly Gates

Lone Star Life Insurance Co.
4201 Spring Valley Rd.
Dallas, TX 75244
(214) 702-6400
Personnel: Neole Warsitz

Millers Insurance Group
300 Burnett St.
Fort Worth, TX 76103
(817) 332-7761
Supervisor of Personnel Services: Elaine Hargett

Mutual of Omaha Insurance Co.
6263 Harry Hinds Blvd.
Dallas, TX 75235
(214) 363-7465
Personnel Department

National Financial Life Insurance
403 S. Akard St.
Dallas, TX 75202
(214) 670-9700
Manager of Personnel and Payroll: Dot Pryer

National Foundation Life
777 Main St.
Fort Worth, TX 76102
(817) 878-3300
Manager of Human Resources: Paula Hunter

National Health Insurance Co.
P.O. Box 619999
D/FW Airport, TX 75261
Metro (817) 640-1900
Personnel Assistant: Sandra Harris

J.C. Penny Life Insurance Co.
2700 W. Plano Pkwy.
Plano, TX 75074
(214) 881-6513
Personnel Department

Philadelphia Life Insurance Co.
Lincoln Plaza, 6th Floor
500 N. Akard St.
Dallas, TX 75201
(214) 954-7111
Human Resources Recruiter: Chris Babler

Republic Insurance
2727 Turtle Creek Blvd.
Dallas, TX 75219
(214) 559-1271
Director of Human Resources: Larry Westerfield

William Rigg Co.
309 W. 7th St., Suite 200
Fort Worth, TX 76102
Metro (817) 429-0040
Controller: James Couch

Southwestern Life Insurance Co.
500 N. Akard St., 6th Floor
Dallas, TX 75201

Metro (214) 954-7703
Contact Personnel Department

States General Life Insurance Co.
P.O. Box 140500
Dallas, TX 75214
(214) 823-7450
Secretary/Treasurer: Don Morris

Texas Credit Union League and Affiliates
4455 LBJ Frwy., Suite 917
Dallas, TX 75244
(214) 980-5441
Recruiter: Perry Nelson

Transport Insurance Co.
4100 Harry Hines Blvd.
Dallas, TX 75219
(214) 526-3876
Human Resources Associate: Eva Mayberry

Transport Life Insurance Co.
714 Main St., 20th Floor
Fort Worth, TX 76102
Metro (817) 429-1620
Assistant Personnel Director: Audrey Bradford

Travelers Insurance Co.
2270 Lakeside Blvd.
Richardson, TX 75081
(214) 470-8920
Contact: Personnel Department

Trinity Universal Insurance
2000 Ross Ave.
Dallas, TX 75201
(214) 360-8000
Assistant Manager of Human Resources: Valorie Cordes

Union Bankers Insurance Co.
2551 Elm St.
Dallas, TX 75226
(214) 939-0821
Personnel Manager: Kay Reneau

United American Insurance
2909 N. Buckner Blvd.
Dallas, TX 75228
(214) 328-2841
Contact: Personnel Department

US Life Corporation
1380 River Bend Dr.
Dallas, TX 75247
(214) 631-2422
Personnel Manager: Jan Creel

Wausau Insurance Co.
1333 Corporate Dr., Suite 300
Irving, TX 75015
Metro (214) 550-1615
Personnel Director: Mark Foster

Investment Bankers/Stock Brokers

You may also want to look at the sections on **Accounting** and **Banking.**

For networking in **finance** and related fields, you can contact:

PROFESSIONAL ORGANIZATIONS:

Association for Investment Management & Research
200 Park Ave.
New York, NY 10166
(212) 957-2860

Financial Analysts Federation
5 Boar's Head Lane
P.O. Box 3668
Charlottesville, VA 22903
(804) 977-6600

International Asscociation of Financial Planning
2 Concourse Pkwy.
Atlanta, GA 30328
(404) 395-1605

Investment Counsel Association of America
20 Exchange Pl.
New York, NY 10005
(212) 344-0999

National Association of Private Placement Syndicators
P.O. Box 19074
Anaheim, CA 92817
(714) 730-6100

National Association of Securities Dealers
9513 Key West Ave.

Rockville, MD 20850
(301) 590-6500

National Venture Capital Association
1655 N. Fort Myer Dr., #700
Arlington, VA 22209
(703) 528-4370

Securities Industry Association
120 Broadway
New York, NY 10271
(212) 608-1500

Security Traders Association
1 World Traders Center, #4511
New York, NY 10048
(212) 524-0484

PROFESSIONAL PUBLICATIONS:

Business Credit
CFO
Commodity Perspective
Corporate Finance
Dun's Business Month
Finance
Financial Analysts Journal
Financial Executive
Financial World
Institutional Investor
Investment Dealers Digest
Market Chronicle
Mergers & Acquisitions
Registered Representative
Securities Week
Traders Magazine
Wall St. Transcript

DIRECTORIES:

Corporate Finance Sourcebook (National Register, Wilmette, IL)
Directory of Registered Investment Advisors (Money Market Directories,
    Charlottesville, VA)
ERISA Red Book of Pension Funds (Duns Marketing Services, Mountain
    Lakes, NJ)
*Money Magazine Special Issue: The Best Financial Planners, Money Managers
    & Stock Brokers* Fall Issue (Time, Inc., New York, NY)
Money Market Directory (Money Market Directories, Inc.,
    Charlottesville, VA)

Securities Dealers of North America (Standard and Poor's, New York, NY)
Who's Who in the Securities Industry (Economist Publishing Co., New
   York, NY)

EMPLOYERS:

Bear, Stearns & Co.
1601 Elm St., 40th Floor
Dallas, TX 75201
(214) 754-8300
Office Manager: Paula Castonguay

Cullum & Sandow
2001 Bryan Tower, Suite 1360
Dallas, TX 75201
(214) 754-0111
President: Richard Sandow

Dallas Securities Investment Corp.
4851 LBJ Freeway, 4th Floor
Dallas, TX 75244
(214) 239-2150
Office Manager: Cindy Penton

Dean Witter Reynolds
2300 Lincoln Plaza
500 N. Akard St.
Dallas, TX 75201
(214) 740-2000
Assistant Branch Manager: Pam Graig

Donaldson, Lufkin & Jenrette Securities Corp.
2200 Ross Ave., Suite 2900
Dallas, TX 75201
(214) 979-4000
Contact: Branch Manager Rhodes Bobbitt for sales positions and
Office Manager Helen Cohn for support staff positions

A.G. Edwards & Sons
One Main Place, Suite 100
Dallas, TX 75250
(214) 741-7911
Assistant Branch Manager: Chet Young or individual branches

Eppler, Guerin & Turner
1445 Ross Ave.
Dallas, TX 75202
(214) 880-9000
Personnel Director: Tanya McCann

First Southwest Co.
1700 Pacific Ave., Suite 500

Dallas, TX 75201
(214) 953-4000
Executive Vice President: Daniel Son

IDS Financial Services
801 E. Campbell Rd., Suite 150
Richardson, TX 75081
(214) 437-9311
Assistant to Division Manager: Leann Dickson

Paine Webber
Thanksgiving Square
1601 Elm St., Suite 2000
Dallas, TX 75201
(214) 978-6000
Branch Manager

Prudential Securities
10440 N. Central Expwy., Suite 1600
Dallas, TX 75231
(214) 373-2700
Branch Manager: Michael McClain

Rauscher Pierce Refsnes
Plaza of the Americas, Suite 2500
RPR North Tower, L.B. 331
Dallas, TX 75201
(214) 978-0111
Employment Specialist: Carie Elston

Rotan Mosle
1201 Elm St., Suite 2600
Dallas, TX 75270
(214) 651-6000
Administrative Manager: Pat Rawson

Shearson Lehman Hutton
1999 Bryan St., Suite 2600
Dallas, TX 75201
(214) 979-7000
Contact: Personnel Director

Smith, Barney, Harris, Upham & Co.
200 Cresent Court, Suite 1200
Dallas, TX 75201
(214) 855-7900
Contact: Arlene Jolly

Southwest Securities
1201 Elm St., Suite 4300
Dallas, TX 75270

(214) 651-1800
Contact: Personnel Administrator

H.D. Vest Financial Services
433 E. Las Colinas Blvd., 3rd Floor
Irving, TX 75039
(214) 556-1651
Contact: Department Head

Weber Investment Corporation
1525 Elm St., Suite 1800
Dallas, TX 75201
(214) 954-9472
Treasurer: Terry Rader

Law Firms

For networking in **law** and related fields, check out the following professional organizations listed in Chapter 5:

PROFESSIONAL ORGANIZATIONS:

Dallas Association of Black Women Attorneys
Dallas Association of Law Librarians
Dallas Association of Legal Secretaries
Dallas Association of Young Lawyers
Dallas Bar Association
Dallas Business League
Dallas Women Lawyers Association
Fort Worth/Tarrant County Young Lawyers Association
North Dallas Bar Association
Professional Services Marketing Association
Tarrant County Bar Association
Tarrant Conty Women's Bar Association

For more information about the legal profession, you can contact the following organizations:

American Bar Association
750 N. Lake Shore Dr.
Chicago, IL 60611
(312) 988-5000

Association of Trial Lawyers of America
1050 31st St., NW
Washington, DC 20007
(202) 965-3500

National Bar Association (minority attorneys)
1225 11th St., NW
Washington, DC 20001
(202) 842-3900

National Paralegal Association
P.O. Box 406
Solebury, PA
(215) 297-8333

PROFESSIONAL PUBLICATIONS:

ABA Journal
American Lawyer
Banking Law Journal
Criminal Law Bulletin
Lawyers' Weekly
The Paralegal
Texas Lawman
Trial

DIRECTORIES:

ABA Directory (American Bar Association, Chicago, IL)
Directory of Local Paralegal Clubs (National Paralegal Association, Solebury, PA)
Martindale-Hubbell Law Directory (Martindale-Hubbell, Summit, NJ)

EMPLOYERS:

Akin, Gump, Strauss, Hauer & Feld
4100 First City Center
1700 Pacific Ave.
Dallas, TX 75201
(214) 969-2800
Contact: Personnel Department

Arter, Hadden & Witts
1717 Main St., Suite 4100
Dallas, TX 75201
(214) 741-7561
Contact: Lori Swalm

Barlow, Garsek & Bowlers
3815 Lisbon St.
Fort Worth, TX 76107
(817) 731-4500
Office Manager for support positions: Marsha Stewart

Bishop, Payne, Lamsens & Brown
500 W. 7th St., Suite 1800
Fort Worth, TX 76102
(817) 335-4911
Office Manager: Tim Harvard

Brown, Herman, Scott, Dean & Miles
203 Fort Worth Club Building
306 W. 7th St.,
Fort Worth, TX 76102
(817) 332-1391
Contact: Partners for attorney's positions
Office Administrator: Debra Bales for support positions

Carrington, Coleman, Sloman & Blumenthal
200 Crescent Court, Suite 1500
Dallas, TX 75201
(214) 855-3000
Personnel Director: Candy Dickey

Cowles & Thompson
4000 NCNB Plaza
901 Main St.
Dallas, TX 75202
(214) 670-1100
Recruiting Coordinator: Brent Cooper
Personnel Director: Shirly Sinks

Decker, McMackim & McClain
3200 Continental Plaza
Fort Worth, TX 76102
Metro (817) 429-2740
Office Administrator: Jerry Prader

Dushman & Friedman
2620 Airport Frwy.
Fort Worth, TX 76111
(817) 834-8851
Office Manager: Larry Forderhause

Gandy, Michener, Swindle, Whitaker & Pratt
3500 City Center, Tower II
Fort Worth, TX 76102
Metro (817) 429-6268
Managing Partner: John Michener

Gardere & Wynne
1601 Elm, Suite 3000
Dallas, TX 75201
(214) 999-3000
Contact: Becky McCoy

Geary, Glast and Middleton
500 Trammell Crow Center
2001 Ross Ave.
Dallas, TX 75201
(214) 220-8200
Managing Director: Sam Glast

Godwin, Carlton & Maxwell
3300 NCNB Plaza
901 Main St.
Dallas, TX 75202
(214) 939-4400
Personnel Director: Gayle Hannah

Harris, Finley & Bogle
3100 Continental Plaza
Fort Worth, TX 76102
(817) 335-5050
Partner: Roland Johnson

Hartley, Bodennhamer and O'Neil
1300 S. University, Suite 306
301 Commerce St.
Fort Worth, TX 76107
Metro (817) 335-4275
Managing Partner: Dwight Hartley

Haynes & Boone
3100 NCNB Plaza
901 Main St.
Dallas, TX 75202
(214) 651-5000
Human Resources Manager: Tom Stewart

Hudson, Keltner, Smith, Brants & Sparks
2300 Texas American Bank Bldg.
Fort Worth, TX 76102
(817) 336-2300
Senior Partner: Harry Brants

Hughes & Luce
2800 Momentum Place
1717 Main St.
Dallas, TX 75201
(214) 939-5500
Personnel Director: Denni Washington

Jackson & Walker
6000 NCNB Plaza
901 Main St.
Dallas, TX 75202

(214) 953-6000
Personnel Coordinator: Gail Richardson

Jenkins & Gilchrist
1445 Ross Ave., Suite 3200
Dallas, TX 75202
(214) 855-4500
Personnel Director: Terry Turner

Johnson, Bromberg & Leeds
Lincoln Plaza, Suite 2600
Dallas, TX 75201
Metro (214) 740-2600
Personnel Director: Anne Pertzborn

Johnson & Gibbs
100 Founders Square
900 Jackson St.
Dallas, TX 75202
(214) 977-9000
Recruiting Administrator: Kaye Scoggin

Jones, Day, Reavis & Pogue
2001 Ross Ave., Suite 2300
Dallas, TX 75201
(214) 220-3939
Paralegals: Jerrie Hawley; Office Staff: Paula Inderwish

Kelly, Hart & Hallman
2500 First City Bank Tower
201 Main St.
Fort Worth, TX 76102
Metro (817) 429-2500
Personnel Director: Donna Gilley

Law, Snakard & Gambill
3200 Texas American Bank Bldg.
Fort Worth, TX 76102
Metro (817) 429-2991
Recruiting Coordinator: Sarah Jubela

Locke Purnell Rain Harrell
2200 Ross Ave., Suite 2200
Dallas, TX 75201
(214) 740-8000
Attornies: Joruth Oden; Office Staff: Mark Hounce

Mankoff & Hill
300 Crescent Court, Suite 700
Dallas, TX 75201
(214) 855-3700
Director of Human Resources: Mickey Held

Murphey, Moore & Bell
1300 S. University Dr., Suite 500
Fort Worth, TX 76107
(817) 336-4456
Managing Partner: Franklin Moore

Renfro, Mack & Hudman
1800 First City Bank Tower
201 Main St.
Fort Worth, TX 76102
(817) 335-6261
Office Manager: Mable Peterson

Ross and Hartley
500 E. Border St., Suite 517
Arlington, TX 76010
Metro (817) 261-7711
Firm Administrator: Linda Douglas

Shank, Irwin, Conant, Lipshy & Casterline
2100 Lincoln Plaza
500 N. Akard St.
Dallas, TX 75201
(214) 720-9700
Recruiting Coordinator: Cherie Walker

Shannon, Gracey, Ratliff & Miller
2200 First City Bank Tower
201 Main St.
Fort Worth, TX 76102
(817) 336-9333
Partner: John Bonds

Simon, Anisman, Doby, Wilson & Skillern
303 W. 10th St., Suite 400
Fort Worth, TX 76102
Metro (817) 429-3245
Personnel Manager: Suzy Stark

Strasburger & Price
901 Main St., Suite 4300
Dallas, TX 75202
(214) 651-4300

Thompson, Coe, Cousins & Irons
200 Crescent Court, 11th Floor
Dallas, TX 75201
(214) 871-8288
Partner: Jon Petterson

Vial, Hamilton, Koch & Knox
1717 Main St., Suite 4400

Dallas, TX 75201
(214) 922-9393
Attorney: Stephen Baskind

Winstead, McGuire, Sechrest & Minick
5400 Renaissance Tower
1201 Elm St.
Dallas, TX 75270
(214) 745-5406
Recruitment Director: Dominique Anderson

Worsham, Forsythe, Samples & Wooldridge
2001 Bryan Tower, Suite 3200
Dallas, TX 75201
(214) 979-3000
Office Administrator: Frances Mendoza

Management Consultants

For networking in **management consulting** and related fields, you can contact:

PROFESSIONAL ORGANIZATIONS:

Association & Institute of Management Consultants

For additional information, you can contact:

ACME-The Association of Management Consulting Firms
230 Park Ave.
New York, NY 10169
(212) 949-6571

Institute of Management Consultants
230 Park Ave.
New York, NY 10169
(212) 697-8262

Society of Professional Consultants
95 Sawyer Rd.
3 University Park Office, #400
Waltham, MA 02154
(617) 894-2547

PROFESSIONAL PUBLICATIONS:

ACME Newsletter
Academy of Management Review

Consultant News
Harvard Business Review
Journal of Management
Management Review

DIRECTORIES:

ACME Directory (ACME-Association of Management Consultants, New
    York, NY)
Association of Management Consulting Firms–Directory of Members (Council of
    Consulting Organizations, New York, NY)
Consultants & Consulting Organizations (Gale Research, Detroit, MI)
Directory of Management Consultants (Kennedy Publications,
    Fitzwilliam, NH)
Dun's Consultants Directory (Dun & Bradstreet Corp., Parsippany, NJ)
IMC Directory (Institute of Management Consultants, New York, NY)
Management Consulting (Harvard Business School Press, Cambridge, MA)

EMPLOYERS:

Booz, Allen & Hamilton
901 Main St., Suite 6500
Dallas, TX 75202
(214) 746-6500
Recruiting: Marshall Anderson

Challenger, Gray & Christmas
5501 LBJ Frwy., Suite 1000
Dallas, TX 75244
(214) 788-1816
President: Dennis G. Simon
Specialty: Outplacement and transplacement for helping spouses of
transferred employees.

Mok-Bledsoe International
14455 Webb Chapel Rd., Suite 102
Dallas, TX 75234
(214) 484-4444
President: Larry Bledsoe

RCM Corp.
1140 Fort Worth Club Tower
Fort Worth, TX 76102
(817) 335-9951
Owner: John W. Ratliff
Specialty: Mergers and acquisitions.

Taylor Management Systems
9242 Markville Dr., Suite B
Dallas, TX 75243
(214) 690-4333

President: David Taylor
Small business consulting.

Towers Perrin
12377 Merit Dr., Suite 1200
Dallas, TX 75251
(214) 233-5561
Personnel Manager: Liz Malloy

Manufacturers

To learn more about **manufacturing,** you can contact:

PROFESSIONAL ORGANIZATION:

National Association of Manufacturers
1331 Pennsylvania Ave.
Washington, DC 20004

PROFESSIONAL PUBLICATIONS:

Assembly Engineering
Design News
Iron Age
Manufacturing Engineering
Manufacturing Systems
Manufacturing Week

DIRECTORIES:

Directory of Texas Manufacturers (Bureau of Business Research, Austin, TX)
Thomas Register of Manufacturers (Thomas Publishing, New York, NY)
US Industrial Directory (Cahners Publications, Stamford, CT)

EMPLOYERS:

American Permanent Ware Co.
729 3rd Ave.
Dallas, TX 75226
(214) 421-7366
Personnel Manager: Barbara Asbury
Restaurant equipment.

Atlas Match Corp.
1801 S. Airport Circle
Euless, TX 76040
Metro (817) 267-1500

Assistant Controller: Regina Clark
Advertising matchbooks.

Baker Hughes Mining Tools
1600 S. Great Southwest Pkwy.
Grand Prairie, TX 75051
Metro (214) 988-3322
Personnel Director: Pat Morris
Rock drilling bits.

Beckett Co.
2521 Willowbrook Rd.
Dallas, TX 75220
(214) 357-6421
Secretary/Treasurer: Wingate Sung
Float valves, drinking fountains, and submergible water pumps.

Brinkman Corp.
4215 McEwen Rd.
Dallas, TX 75244
(214) 387-4939
Personnel Director: Sandra Scott
Metal detectors, meat smokers, spotlights, flashlights, and radar detectors.

Cook Machinery Co.
4301 S. Fitzhugh Ave.
Dallas, TX 75210
(214) 421-2135
Contact: Department Head
Commercial laundry equipment.

Susan Crane
8107 Chancellor Row
Dallas, TX 75247
(214) 631-6490
Human Resources: Janice Calder
Display materials, artificial flowers, and gift wrappings.

Dahlgren Manufacturing Co.
1725 Sandy Lake Rd.
Carrollton, TX 75006
(214) 245-0035
Contact: Wayne Rich
Dampening systems and printing press equipment.

Dallas Corp.
6750 LBJ Frwy., Suite 1200
Dallas, TX 75240
(214) 233-6611
Overhead doors.

Dallas Lighthouse for The Blind
P.O. Box 64420
Dallas, TX 75206
(214) 821-2375
Personnel Department: Dohn Taylor
Household items and commissary items for the government.

Dallas Woodcraft/Division of Bomar Manufacturing
2829 Sea Harbour Rd.
Dallas, TX 75212
(214) 638-2270
General Manager: James Johnson
Picture frames.

Esco Elevators
4720 Esco Dr.
Fort Worth, TX 76140
Metro (817) 478-4251
Hydraulic passenger and freight elevators.

Fojtasek Companies
2101 Union Bower Rd.
Irving, TX 75061
(214) 438-4787
Plant: Georgia Delatorri
Office: Shirley Crutcher
Aluminum extrusions, shapes, forms, windows, and patio doors.

Forney International
3405 Wiley Post Rd.
Carrollton, TX 75006
(214) 233-1871
Contact: Human Resources
Manufactures industrial boiler burners and process control systems.

Fruehauf Corp.
4800 Blue Mound Rd.
Fort Worth, TX 76106
(817) 625-2189
Contact: Personnel Department
Semi-trailers

Gifford-Hill American
1004 Meyers Rd.
Grand Prairie, TX 75050
Metro (214) 263-1990
Personnel Assistant: Billie Amick
Concrete pressure pipe and pipe fittings.

Hobart Corp.
4407 Alpha Rd.
Farmers Branch, TX 75244

How To Get a Job

(214) 233-7781
Contact: Department Head
Food equipment.

Ben Hogan Co.
2912 W. Pafford St.
Fort Worth, TX 76110
(817) 921-2661
Contact: Personnel Department
Golf clubs, golf balls, and golf apparel.

Johnson Controls
1111 Shiloh Rd.
Garland, TX 75042
(214) 494-2461
Personnel Assistant: Susan Richardson
Auto, marine, and commercial storage batteries.

Justin Industries
2821 W. 7th St.
Fort Worth, TX 76107
(817) 336-5125
Contact: Personnel Department
Diversified products, including Acme brick, Justin and Nocona boots,
ceramic cooling towers, and concrete products.

LTV Energy Products, Oil States Industries Division
7701 S. Cooper St.
Arlington, TX 76004
(817) 468-1400
Contact: Personnel Department
Rubber molded products and drilling equipment.

Lasko Metal Products
1700 Mecham Blvd.
Fort Worth, TX 76106
(817) 625-6381
Contact: Texas Employment Commission
Plastic electric fans.

MPI
1301 Cold Springs Rd.
Fort Worth, TX 76113
(817) 347-7200
Personnel: Gary Tallaut
Carpet underlay.

Otis Engineering Corp.
2601 Belt Line Rd.
Carrollton, TX 75006

(214) 418-3451
Valves and controls used in oil and gas, marine, and other large industries.

PVI Industries
3209 Galvez St.
Fort Worth, TX 76111
Metro (817) 429-1313
Human Resources Manager: Tom Lynch
Commercial, institutional, and industrial water heaters and heat exchangers.

Publishers Equipment Corp.
16660 Dallas Pkwy., Suite 1100
Dallas, TX 75248
(214) 931-2312
Contact: Personnel Office at (815) 874-8877
Newspaper printing presses.

Redman Industries
2550 Walnut Hill Lane, Suite 200
Dallas, TX 75229
(214) 353-3600
Personnel: Carolyn Pannell
Mobile homes.

Rochester Gauges of Texas
11616 Harry Hines Blvd.
Dallas, TX 75229
(214) 241-2161
Personnel Administrator: Karen Knox
Industrial gauges.

Samsill Corp.
4301 Mansfield Hwy.
Fort Worth, TX 76119
(817) 535-0203
Contact: Personnel
Office products.

Sargent-Sowell
1185 108th St.
Grand Prairie, TX 75050
(214) 647-1525
Street signs.

Shoreline Products
921 W. Mayfield Rd.
Arlington, TX 76015
Metro (817) 467-7871
President: Don Staines
Boat trailers and other pleasure trailers.

Snapper Power Equipment
5000 South Frwy.
Fort Worth, TX 76115
(817) 921-3611
Personnel Director: Maggie Grinstead
Garden and lawn equipment.

Snow Corp.
3817 Rutledge St.
Fort Worth, TX 76107
(817) 732-5554
Comptroller: Monty Rockwell
Plastic process machinery and molded plastic products.

Southwestern Petroleum Corp.
534 N. Main St.
Fort Worth, TX 76101
(817) 332-2336
Contact: Personnel Department
Building products, roofing materials, and lubricants.

Telsco Industries
3301 W. Kingsley Rd.
Garland, TX 75041
(214) 278-6131
Contact: Texas Employment Commission
Lawn sprinklers compression systems.

Texas Industries
7610 N. Stemmons Frwy.
Dallas, TX 75247
Toll Free (214) 647-3902
Contact: Personnel Department
Cement, concrete products, and related materials.

Texstar
802 Ave. J East
Grand Prairie, TX 75050
Metro (214) 647-1366
Personnel Administrator: Gayle Landers
Plastic molders and fabricators.

Trane Co.
13821 Diplomat Dr.
Dallas, TX 75234
(214) 406-6000
Contact: Department Head
Air-conditioning equipment for buildings, buses, trucks, and mass
transit vehicles.

Triangle Pacific Corp.
16803 Dallas Pkwy.

Dallas, TX 75266
(214) 931-3000
Personnel Assistant: Carey Johnson
Cabinet and hardwood floors.

Universal Manufacturing Co.
900 S. Cedar Ridge Rd.
Duncanville, TX 75137
(214) 298-0531
Contact: Department Head
Metal enclosures for electrical wiring.

Media: Print

For networking in the **magazine and newspaper** publishing business, check out the following professional organizations listed in Chapter 5:

PROFESSIONAL ORGANIZATIONS:

American Society of Magazine Photographers
Dallas/Fort Worth Association of Black Communicators
Dallas Professional Photographers Association
Network of Hispanic Communicators
Newspaper Advertising Sales Association
Press Club of Dallas
Society of Professional Journalists
Women in Communications

For additional information, you can contact:

American Newspaper Publishers Association
Dulles International Airport
P.O. Box 17407
Washington, DC 20041
(703) 648-1000

Magazine Publishers Association
575 Lexington Ave.
New York, NY 10022
(212) 752-0055

National Newspaper Association
1627 K St., NW, #400
Washington, DC 20006
(202) 466-7200

Suburban Newspapers of America
401 N. Michigan Ave.

Chicago, IL 60611
(312) 644-6610

PROFESSIONAL PUBLICATIONS:

Columbia Journalism Review
Editor & Publisher Market Guide
Folio
Publishers Auxiliary
Suburban Publisher
The Writer
Writer's Digest

DIRECTORIES:

Editor & Publisher International Yearbook (Editor & Publisher, New York, NY)
Hispanic Media and Markets Directory (Standard Rate & Data Service, Wilmette, IL)
Magazine Industry Marketplace (R.R. Bowker, Inc., New York, NY)
Media Review Digest (Pierian Press, Ann Arbor, MI)
SNA Membership Directory (Suburban Newspapers of America, Chicago, IL)

EMPLOYERS:

Adweek/Southwest
2909 Cole Ave., Suite 220
Dallas, TX 75204
(214) 871-9550
Editor: Monica Reeves
Weekly trade publication for the advertising, marketing, and public relations industries.

Arlington Citizen-Journal
1111 W. Abram St.
Arlington, TX 76010
Metro (817) 261-1191
Contact: *Fort Worth Star-Telegram* personnel office, (817) 390-7459
Community newspaper published twice weekly.

Associated Press
4851 LBJ Frwy., Suite 30
Dallas, TX 75244
(214) 991-2100
A.C.O.B.: Dave Sedeno
Wire service.

Aura of Fort Worth
2917 Morton
Fort Worth, TX 76107

(817) 336-7453
Editor: John Paschal
Publisher: Doug Jumper
Bimonthly city lifestyle magazine.

Carrollton Chronicle
102 Lakeland Plaza
Lewisville, TX 75067
(214) 446-0303
Executive Editor: Wayne Esperson
Weekly newspaper.

D Magazine
3988 N. Central Expwy., Suite 1200
Dallas, TX 75204
(214) 827-5000
Editor: Melissa Houtte
Monthly city magazine.

D/FW People
400 Fuller-Wiser Rd., Suite 125
Euless, TX 76039
Metro (817) 540-4666
General Manager: Jamie Ross
Weekly newspaper.

Dallas Business Journal
4131 N. Central Expwy., Suite 310
Dallas, TX 75204
Metro (214) 263-0449
Contact: Department Head
Weekly business newspaper.

Dallas/Fort Worth Suburban Newspapers
1000 Ave. H East
Arlington, TX 76011
Metro (817) 695-0500
Editor: Banks Disham
Chain of community newspapers owned by the Belo Corporation
that publishes the *Arlington Daily News, Garland Daily News, Grand
Prairie Daily News, Irving Daily News, Mesquite Daily News, Mid-Cities
Daily News,* and *Richardson Daily News.*

The Dallas Morning News
Communications Center
Dallas, TX 75265
(214) 977-8222
Contact: Personnel Department
Major daily newspaper with a morning edition.

Dallas Observer
3211 Irving Blvd., Suite 110

Dallas, TX 75247
(214) 637-2072
Weekly entertainment and features publication.

Dallas Times Herald
1101 Pacific Ave.
Dallas, TX 75202
(214) 720-6111
Contact: Human Resources Department
Major daily newspaper with morning and evening editions.

Duncanville Suburban
606 Oriole Blvd.
Duncanville, TX 75116
(214) 298-4211
Personnel Manager: Cathy Ramsy
Weekly newspaper.

El Sol De Texas
4260 Spring Valley Rd.
Dallas, TX 75244
(214) 386-9120
V.P. of Telemarketing: Jaime Montano
Weekly Spanish-language newspaper with news about Dallas, Fort
Worth, and Latin countries

Farmers Branch Times
1712 Belt Line Rd.
Carrollton, TX 75006
(214) 446-0303
Executive Editor: Wayne Epperson
Weekly newspaper.

Fort Worth Star-Telegram
400 W. 7th St.
Fort Worth, TX 76101
Metro (817) 429-2655
Contact: Personnel Department
Fort Worth's major daily newspaper with morning and evening
editions.

Grapevine Sun
322 S. Main St.
Grapevine, TX 76051
(214) 434-2300
Personnel Director: Carol Puckett
Newspaper published twice weekly.

Lancaster News
330 W. Pleasant Run Rd.
Lancaster, TX 75146
(214) 227-6033

Publisher: Linda Ball
Weekly newspaper.

Lewisville Daily Leader
Professional Building, Suite 100
Lakeland Plaza
Lewisville, TX 75067
(214) 436-3566
Editor: Wayne Epperson
Newspaper published five times a week.

Lewisville News
131 W. Main St.
Lewisville, TX 75067
(214) 436-5551
Contact: Editor
Newspaper published three times a week.

Metrocrest News
1430 Valwood Pkwy., Suite 125
Carrollton, TX 75006
(214) 243-0194
Personnel Director: Phyllis Masalkoski
Weekly newspaper.

Park Cities News
8115 Preston Rd., Suite 120
Dallas, TX 75225
(214) 369-7570
Publisher: Marj Waters
Weekly newspaper.

Park Cities People
8115 Preston Rd., Suite 120
Dallas, TX 75225
(214) 739-2244
Executive V.P.: Jim Wilson
Weekly newspaper.

Plano Daily Star-Courier
801 E. Plano Parkway
Plano, TX 75074
(214) 424-6565
Editor: Wayne Epperson
Daily newspaper.

The Texas Lawyer
1 Ferris Plaza
400 S. Record St., Suite 1400
Dallas, TX 75202
(214) 744-9300

Publisher/Editor: Mark Obbie
Weekly publication for the legal profession.

Travelhost Magazine
8080 N. Central Expwy., 14th Floor
Dallas, TX 75206
(214) 691-1163
Office Manager: Nancy E. Chaussee
Weekly travel magazine.

United Press International
13900 Midway Rd.
Dallas, TX 75244
(214) 980-8300
Personnel Coordinator: Christa Clark at main ofice in Fairfax, VA,
(703) 359-6262
Wire service.

The Wall Street Journal
1233 Regal Row
Dallas, TX 75247
(214) 631-7250
Personnel Manager: Lisa Charles in South Brunswick, New Jersey
(609) 520-4128
Publishing office for the Southwest edition of this leading financial
newspaper, published Monday through Friday.

**Trials of the
trailing spouse**

For years Taunne Besson has helped spouses who are out of work because their mates have been transferred settle into the D/FW area and find new careers. As part of several national networks, she works with clients who are moving from anywhere in the U.S. and often abroad.

Besson recognizes that most relocating people feel uprooted and really miss the support system they have developed in their former cities. Consequently, "plugging into" D/FW will be as important as finding a new job. To accomplish both goals simultaneously, Taunee says, talk to the people you already know in your present town. Ask friends, colleagues at work and in professional organizations, fellow church members, school and fraternity alums, etc., who they know in D/FW. This can serve as the basis for an excellent network of people with like interests who are genuinely concerned about facilitating your job search and making you feel welcome when you arrive.

Also be sure to check with your spouse's (partner's) company to see if they provide job-search counseling or a resume exchange with other firms. Take advantage of every resource available.■

Metal Products

Major trade publications read by **metal products** manufacturers include:

PROFESSIONAL PUBLICATIONS:

Assembly Engineering
Design News
Iron Age
Manufacturing Systems

DIRECTORY:

Dun's Industrial Guide: The Metalworking Directory (Dun's Marketing
   Services, Parsippany, NJ)

EMPLOYERS:

A.S.C. Pacific
404 E. Dallas Rd.
Grapevine, TX 76051
Metro (817) 481-3521
Contact: Department Head
Sheet belting components.

Anchor Crane & Hoist Service Co.
2020 E. Grauwyler Rd.
Irving, TX 75061
(214) 438-5100
Contact: Department Head
Manufactures overhead cranes and hoists.

Austin Steel Co.
1815 Coombs St.
Dallas, TX 75215
(214) 421-2141
Corporate Secretary: Paul Davenport
Steel fabricators.

Barker & Bratton Steel
10733 Newkirk St.
Dallas, TX 75220
(214) 556-1951
Contact: J.W. Bratton for shop positions and David Bratton for office positions
Steel fabricators.

Commercial Metals Co.
7800 Stemmons Frwy.
Dallas, TX 75247
(214) 689-4300
Corporate Personnel Director: Jesse Barnes
Secondary metals processing, steel manufacturing, and trading.

Cronus Industries
12700 Park Central Dr., Suite 300
Dallas, TX 75251
(214) 386-2900
Contact: Personnel Department
Manufactures heat transfer equipment.

General Aluminum Corp.
1001 W. Crosby Rd.
Carrollton, TX 75006
(214) 242-5271
Professional positions: Hal Giddens; Industrial and office personnel: Linda Boustos
Manufactures aluminum windows and sliding glass doors.

Glitsch
4900 Singleton Blvd.
Dallas, TX 75212
(214) 631-3841
Employee Relations: Peggy White
Heavy metal fabricator that manufactures metal plates, petroleum refinery processing equipment, and pollution control devices.

G. H. Hensley Co.
2108 Joe Field Rd.
Dallas, TX 75229
(214) 241-2321
Personnel Manager: Tom McKormick
Steel foundry, producing steel castings and construction equipment parts.

Keystone Consolidated Industries
5430 LBJ Frwy., Suite 1700
Dallas, TX 75234
(214) 458-0028

Contact: Personnel Manager
Manufactures wire products and locks.

M&M Manufacturing Co.
200 Adolph St.
Fort Worth, TX 76107
(817) 336-2311
Shop Supervisor: Don Colley
Manufactures air-conditioning ducts and pipes and sheet metal products.

Martin Sprocket & Gear & Fairmount Tools
3600 McCart St.
Fort Worth, TX 76101
Metro (817) 654-4505
Contact: Personnel Department
Manufactures mechanical power transmission and bulk materials handling equipment.

Mesco Metal Buildings Corp.
Hwy. 114 and N. Kimball Rd.
Southlake, TX 76051
Metro (817) 481-2501
Contact: Department Heads
Manufactures metal building systems.

Nasco Steel
1909 Northpark Dr.
Fort Worth, TX 76102
(817) 332-7069
President: Val Martin
Steel fabrication company.

North Texas Steel Co.
412 W. Bolt St.
Fort Worth, TX 76110
Metro (817) 654-3328
Controller: Bill Fudge
Fabricated structural steel.

RSR Corp.
1111 W. Mockingbird Lane
Dallas, TX 75247
(214) 631-6070
Industrial Relations Manager: Rod Pestinger
Secondary lead smelter.

Skotty Aluminum Products Co.
2100 E. Union Bower Rd.
Irving, TX 75061

(214) 445-0040
Office Manager: Shirly Crutcher
Manufactures aluminum windows.

Temtex Industries
3010 LBJ Frwy., Suite 650
Dallas, TX 75234
(214) 484-1845
Vice President of Finance: Roger Stibers
Manufactures fabricated metal and structural clay products.

Texas Steel Co.
3901 Hemphill St.
Fort Worth, TX 76110
(817) 923-4611
Industrial Relations Manager: Wendall Pender
Manufactures steel castings for machinery parts.

Thornton Industries
2700 W. Pafford St.
Fort Worth, TX 76110
(817) 926-3321
Contact: Department Head
Structural steel fabricators.

Trinity Industries
501 Maple Ave.
Dallas, TX 75235
(214) 631-4420
Human Resources: Bobbie Carol
Produces fabricated structural steel and steel platework.

Trinity Industries
2548 NE 28th St.
Fort Worth, TX 76110
Metro (817) 429-3453
Contact: Personnel Department
Steel fabricators.

Museums and Art Galleries

To learn more about running **museums and art galleries,** you can
contact:

PROFESSIONAL ORGANIZATIONS:

American Association of Museums
1225 I St., NW

Washington, DC 20005
(202) 289-1818

National Assembly of Local Art Agencies
1420 K St., NW
Washington, DC 20005
(202) 371-2830

National Assembly of State Arts Agencies
1010 Vermont Ave., NW
Washington, DC 20005
(202) 347-6352

PROFESSIONAL PUBLICATIONS:
Art Forum
Art World
Aviso
Connections Monthly
Museum News
NASAA News

DIRECTORIES:

Artsource Texas (Dallas Public Library, Dallas, TX)
NASAA Directory (National Assembly of State Arts Agencies, Washington, DC)
Official Museum Directory (American Association of Museums, Washington, DC)
Texas Museum Directory (Texas Historical Commission, Austin, TX)

EMPLOYERS:

Amon Carter Museum
3501 Camp Bowie Blvd.
Fort Worth, TX 76107
(817) 738-1933
Personnel Services Coordinator: Kathy Goodale
Western art collection with special exhibits.

Biblical Arts Center
7500 Park Lane
Dallas, TX 75225
(214) 691-4661
Director: Ronnie Roesy
Religious-theme exhibits, including Miracle at Pentacost.

Dallas Fire Fighters Museum
3801 Parry Ave.
Dallas, TX 75226
(214) 821-1500

Director: James L. Clay
Display of antique fire trucks and firefighting equipment in historic setting.

Dallas Museum of Art
1717 N. Harwood St.
Dallas, TX 75201
(214) 922-1200
Personnel Director: Scott Gensemer
Dallas' largest fine arts museum, with Old Masters, modern, pre-Columbian, and American art.

Fort Worth Museum of Science & History
1501 Montgomery St.
Fort Worth, TX 76107
Metro (817) 654-1356
Contact: Department Head
Hall of Texas history exhibit, planetarium, and Omni Theater.

Kimbell Art Museum
3333 Camp Bowie Blvd.
Fort Worth, TX 76107
Metro (817) 654-1034
Associate Director for Administration: Barbara White
Fort Worth's largest fine arts museum, with extensive permanent collection and special exhibits.

Meadows Museum
Owen Fine Arts Center
SMU Campus
Dallas, TX 75275
(214) 692-2516
Acting Director: Samuel K. Heath
Spanish drawings and prints.

Modern Art Museum of Fort Worth
1309 Montgomery St.
Fort Worth, TX 76107
(817) 738-9215
Contact: Personnel Department
Modern art museum, with special exhibits.

Old City Park
1717 Gano St.
Dallas, TX 75215
(214) 421-5141
Director: Dr. Tom Smith
Historical buildings and exhibits located in park near downtown Dallas.

Sid Richardson Collection of Western Art
309 Main St.

Fort Worth, TX 76102
(817) 332-6554
Director: Jan Brenneman
Western art and special exhibits.

Science Place
Fair Park
1318 2nd Ave.
Dallas, TX 75210
(214) 428-7200
Contact: Personnel Department
Museum with permanent and special science and energy exhibits and planetarium shows

Paper/Packaging/Allied Products

For more information about the **paper industry,** you can write to:

PROFESSIONAL ORGANIZATIONS:

American Paper Institute
260 Madison Ave.
New York, NY 10016

Paper Industry Management Association
2400 E. Oakton St.
Arlington Hts., IL 60005

PROFESSIONAL PUBLICATIONS:

Good Packaging Magazine
Packaging
Paper Trade Journal
Pulp and Paper
Pulp and Paper Week
TAPPI Journal
World Wood

DIRECTORIES:

American Papermaker—Mill and Personnel Issue (MacClean/Hunter
     Publishing, Atlanta, GA)
Lockwood-Post's Directory of the Pulp, Paper and Allied Trades (Miller
     Freeman, New York, NY)
Official Container Directory (Edgall Communications, Chicago, IL)

Secondary Wood Products Manufacturers Directory (Miller Freeman, New York, NY)
TAPPI Directory (Technical Association of the Pulp and Paper Industry, Atlanta, GA)

EMPLOYERS:

American Excelsior Co.
900 Ave. H East
Arlington, TX 76011
Metro (817) 640-2161
Branch Manager: Bob Landon
Manufactures protective shipping pads, fabricated polyurethane foam, and related products.

Arrow Industries
2625 Belt Line Rd.
Carrollton, TX 75006
(214) 620-2902
Contact: Personnel Department
Manufactures paper plates and packaged dry food products.

Bates Container
6433 Davis Blvd.
North Richland Hills, TX 76180
Metro (817) 498-3200
Personnel Manager: Sally Hackfeld
Manufactures corrugated board.

Campbell Paper Co.
5300 W. Vickery Blvd.
Fort Worth, TX 76107
Metro (817) 429-8471
President: Jerry Whittacker
Distributor of paper for food service, retail, janitorial supplies, and computers.

Champion International Corp.
1901 Windsor Place
Fort Worth, TX 76110
(817) 926-6661
Contact: Texas Employment Commission
Manufactures milk cartons.

Clampitt Paper Co.
2101 Franklin Dr.
Fort Worth, TX 76106
Metro (817) 988-7192
Contact: Duane Pelvel or Steve Romaine
Paper distribution company.

Container Corp. of America
6701 South Frwy.
Fort Worth, TX 76134
(817) 568-3420
Personnel: Bess Miller
World's largest producer of paperboard packaging, including folding
cartons, sanitary food containers, and sales promotional products.

Dixico
1300 Polk St.
Dallas, TX 75224
(214) 943-0740
Human Resource Manager: Christine Hunt
Manufactures snack food packaging.

Kimberly-Clark Corp.
545 E. John W. Carpenter Frwy.
Irving, TX 75062
(214) 830-1483
Human Resources: Barbara Kents
World headquarters for producers of household, personal care,
business, and health care paper products.

Olmsted-Kirk Paper Co.
2420 Butler St.
Dallas, TX 75235
(214) 637-2220
Personnel Director: Tom Harmon
Wholesale paper distributor for specialty products and industrial
papers. Operates graphic arts and retail centers. Branch office in Fort
Worth.

Packaging Corp. of America
1001 113th St.
Arlington, TX 76011
Metro (817) 640-1888
Contact: Personnel Department
Manufactures corrugated containers.

Princeton Packaging
14240 Proton Rd.
Dallas TX 75244
(214) 387-0700
Director of Human Resources: T.M. Foran
Manufactures flexible packaging products.

Rock-Tenn Co.
1120 E. Clarendon Dr.
Dallas, TX 75203
(214) 941-3400
Personnel: Kent Southerland
Manufactures paperboard and paperboard packing products.

Stone Container Corp.
2302 W. Marshall Dr.
Grand Prairie, TX 75051
(214) 647-1333
Personnel Administrator: May Hanke
Manufactures corrugated boxes.

Westvaco Corp.
10700 Harry Hines Blvd.
Dallas, TX 75220
(214) 352-9791
Personnel: Sandy Tuel
Manufactures envelopes.

Printers

For networking in **printing** and related fields, you can check out the following professional organization listed in Chapter 5:

PROFESSIONAL ORGANIZATIONS:

Printing Industries Association of Texas

For more information, you can write to:

National Association of Printers and Lithographers
780 Palisade Ave.
Teaneck, NJ 07666

Technical Association of the Graphic Arts
Box 9887
Rochester, NY 14614

PROFESSIONAL PUBLICATIONS:

American Printer
Graphic Arts Monthly
Print
Printing News

DIRECTORIES:

Design Firms Directory (Wefler and Associates, Evanston, IL)
Graphic Arts Monthly Buyer's Guide/Directory Issue (Cahners Publishing, New York, NY)
Graphic Arts Blue Book (A.F. Lewis & Co., New York, NY)

EMPLOYERS:

Allied Printing Co.
501 N. Good-Latimer Expwy.
Dallas, TX 75204
(214) 827-5151
Contact: Department Head
Printing and publishing company.

American Signature Graphics
6320 Denton Dr.
Dallas, TX 75235
(214) 358-1371
Contact: Department Head
Prints periodicals.

Anchor Press
820 N. Main St.
Fort Worth, TX 76106
(817) 335-4861
Office Manager: Cindy Ford
Commercial printing.

Bennett Printing Co.
990 S. St. Paul St.
Dallas, TX 75201
(214) 741-7751
Contact: Joyce Adam
Commercial printing.

Blanks Engraving
2343 N. Beckley Ave.
Dallas, TX 75208
(214) 741-3905
Personnel Manager: Elaine Grant
Four-color separations, flexo-separations, stripping, photopolymer
plates.

Branch-Smith
120 St. Louis Ave.
Fort Worth, TX 76104
(817) 332-6306
Contact: Department Head
Advertising, printing, and publishing of trade magazines.

Buchanan Printing Co.
2330 Jett St.
Dallas, TX 75234
(214) 241-3311
Contact: Department Head
Commercial printing.

Deluxe Check Printers
9125 Viscount Row
Dallas, TX 75247
(214) 631-7780
Personnel Manager: Lisa Shinn
Check printing company.

Evans Press
5133 Northeast Pkwy.
Fort Worth, TX 76106
(817) 626-1901
Plant Manager: Bill Haley
Prints college handbooks.

Horticulture Printers
3638 Executive Blvd.
Mesquite, TX 75149
(214) 289-0705
Vice President: Vera Rhodes
Commercial and horticultural printing.

Printing Center of Texas
701 E. 5th St.
Fort Worth, TX 76102
Metro (817) 429-2320
Contact: Personnel Department
Prints books, newspapers, circulars, and college catalogs.

Retail Graphics Printing Co.
8000 Ambassador Row
Dallas, TX 75247
(214) 630-9900
Personnel: Margrett Kemp
Newspaper insert printing.

Riverside Press
4901 Woodall St.
Dallas, TX 75247
(214) 631-1150
Contact: Personnel Department
Commercial printing.

VIP Printing
2800 112th St.
Grand Prairie, TX 75050
Metro (214) 647-8888
Personnel: Lori Fabic
Commercial printing.

Williamson Printing Corp.
6700 Denton Dr.
Dallas, TX 75235

(214) 352-1122
Vicew President of Personnel: Tony LaLumia
Commercial printing

Real Estate

You may also want to look at the section on **Architecture.**

For networking in **real estate** and related fields, check out the following professional organizations listed in Chapter 5:

PROFESSIONAL ORGANIZATIONS:

National Society of Real Estate Appraisers
Society of Industrial and Office Realtors

For additional information, you can contact:

American Association of Certified Appraisers
800 Compton Rd.
Cincinnati, OH 45231
(513) 729-1400

American Society of Appraisers
535 Herndon Pkwy., #150
Herndon, VA 22070
(703) 478-2228

Building Owners & Managers Association International
1201 New York Ave., NW
Washington, DC 20006
(202) 223-9669

National Association of Realtors
430 N. Michigan Ave.
Chicago, IL 60611
(312) 329-8200

National Network of Commercial Real Estate Women
808 17th St., NW, #3200
Washington, DC 20006
(202) 223-9669

PROFESSIONAL PUBLICATIONS:

Banker & Tradesman
National Real Estate Investor
Real Estate News

Realty & Building
Southwest Real Estate News

DIRECTORIES:

American Real Estate Guide (LL&IL Publishing, Marhasset, NY)
American Society of Real Estate Counselors Directory (ASREC, Chicago, IL)
Construction Users Guide & Directory (Associated Builders & Contractors, Burlington, MA)
Directory of Certified Residental Brokers (Retail National Marketing Institute, Chicago, IL)

EMPLOYERS:

BEI Real Estate Services
5400 LBJ Frwy., Suite 900
Dallas, TX 75240
(214) 385-8333
Personnel Director: Jean Higgens

Blackland Properties
P.O. Box 2129
Dallas, TX 75221
(214) 954-0099
Contact: Mail resume to Personnel Department

Bramalea Texas
901 Main St., Suite 5000
Dallas, TX 75202
(214) 761-6200
Office Manager: Debra DeCathelineau

Centennial Homes
5720 LBJ Frwy., Suite 610
Dallas, TX 75240
(214) 458-9909
Personnel Director: Thelma Wallace

Century 21 Real Estate of Northern Texas
420 Decker Rd., Suite 200
Irving, TX 75062
(214) 541-0221
Contact: Department Head

Coldwell Banker Commercial Real Estate Co.
5400 LBJ Frwy., Suite 1100
Dallas, TX 75240
(214) 458-4800
Sales Manager: Jana Thays

Trammell Crow Co.
3500 Trammell Crow Center
2001 Ross Ave.
Dallas, TX 75201
(214) 979-5404
Contact: Staff Recruiter

Cushman & Wakefield of Texas
5430 LBJ Frwy., Suite 1100
Dallas, TX 75240
(214) 770-2500
Contact: Department Head or Branch Manager

Dal-Mac Development Corp.
111 W. Spring Valley Rd.
Richardson, TX 75083
(214) 238-0401
Personnel Manager: Jenny Espino

Hank Dickerson & Co.
5950 Berkshire Lane, Suite 1500, L.B. #5
Dallas, TX 75225
(214) 360-4500
Contact: Personnel Manager

ERA Real Estate
Southwest Regional Headquarters
400 E. Las Colinas Blvd., Suite 1035
Irving, TX 75039
(214) 556-0362
Contact: Office managers at ERA offices

Folsom Investments
16475 Dallas Pkwy., Suite 800
Dallas, TX 75248
(214) 931-7400
Contact: Department Head

Fox & Jacobs/Centex
3333 Lee Pkwy.
Dallas, TX 75219
(214) 559-6500
Coordinator: Jane Mongiafico

Gemcraft Homes
605 Perry Ct.
Bedford, TX 75104
Metro (214) 299-9393
Contact: Personnel Department

General Homes Corp.
14800 Quorum, Suite 370

Dallas, TX 75240
(214) 392-9200
Manager: Margie McGee

Ebby Halliday Realtors
4455 Sigma Rd.
Dallas, TX 75244
(214) 980-6600
Personnel Director: Florence Willess

JPI Realty
5215 N. O'Connor Rd.
Irving, TX 75039
(214) 556-0300
Contact: Department Head

Lehndorff Management USA
2501 Cedar Springs Rd., Suite 340
Dallas, TX 75201
(214) 855-5800
Employment and Records Supervisor: Shannon Northcutt

Lincoln Property Co.
3300 Lincoln Plaza
500 N. Akard St.
Dallas, TX 75201
(214) 740-3300
Vice President of Personnel: David McCoy

Henry S. Miller Real Estate Co.
2001 Bryan Tower, Suite 3000
Dallas, TX 75201
(214) 748-9171
Personnel: Theresa Tucker

Raymond D. Nasher Co.
8950 N. Central Expwy., Suite 400
Dallas, TX 75231
(214) 369-1234
Contact: Personnel Department

Paragon Group
7557 Rambler Rd., Suite 1200
Dallas, TX 75231
(214) 891-2000
Contact: Department Head

Prentiss Properties
1717 Main St., Suite 5000
Dallas, TX 75201
(214) 761-1440
Personnel: John Shasteen or Kathy Murphy

Pulte Home Corp. of Texas
2221 E. Lamar Blvd., Suite 700
Arlington, TX 76006
Metro (817) 640-7227
Contact: Personnel Department

The Swearingen Co.
3811 Turtlecreek Blvd., Suite 1400
Dallas, TX 75219
(214) 443-2700
Contact: Employee Benefits Coordinator

Vantage Companies
2777 Stemmons Frwy., Suite 1902
Dallas, TX 75207
(214) 631-0600
Vice President of Human Resources: Joe McFadin

Woodbine Development Corp.
1445 Ross at Field
Dallas, TX 75202
Metro (214) 263-2724
Contact: Personnel

Recreation/Sports/Fitness

For networking in **recreation/sports/fitness** and related fields, check out this professional organization listed in Chapter 5:

PROFESSIONAL ORGANIZATIONS:

Texas Recreation & Park Society

For additional information, you can contact:

Aerobics & Fitness Association of America
15250 Ventura Blvd., #310
Sherman Oaks, CA 91403
(818) 905-0040

National Association of Sporting Goods Wholesalers
Box 11344
Chicago, IL 60611
(312) 565-0233

National Collegiate Athletic Association
66201 College Blvd.
Overland Park, KS 66211
(913) 339-1906

National Recreation & Parks Association
3101 Park Center Dr.
Alexandria, VA 22302
(703) 820-4940

National Sporting Goods Association
1699 Wall St.
Mt. Prospect IL 60056
(703) 439-4000

PROFESSIONAL PUBLICATIONS:

American Fitness
NCAA News
Parks & Recreation
Sporting Goods Dealer
Sporting Goods Trade
Sporting Goods Wholesaler
Team Lineup

DIRECTORIES:

Health Clubs Directory (American Business Directories, Omaha, NE)
NCAA Directory (NCAA, Overland Park, KS)
New American Guide to Athletics, Sports, and Recreation (New American
     Library, New York, NY)
Salesman's Guide to Sporting Goods Buyers (Salesman's Guides, New York, NY)
Sporting Goods Directory (Sporting Goods Dealer, St. Louis, MO)
Sports Administration Guide & Directory (National Sports Marketing
     Bureau, New York, NY)
Sports Marketplace (Sportsguide, Princeton, NJ)

EMPLOYERS:

Aerobics Activity Center
12100 Preston Rd.
Dallas, TX 75230
(214) 233-4832
Contact: Jenny Seamster or Sheri Pearce
Fitness center.

Bent Tree Country Club
5201 Westgrove Dr.
Dallas, TX 75248
(214) 931-7326
Contact: Personnel
Private country club.

Brookhaven Country Club
3333 Golfing Green Dr.

Farmers Branch, TX 75234
(214) 243-6151
Personnel Director: Deborah Travis
Private country club.

Colonial Country Club
3735 Country Club Circle
Fort Worth, TX 76109
(817) 927-4200
Personnel Director: Colleen McGrath
Private country club.

Cosmopolitan Lady
221 Bedford Rd., Suite 300
Bedford, TX 76022
(817) 282-2941
Contact: Personnel Director
Fitness center.

Dallas Country Club
4100 Beverly Dr.
Dallas, TX 75205
(214) 521-2151
Contact: Rosemary Burke
Private country club.

Dallas Cowboys
1 Cowboy Pkwy.
Irving, TX 75063
(214) 556-9900
Mail resume to Director of Administration
Headquarters for professional football team.

Dallas Mavericks
777 Sports St.
Dallas, TX 75207
(214) 748-1808
Contact: Accounting Division
Headquarters for professional basketball team.

Dallas Sidekicks
6116 N. Central Expwy., Suite 250
Dallas, TX 75206
(214) 361-5425
President: Gordon Jago
Headquarters for professional soccer team.

Exchange Athletic Club
700 N. Harwood St., Lock Box 11
Dallas, TX 75201
(214) 953-1144

Assistant General Manager: Scott LaCroix
Fitness center.

International Athletic Club of North Dallas
13701 N. Dallas Pkwy.
Dallas, TX 75240
(214) 458-2582
Club Director: Mike Chandler
Fitness center.

Las Colinas Country Club
4900 N. O'Connor Rd.
Irving, TX 75062
(214) 541-1141
Manager: Ed Schweykowski
Private country club.

Premier Club
5910 N. Central Expwy.
Dallas, TX 75206
(214) 891-6600
Contact: Department Head
Fitness center.

President's Health and Racquetball Clubs
13714 Gamma Rd., Suite 100
Dallas, TX 75224
(214) 239-7190
Contact: Department Head
Fitness center.

Prestonwood Country Club
15909 Preston Rd.
Dallas, TX 75248
(214) 239-7111
General Manager: Tonie Tony
Private country club.

Ridglea Country Club
3700 Bernie Anderson Ave.
Fort Worth, TX 76116
(817) 732-8111
Contact: Department Head
Private country club.

Riverbend Athletic Club
2201 E. Loop 820 North
Fort Worth, TX 76118
(817) 284-3553
Contact: Business Office
Fitness center.

Texas Rangers
1250 Copeland Rd., Suite 1100
Arlington, TX 76011
(817) 273-5222
Contact: Department Head
Headquarters for professional baseball team.

University Club of Dallas/Galleria
13350 Dallas Pkwy., Suite 4000
Dallas, TX 75240
(214) 239-0050
Contact: Department Head
Private club with restaurant and fitness center.

Willow Bend Polo & Hunt Club
5845 W. Park Blvd.
Plano, TX 75093
(214) 248-6298
General Manager: Robert Payne
Private polo club.

Woodhaven Country Club
913 Country Club Lane
Fort Worth, TX 76112
(817) 457-5150
Comptroller: Pat Wagner
Private country club.

YMCA/Metropolitan Branch
Dallas headquarters
601 N. Akard St.
Dallas, TX 75201
(214) 880-9622
V.P. Human Resources: Zera Mackie
Fitness center and special programs.

YMCA/Metropolitan Branch
Fort Worth headquarters
540 Lamar St.
Fort Worth, TX 76102
(817) 335-6147
Personnel Director: Patsy Green
Fitness center and special programs.

Restaurants

For networking in the **restaurant industry** and related fields, check out the following organization listed in Chapter 5:

PROFESSIONAL ORGANIZATIONS:

Dallas Restaurant Association

For more information, you can contact:

National Restaurant Association
1200 17th St., NW
Washington, DC 20036
(202) 331-5900

PROFESSIONAL PUBLICATIONS:

Beverage Media
Food and Beverage Marketing
Food Industry Newsletter
Food Management
Food and Wine
Foodservice Product News
Nation's Restaurant News
Restaurant Business
Restaurant Hospitality
Restaurants & Institutions
Signature Magazine

DIRECTORIES:

Directory of Chain Restaurant Operators (Chain Store Guide, New York, NY)
Directory of Food Service Distributors (Information Services, New York, NY)
Restaurant Hospitality: Restaurant Industry Hospitality Issue (Penton Publishing, Columbus, OH)
Restaurants & Institutions: 400 Issue, July Issue (Cahners Publishing, Des Plaines, IL)

EMPLOYERS:

Bennigan's
12404 Park Central Dr.
Dallas, TX 75251
(214) 404-5912
Contact: Hank Simpson

Burger King Corp.
4965 Preston Park Blvd.
Plano, TX 75086
(214) 964-3616
Contact: Personnel Department

Chili's
6820 LBJ Frwy., Suite 200
Dallas, TX 75229
(214) 980-9917
Contact: Human Resources Department

Denny's Restaurant
Regional Office
801 E. Ave. H, Suite 104
Arlington, TX 76011
Metro (817) 640-0731
Contact: Personnel Department

Domino's Pizza
Regional Office
1 Galleria Tower
13355 Noel Rd., Suite 455
Dallas, TX 75240
(214) 392-3030
Contact: Personnel Department

El Chico Corp.
12200 Stemmons Frwy., Suite 100
Dallas, TX 75234
(214) 241-5500
Contact: Director of Recruiting

Grandy's
Corporate Office
997 Grandy's Lane
Lewisville, TX 75067
(214) 317-8000
Contact: Recruiting Department

Jack-In-The-Box Drive-Thru
Administrative Office
3010 LBJ Frwy., Suite 1000
Dallas, TX 75234
(214) 247-8622
Personnel Director: Mary Dixon

Kentucky Fried Chicken
District Office
5605 N. MacArthur, Suite 610
Dallas, TX 75038

(214) 751-8300
Contact: Personnel Department

Long John Silver's Seafood Shoppes
Regional Office
3030 LBJ Frwy., Suite 1140
Dallas, TX 75234
(214) 247-9801
Contact: Personnel

McDonald's
Regional Office
511 E. John W. Carpenter Frwy., Suite 375
Dallas, TX 75062
(214) 869-1888
Contact: Personnel Department

Pancho's Mexican Buffet
3500 Noble St.
Fort Worth, TX 76111
(817) 831-0081
V.P. of Human Resources: David Dixon

Pizza Hut
Regional Personnel
3612 Forest Lane
Dallas, TX 75234
(817) 357-6363
Contact: Personnel Department

Pizza Inn
International Headquarters
5050 Quorum Dr., Suite 500
Dallas, TX 75240
(214) 701-9955
Personnel Department: Cathy Breedlove

Pulido Associates
4924 Old Benbrook Rd.
Fort Worth, TX 76116
(817) 731-4241
General Manager: John Rodriguez

Prufrock Restaurants
8115 Preston Rd., Lock Box 7
Dallas, TX 75225
(214) 363-9514
V.P. of Human Resources: Rosemary Maellaro

S&A Restaurant Corp.
12404 Park Central Dr.
Dallas, TX 75251

Metro (214) 404-5000
Recruiter: Phil Sweeny

Sky Chefs
601 Ryan Plaza Dr., Bldg. B
Arlington, TX 76011
Metro (817) 792-2123
Contact: Human Resources Department

TGI Friday's
14665 Midway Rd.
Dallas, TX 75244
(214) 450-5400
Corporate Recruiter: Sherry Young

Wyatt Cafeterias
10726 Plano Rd.
Dallas, TX 75238
(214) 349-0060
Personnel Recruiter: Paul Grey

Jobs for younger workers

Younger workers who are looking for summer or part-time work face a common dilemma: how do you get a job when you haven't had much work experience?

Special employment programs assist youths in overcoming this problem. College placement services are also good sources for job leads. You can also check with employers in the restaurant, hotel, recreation, and entertainment fields, who traditionally hire younger workers.

Six Flags Over Texas is the area's largest employer of youths. More than 2,400 seasonal staff members are hired to work full-time during the summer and on weekends during the spring and fall. The best time to apply is in January when the theme park begins hiring for the new season. You can apply later in the year, too.

The secret is to get a jump on everyone else and not wait until the last day of school to begin looking for a summer job. You want the odds to be in your favor, considering that the number of applicants always outnumbers the openings.■

Retailers/Wholesalers

For networking in **retailing and wholesaling,** check out the following professional organizations listed in Chapter 5:

PROFESSIONAL ORGANIZATIONS:

Association of Executive Saleswomen
Dallas Business League
Fort Worth Florist's Association
New Car Dealers of Metropolitan Dallas
Sales and Marketing Executives of Fort Worth
Southwest Homefurnishings Association

For additional information, you can contact:

American Pharmaceutical Association
2215 Connecticut Ave., NW
Washington, DC 20037
(202) 628-4410

Manufacturers' Agents National Association
23016 Mill Creek Rd.
Laguna Hills, CA 92653
(714) 859-4040

National Association of Chain Drug Stores
413 N. Lee St.
Box 1417-D49
Alexandria, VA 22314
(703) 549-3001

National Association of Convenience Stores
1605 King St.
Alexandria, VA 22314
(703) 684-3600

National Association of Wholsaler Distributors
1725 K St., NW
Washington, DC 20006
(202) 872-0885

National Grocers Association
1825 Samuel Morse Dr.
Reston, VA 22090
(703) 437-5300

National Retail Federation
100 W. 31st. St.
New York, NY 10001
(212) 244-8780

National Retail Hardware Association
5822 W. 74th St.
Indianapolis, IN 46278
(317) 290-0338

PROFESSIONAL PUBLICATIONS:

Chain Store Age
DIY Retailing
Merchandiser
National Grocer
Pharmacy Weekly
Stores
Women's Wear Daily

DIRECTORIES:

Chain Drug Stores Membership Directory (National Assoc. of Chain Drug
    Stores, Alexandria, VA)
Convenience Stores Membership Directory (National Assoc. of
    Convenience Stores, Alexandria, VA)
Fairchild's Financial Manual of Retail Stores (Fairchild Books, New York,
    NY)
Nationwide Directory-Mass Market Merchandisers (Salesman's Guides,
    New York, NY)
Sheldon's Department Stores (PS & H Inc., Fairview, NJ)

EMPLOYERS:

Ace Hardware Stores
Southwest Distribution Center
2257 Commerce Dr.
Arlington, TX 76011
(817) 649-5118
Contact: Human Resources Department
Dealer-owned hardware cooperative.

Ted Arendale Ford
201 E. Division St.
Arlington, TX 76011
Metro (817) 261-4261
Contact: Department Head
Automobile dealership.

Army Air Force Exchange Service
3911 S. Walton Walker Blvd.
Dallas, TX 75236
(214) 312-2278
Contact: Application Center open 8 a.m.-noon Wednesday
Headquarters for retail and food services located in army and air force
bases throughout the world.

Barber's Book Stores
215 W. 8th St.
Fort Worth, TX 76102
(817) 335-5469
Owner: Brian Perkins
Fort Worth's oldest bookstore.

BeautiControl Cosmetics
2121 Midway Rd.
Carrollton, TX 75006
(214) 458-0601
Human Resources Director: Sandra Egland
Direct sales cosmetics retailer.

Bedroom Shop
2012 W. Pioneer Pkwy.
Arlington, TX 76013
Metro (817) 261-2244
Personnel: Stan McCants or Udell Bell
Retailer of mattresses, box springs, and bedding accessories.

Bookstop
5400 E. Mockingbird Lane
Dallas, TX 75206
(214) 828-4210
Contact: Store Manager
Discount bookstore.

Henry Butts Daihatsu, Hyundai, Oldsmobile
4000 Midway Rd.
Carrollton, TX 75007
(214) 931-8686
Personnel Director: Mary Ann Butts
Automobile dealership.

Cokesbury
19200 Preston Rd.
Dallas, TX 75252
(214) 328-8850
Manager: Sam Albright
Christian bookstore.

Color Tile
515 Houston St.

Fort Worth, TX 76102
(817) 870-9400
Director of Human Resources: Dick Andrews
Retail home improvement outlet.

Contempo Casuals
715 NorthPark Center
Dallas, TX 75231
(214) 739-4106
Contact: Personnel
Women's apparel.

B. Dalton Bookseller
1526 Main St.
Dallas, TX 75201
(214) 742-7232
Contact: individual store manager
National chain of bookstores.

Don Davis Oldsmobile
1901 N. Collins St.
Arlington, TX 76010
Metro (817) 461-1000
Contact: Department Head
Automobile dealership.

Dillard Department Stores
4501 N. Beach St.
Fort Worth, TX 76137
(817) 831-5111
Personnel Manager: Carol Gardner
Retail department store.

Eagle Lincoln Mercury
6116 Lemmon Ave.
Dallas, TX 75209
(214) 357-0461
Contact: Department Head
Automobile dealership.

Eckerd Drugs
4409 Action St.
Garland, TX 75046
(214) 272-0411
Personnel Manager: Bill Hofrichter
Large specialty store with pharmacy and photo finish services,
cosmetics, drugs, and general merchandise.

Foley's
Contact: Houston headquarters for managerial positions
at 1100 Main St., Houston, TX 77002, (713) 651-7038.

Contact store manager for hourly positions.
Department store chain.

Fox Photo
Contact: San Antonio headquarters for managerial positions
at 70 North East Loop 410, Suite 1100, San Antonio, TX 78216.
Contact photo lab manager for hourly positions.
Photo lab chain.

Friendly Chevrolet
5601 Lemmon Ave.
Dallas, TX 75209
(214) 526-8811
Contact: Department Head
Automobile dealership.

Charlie Hillard
1400 S. University Dr.
Fort Worth, TX 76107
(817) 336-9811
Contact: Department Head
Automobile dealership.

Home Interiors & Gifts
4550 Spring Valley Rd.
Dallas, TX 75244
(214) 386-1000
Personnel Manager: George Burton
Decorative accessories sold through home demonstrations.

Horchow Collection
13800 Diplomat Dr.
Dallas, TX 75234
(214) 888-9700
Contact: Personnel Department
Mail order clothing and furniture.

K-Mart Corp.
199 Planters Rd.
Dallas, TX 75182
Metro (214) 226-0295
Contact: Personnel Department
General discount merchandiser.

Macy's
13375 Noel Rd.
Dallas, TX 75240
(214) 851-3300
Contact: Personnel Department
General retail store.

Mary Kay Cosmetics
8787 Stemmons Frwy.
Dallas, TX 75247
(214) 630-8787
Contact: Personnel Department
International headquarters for cosmetics sold through home demonstrations.

David McDavid Pontiac
3700 W. Airport Frwy.
Irving, TX 75062
(214) 790-6000
Contact: Department Head
Automobile dealership.

Mervyn's Department Stores
South Central Headquarters
1600 E. Plano Pkwy.
Plano, TX 75074
(214) 578-9536
Contact: Personnel Department
Softgoods department store.

Michaels/MJDesigns
9015 Sterling St.
Irving, TX 75063
(214) 929-8595
Personnel Director: Bolinda Neal
Arts, crafts, and framing store.

Miller Business Systems
916 113th St.
Arlington, TX 76011
Metro (817) 640-1541
Contact: Human Resources Department
Office supplies and furniture.

Mitchells Department Stores
318 E. Long Ave.
Fort Worth, TX 76106
(817) 626-3726
District Manager: Ron Wells
Corporate headquarters for retail clothing and housewares chain.

Montgomery Ward & Co.
2700 E. Pioneer Pkwy.
Arlington, TX 76010
(817) 649-4903
Contact: Personnel Department
National mass market retail chain.

Neiman Marcus
1618 Main St.
Dallas, TX 75201
(214) 741-6911
Contact: Executive Personnel Departments
Major national specialty store with several area locations.

Page Drug
General Offices
14303 Inwood Rd.
Dallas, TX 75244
(214) 661-9700
Contact: Marlyn Smith for management positions; contact Human
Resources Department for warehouse and office positions
Drug store and pharmacy chain.

Frank Parra Chevrolet
1000 E. Airport Frwy.
Irving, TX 75062
(214) 721-4300
Contact: Department Head
Automobile dealership.

Pearle Vision
2534 Royal Lane
Dallas, TX 75229
(214) 241-3381
Contact: Deborah Flaherty for management positions; contact
Deedee Carr for hourly positions
Retail eyewear.

J. C. Penney Co.
14841 Dallas Pkwy.
Dallas, TX 75251
(214) 591-2300
Contact: Personnel Department
National headquarters for retail merchandise sales and service stores,
with several area locations.

Pier 1 Imports
301 Commerce St., Suite 600
Fort Worth, TX 76102
(817) 878-8000
Vice President of Human Resources: Mitch Weatherly
Imported merchandise with several area stores.

Radio Shack
500 One Tandy Center
Fort Worth, TX 76102
(817) 390-3011

V.P. of Human Resources: George Berger
National headquarters for retailer of electronic equipment and computers.

Sears, Roebuck & Co.
5334 Ross Ave.
Dallas, TX 75206
(214) 841-2307
Personnel Manager: Craig Hibbison
One of world's largest retailers and catalog merchandisers, with subsidiaries in insurance and real estate. Several area locations.

Sherwin-Williams Co.
10440 E. Northwest Hwy.
Dallas, TX 75238
(214) 553-2979
Personnel Director: Con Barthell
Retail and wholesale paint, wallpaper, and floor covering.

Sound Warehouse
10911 Petal St.
Dallas, TX 75238
(214) 343-4700
Contact: Department Head
One of area's largest record and tape chains.

Sunbelt Nursery Group
6500 West Frwy., Suite 600
Fort Worth, TX 76116
(817) 738-8111
Personnel Director: Tim Hinaman
Retail garden centers and nurseries.

Suzanne Shops
3236 Skyline Dr.
Carrollton, TX 75006
(214) 634-0311
Contact: Department Head
Women's discount dress shop chain.

Tandycrafts
1400 Everman Pkwy.
Fort Worth, TX 76140
(817) 551-9600
Contact: Patsy Brantley
Home office for leather crafts, Christian books, and cargo furniture.

Target Stores
555 Republic Dr., Suite 500
Plano, TX 75074
(214) 422-7400

Regional Personnel Director: Dave Biron
General discount.

Taylors Bookstores
10495 Olympic Dr., Suite 100
Dallas, TX 75220
(214) 357-1700
Contact: Store Manager
Large bookstore with several area locations.

Tuesday Morning
14621 Inwood Rd.
Dallas, TX 75244
(214) 387-3562
Payroll: Debra Steenrod
Discount linens, towels, and other household merchandise.

Vandergriff Chevrolet Co.
901 E. Division St.
Arlington, TX 76011
Metro (817) 860-7171
Vice President: Victor Vandergriff
Automobile dealership.

Waldenbooks
1084 Prestonwood Town Center
5301 Belt Line Rd.
Dallas, TX 75240
Contact: individual store manager
National retail bookstore chain.

James K. Wilson
Service Center
2503 Butler St.
Dallas, TX 75235
(214) 638-6350
Contact: Store Manager or corporate office at 101 N. Wacker Dr.,
Chicago, IL 60606
Men's and women's clothing store chain.

Zale Corp.
Employment Center: 901 W. Walnut Hill Lane
Irving, TX 75038
(214) 580-4172
Staffing Manager: Joan Shaw
Retail jewelry chain.

Retailing jobs overseas

Here's an opportunity to see the world and work for one of America's largest retailers—the Army and Air Force Exchange Service.

AAFES's international headquarters is located in Dallas. Associates have the option of being mobile, which allows them to relocate with AAFES worldwide, as opposed to remaining in the same location for the duration of their AAFES career.

One advantage of working for AAFES is an opportunity for people to advance quickly and assume greater responsibility. There are more than 78,000 positions worldwide that include working in retail stores, cafeterias, fast food operations, and movie theaters.

Associates are selected for AAFES employment based on their ability to meet the job qualifications. Competition for the jobs is stiff. Applications for Hourly Pay Plan positions are kept on file for three months, and applications for management positions are forwarded to the Career Management Division for review and consideration. Applications are taken from 8 a.m. to noon, Wednesdays at the headquarters Recruitment Center, located at 3911 S. Walton Walker Blvd., and from 8 a.m. to noon, Thursdays at the AAFES Operations Center, located at 2727 LBJ Freeway in Dallas.

Telecommunications

To learn more about the **telecommunications** field, you can write to:

PROFESSIONAL ORGANIZATION:

North American Telecommunications Association
2000 M St., NW
Washington, DC 20036

PROFESSIONAL PUBLICATIONS:

Data Pro Reports on Telecommunications
Technology Review
Telecommunications
Telecommunications Reports
Telecommunications Week
Telephony

DIRECTORIES:

Data Processing Services Directory (American Business Directories, Omaha, NE)
Electrical World Directory of Electrical Utilities (McGraw-Hill, New York, NY)
Sourcebook (North American Telecommunications Association, Washington, DC)

EMPLOYERS:

BNR
1150 Arapaho Rd.
Richardson, TX 75081
(214) 997-4500
Contact: Staffing Department
Designs digital switching systems.

DSC
1000 Coit Rd.
Plano, TX 75075
(214) 519-3000
Contact: Personnel Department
Designs, manufactures, installs, and repairs telecommunications and switching systems.

Electrospace Systems
1301 E. Collins Blvd.
Richardson, TX 75083
(214) 470-2000
Contact: Personnel Department
Designs, manufactures, installs, and repairs telecommunications and switching systems.

Ericsson North America
730 International Pwky.
Richardson, TX 75081
(214) 669-9900
Human Resources Assistant: Pat Gee
Manufactures telecommunications equipment.

International Telecom
13719 Omega

Dallas, TX 75244
(214) 991-9677
Sales Manager: Eric Symula
Sells and sevices telecommunications equipment.

Intervoice
17811 Waterview
Dallas, TX 75252
(214) 669-3988
Senior Personnel Administator: Kathy Hackney
Manufactures voice automation systems.

NAC
1830 N. Greenville Ave.
Richardson, TX 75081
(214) 238-9676
Human Resources Manager: Merrylin Lovelady
Designs and manufactures telecommunication systems.

NEC America
1525 Walnut Hill Lane
Irving, TX 75038
(214) 580-9100
Human Resources Supervisor: Linda Johnson
Manufactures telecommunications equipment.

Northern Telecom
1001 E. Arapaho Rd.
Richardson, TX 75081
(214) 234-5300
Contact: Human Resources Department
Sales office for telecommunications company that offers a complete
line of digital switching and transmissions systems.

Rockwell International Corp.
1200 N. Alma Rd.
Richardson, TX 75081
(214) 996-5434
Contact: Staffing Department
Manufactures electronics and communications systems for commercial
and defense applications.

Rolm Co.
15030 Dallas Pkwy., Suite 1100
Dallas, TX 75248
(214) 980-0098
Contact: Personnel Department
Sells and services telecommunications equipment.

Telinq Systems
1651 N. Glenville Ave.
Richardson, TX 75081

(214) 680-6900
Financial Administration: Regina Smith
Manufactures high-speed digital switches for telecommunications systems.

Travel/Transportation/ Shipping

For networking in **transportation,** check out the following organization listed in Chapter 5:

PROFESSIONAL ORGANIZATIONS:

Women's Transportation Club of Dallas

For additional information, you can contact:

Amercian Society of Travel Agents
1101 King St., #200
Alexandria, VA 22314
(703) 739-2782

Association of Retail Travel Agents
1745 Jefferson Davis Hwy., #300
Arlington, VA 22202
(703) 553-7777

National Association of Rail Shippers
50 F St., NW
Washington, DC 20001
(202) 639-2378

Transportation Brokers Conference of America
60 Revere Dr.
Northbrook, IL 60062
(312) 480-1046

Travel Industry Association of America
1133 21 St, NW
Lafayette Center
Washington, DC 20036

PROFESSIONAL PUBLICATIONS:

Air Travel Journal
ASTA Travel News
The Professional Broker

DIRECTORIES:

Aviation Directory (E.A. Brennan Co., Garden Grove, CA)
Membership Directory (Aviation Distributors & Manufacturers
    Association, Philadelphia, PA)
Moody's Transportation Manual (Moody's Investor Service, New York, NY)
Travel Industry Personnel Directory (Fairchild Publications, New York, NY)
Worldwide Travel Information Contact Book (Gale Research, Detroit, MI)

EMPLOYERS:

ABF Freight System
6814 Harry Hines Blvd.
Dallas, TX 75235
(214) 350-8901
Contact: Personnel
Common freight carrier.

American Airlines
55 Amon Carter Blvd.
Arlington, TX 75261
Metro (817) 963-1234
Contact: Personnel Department
Passenger and air freight services.

American Express Travel Co.
5080 Spectrum Dr., Suite 608W
Dallas, TX 75248
(214) 991-8500
Personnel Supervisor: Lori Larson
Travel agency.

Amtrak, National Railway Passenger Corp.
400 S. Houston St.
Dallas, TX 75202
(214) 653-1101
Contact: Main office at 210 S. Canal St., Chicago, IL 60606
Passenger rail service.

Avis Rent A Car
1 W. N. International Pkwy.
Dallas/Fort Worth Airport, TX 75261
(214) 574-4110
Personnel Supervisor: Chris DeSimmone
Automobile rentals.

Budget Rent-A-Car Systems
1702 Old Minters Chapel Rd.
Grapevine, TX 76051
(817) 329-8700

Contact: Personnel Department
Automobile and truck rentals.

Burlington Northern Railroad Co.
3000 Continental Plaza
777 Main St.
Fort Worth, TX 76102
(817) 878-2000
Contact: Mail resume to Human Resources Department
Freight transporter.

Carlson Travel Company
1112 E. Copeland Rd.
Arlington, TX 76011
Metro (817) 461-9551
Office Manager: Patty Koski
Corporate travel services.

Central Freight Lines
5200 E. Loop 820 South
Fort Worth, TX 76119
(817) 478-8211
Contact: Assistant General Manager
Common freight carrier.

Jack Cooper Co.
2909 E. Abram St.
Arlington, TX 76010
Metro (817) 640-0829
Office Manager: Cheri Wilson
Automobile transporter.

DART
601 Pacific Ave.
Dallas, TX 75202
(214) 573-8550
Contact: Employment Office
Regional transportation authority.

Dallas/Fort Worth International Airport
Dallas/Fort Worth Airport, TX 75261
(214) 574-6031
Contact: Personnel Department
Major international airport.

Delta Air Lines
District Marketing Office
8700 N. Stemmons Frwy., Suite 212
Dallas, TX 75247
(214) 879-6000
Contact: Personnel or headquarters in Atlanta, GA, (404) 765-2501
Passenger and air freight services.

Frozen Food Express Industries
3100 Danieldale Rd.
Lancaster, TX 75207
(214) 428-7661
Contact: Personnel Department
Transporter of general commodities sold in grocery, discount, and department stores.

Greyhound Lines
15110 N. Dallas Parkway
Dallas, TX 75248
(214) 744-6500
Contact: Recruiting Department
Regional division of a national bus line.

Hertz Rent A Car
8505 Freeport Pkwy., Suite 300
Irving, TX 75063
(214) 453-0370
Employee Relations Manager: Robert Salmon
Automobile renting and leasing.

Metro Airlines
8505 Freeport Pkwy.
Irving, TX 75063
(214) 453-4400
Contact: Personnel Department
Airline passenger and cargo service.

Missouri-Kansas-Texas Railroad Co.
701 Commerce St.
Dallas, TX 75202
(214) 651-6746
Contact: Personnel Department
Headquarters for freight railroad, operating in a four-state area.

North Texas Lines
710 E. Davis St.
Grand Prairie, TX 75050
(214) 263-0294
Transportation Supervisor: Ray Gardner
College and university transportation.

Southwest Airlines
8008 Aviation Place
Dallas, TX 75235
(214) 904-4803
Contact: Personnel Department
Headquarters for interstate airline.

State Taxicab Co.
3043 Cedar Crest Blvd.

Dallas, TX 75203
(214) 371-0777
Contact: Department Head
Taxi company.

Sunbelt Motivation & Travel
909 E. Las Colinas Blvd., Suite 200
Irving, TX 75039
(214) 401-0210
Personnel Manager: D'ann Hardy
Travel service.

The T-Fort Worth Transportation Authority
2304 Pine St.
Fort Worth, TX 76102
(817) 871-6220
Personnel Supervisor: Ruth Lyon
Fort Worth's public transportation service.

TNT Bestway
2121 E. Grauwyler
Irving, TX 75061
(214) 721-1901
Contact: Terminal Manager
Common freight carrier.

Interested in becoming a flight attendant?

Tens of thousands of men and women apply each year for American Airlines flight attendant positions. So what are your chances of landing one of these plum positions?

They're good if you possess the qualities Recruitment Manager Kathy Blair looks for in applicants.

"The airline industry has changed so much that this job isn't for everyone," Blair says. "It's very fast-paced and flight attendants are required to deal with full airplanes and a variety of people. These customers expect a lot and we promise it. You need to be very flexibile, prefer a varied work schedule, and not mind waking up in a different city each day."

As for looks, Blair says, "You must be well groomed, but we aren't for cookie-cutter people. We are looking inwardly for individuals who truly care about giving service and selling the company. More and more, our flight attendants are becoming in-flight salespeople. They spend more time with the customer than anyone else."

American Airlines can be selective in hiring because of its low turnover. "We see lots of wonderful people, but the number of positions we have open is very limited," Blair says.

As for basic requirements, applicants must be at least 20 years old and have a high school education or GED. Two years of working experience, preferably one that requires contact with the public, or the same amount of time in college is a plus, Blair says. She says people often ask what type of education is most helpful, and she believes a liberal arts background is one of the best because of the exposure to a broad range of subjects.

Finalists are carefully screened. They are required to write an essay to determine their writing skills. And they are evaluated during group interviews on how well they interact with strangers to determine their poise, sensitivity, maturity, and warmth.

Their weight and height are checked to make sure they fulfill safety requirements of being between 5-feet-1½ -inches and 6-feet tall. Weight must be proportionate to height. Candidates must also take a company physical and pass an eye exam to make sure their vision is at least 20-50 in both eyes.

Those who are accepted for the program attend a 5½ -week training course at the American Airlines Learning Center located several miles south of Dallas/Fort Worth International Airport on Highway 360.

To apply for a position, write American Airlines Flight Service Recruitment, P.O. Box 619410, Mail Drop 4125, Dallas/Fort Worth Airport, TX 75261-4125.■

Utilities

For additional information about **public utilities** you can contact:

American Public Gas Association
Box 1426
Vienna, VA 22183
(703) 281-2910

American Public Power Association
2301 M St., NW
Washington, DC 20037
(202) 467-2900

PROFESSIONAL PUBLICATIONS:

Electric Light & Power
Electrical World
Powerline
Public Power
Public Utilities
Yankee Oilman

DIRECTORIES:

APGA Directory of Municpal Gas Systems (Amer. Public Gas Assoc.,
    Vienna, VA)
Brown's Directory of North American & International Gas Companies
    (Edgel Communications, Cleveland, OH)
Moody's Public Utility Manual (Moody's Investor Service, New York, NY)

EMPLOYERS:

AT&T
2777 Stemmons Frwy., Suite 1425
Dallas, TX 75207
(214) 308-5542
Supplier of communication services and equipment.

AT&T
2501 Parkview Dr., Suite 200
Fort Worth, TX 76102
(817) 870-4420
Contact: Dallas Office
Supplier of communication services and equipment.

GTE Directories Corp.
GTE Place
West Airfield Dr.
D/FW International Airport, TX 75261
(214) 453-7000
Human Resources Recruiter
Telephone directories and listings.

GTE Corp.
290 E. Carpenter Frwy., Suite 700
Irving, TX 75062
(214) 717-7700
Contact: Human Resources Department
National headquarters for diversified telephone company that serves
31 states.

Lone Star Gas Co.
Dallas Office
1817 Wood St., Room 105W
Dallas, TX 75201
(214) 741-3711
Contact: Senior Employment Representative Scott Brock for
managerial positions and Employment Representative Pam Hixon for
support positions
Headquarters for one of the largest natural gas transmission and
distribution companies. Serves Texas and a portion of Oklahoma.

Lone Star Gas Go.
Fort Worth Office
908 Monroe St.
Fort Worth, TX 76102
(817) 336-8381
Personnel Manager: H. Shukers
Natural gas transmission and distribution company.

Southwestern Bell Telephone Co.
Dallas Office
308 S. Akard St., Three Bell Plaza, Room 101
Dallas, TX 75202
(214) 464-3171
Contact: Employment Office
Telephone service.

Southwestern Bell Telephone Co.
Fort Worth Office
1116 Houston St., Room 105
Fort Worth, TX 76102
(817) 338-6537

Contact: Employment Office
Telephone service.

Southwestern Electric Service
1717 Main St., Suite 3300
Dallas, TX 75201
(903) 741-3125
Contact: Personnel Office in Jacksonville, TX (214) 586-9851
Purchase, transmission, distribution, and sale of electric energy.

Texas-New Mexico Power Co.
4100 International Plaza
820 Hulen Tower II
Fort Worth, TX 76109
(817) 731-0099
Employment Coordinator: Susan Overcash
Electrical utility.

TU Electric
115 W. 7th St.
Fort Worth, TX 76102
(817) 336-9411
Contact: Dallas Office
Electric service.

TU Electric
400 N. Olive Rd.
Dallas, TX 75201
(214) 812-8633
Contact: Employment Office
Electric service.

Tri-County Electric Cooperative
600 Northwest Pkwy.
Azle, TX 76020
(817) 444-3201
Office Manager: Tom Weems
Headquarters for electric co-op that serves cities in seven North
Central Texas counties.

US Sprint Communications
1520 E. Rochelle Blvd.
Irving, TX 75039
(214) 506-1000
Recruiter: Debra Goddard
Long distance telephone carrier.

**Tips for landing
your first job
out of college**

Landing that first job out of school is a frightening prospect for many. But there are ways to prepare for the entry into the work world.

We asked directors of college and university career centers for the best advice they could give someone who is starting to look for their first job after graduation. Here are their replies:

Suzanne M. Fields, Tarrant County Junior College Northeast's Director of Counseling and Testing Services: "Try to get work experience while you're in college. If you wait until you get out, you're already behind. Don't worry about low pay because the experience will more than make up for the difference. Later on you will get back what you didn't receive in pay in terms of the extra boost to your career. Work experience also helps you know if you want to enter a field before you waste time. Also be sure to get as much experience in writing and English as you can. I have applications from Ph.D.s who can't write or communicate effectively."

Dr. Don Hankins, Tarrant County Junior College South Campus Director of Counseling and Testing: "One of the most important things is to work on communications skills. People who present themselves well do better in getting a job, and once they get out, they get ahead faster than others."

Linda Foley, Eastfield Community College Coordinator of Career Placement: "To be prepared, learn how to get a job. Preparation and research as well as resume writing and interviewing techniques are what can really help you get a job these days. Many people are unaware of how college centers can help current students as well as past students get help for free or for a nominal fee, which compares favorably with career consulting firms." ■

L

M

Q

R

S

U

V

W

XYZ

General Index

E

F

G

H

I

U,V

W,Y